Woodrow Wilson

Woodrow Wilson

The Essential Political Writings

Ronald J. Pestritto

LEXINGTON BOOKS

A Division of
ROWMAN & LITTLEFIELD PUBLISHERS, INC.
Lanham • Boulder • New York • Toronto • Oxford

LEXINGTON BOOKS

A division of Rowman & Littlefield Publishers, Inc.
A wholly owned subsidiary of The Rowman & Littlefield Publishing Group, Inc.
4501 Forbes Boulevard, Suite 200
Lanham, MD 20706

PO Box 317
Oxford
OX2 9RU, UK

British Library Cataloguing in Publication Information Available

Library of Congress Cataloging-in-Publication Data

Wilson, Woodrow, 1856–1924.
  [Essays. Selections]
  Woodrow Wilson : the essential political writings / [edited by] Ronald J. Pestritto.
    p. cm.
  Includes bibliographical references and index.
  ISBN 0-7391-0945-6 (cloth : alk. paper) — ISBN 0-7391-0951-0 (pbk. : alk. paper)
  1. United States—Politics and government. 2. Political science—United States. I.
  Pestritto, Ronald J. II. Title.
  E660.W714 2005
  973.91'3'092—dc22   2004027468

Published in the United States of America

⊗™ The paper used in this publication meets the minimum requirements of
American National Statndard for Information Sciences—Permanence of Paper
for Printed Library Materials, ANSI/NISO Z39.48-1992.

Contents

Preface and Acknowledgments

This collection is designed to bring together in one volume the most essential works of Woodrow Wilson for students of American political thought and American political institutions. Wilson is best known, of course, for his influence in the realm of foreign policy. This is why his speeches and writings pertaining to foreign policy are numerous and widely available elsewhere, and it is why I have included in this collection just two of the most important foreign policy speeches. The present collection is grounded in the recognition that Wilson's role in the development of American political thought and institutions may be just as important as it was to American foreign policy; yet, no single volume exists that allows convenient access to Wilson's numerous contributions in these fields.

The motivation for this collection came from my experience—and the experiences of many colleagues with whom I spoke—in attempting to put together readings in graduate and undergraduate courses on American political thought, the presidency, Congress, political parties, and public administration, among others. When it came to including readings from Wilson, it was necessary to assemble a multitude of photocopies from various places in order to allow students access to his many relevant writings and speeches. The selections in this volume come from a desire to remedy this defect and are drawn from the exposure to Wilson's works that I gained while writing my book-length treatment of his political thought, *Woodrow Wilson and the Roots of Modern Liberalism* (2005).

With the exception of the sixty-nine-volume collection of Wilson's papers, the only work of Wilson's in print until very recently was his 1885 book *Congressional Government*. Within the last few years, that book has been reprinted with a new introduction by William F. Connolly Jr. Also reprinted recently was *Constitutional Government in the United States* with a new introduction by Sidney A. Pearson Jr. For professors interested in those books as a whole, these are excellent editions, and both new introductions are especially good and worth reading in their own right. But for professors interested only in certain portions of those books, or who would like their students to have access to key chapters from other important books, such as *The State* and *The New Freedom*, or to essays such as "The Study of Administration" and "Leaders of Men," my hope is that they will find this volume useful. I have tried to gather as much of all of these things under one cover as possible, while also trying to include some essays that may not be as well known, but that are of real significance in discerning Wilson's contribution to the American political tradition.

ORGANIZATION

This collection of writings is not presented in a strictly chronological fashion. Instead, I have organized the selections around the primary identifiable themes in Wilson's political thought. The collection begins with Wilson's theory of the state, with writings that show its foundation in historical thinking. Most prominent of these are selected chapters from Wilson's textbook *The State*, which was certainly his most comprehensive treatment of the theory of government and politics. The second part of the collection deals with Wilson's conception of political liberty and the purpose of government, which includes his progressive reinterpretation of the political theory of the American founding in essays on Jefferson and the Declaration of Independence, as well as some of his campaign addresses from 1912. The third part of the collection excerpts Wilson's most important works on reforming American national institutions, including his commentary on Congress, the presidency, and political parties. Part IV addresses Wilson's treatment of leadership, both in politics and administration. The essays "Leaders of Men" and "The Study of Administration" address the question of the connection between public opinion and governing in Wilson's famous separation of politics and administration. The collection concludes with two of Wilson's most famous foreign policy speeches—the "War Message to Congress" and his address on the "Fourteen Points."

A SNAPSHOT OF WILSON'S WORK

Because this collection does not proceed in a strictly chronological fashion, some brief overview of the main periods and works of Wilson's life seems appropriate here. For more details, readers are directed to the appendix, which provides a time line of Wilson's works and the main events of his life.

Wilson's early essays and letters, written during his days in college, law school, and graduate school, largely fall into one of two categories. One of these addresses religious questions, like the brief but interesting series including "Christ's Army" and "Christian Progress" that he penned during the fall and winter of 1876 and 1877. The other concerns Wilson's ideas for reforming American government, ideas that are brought out in his account of British history and important British historical figures. Wilson's reflections on John Bright and William Gladstone (1880) fall into this category, as do his essays like "Cabinet Government in the United States" (1879). Such essays are built into what eventually becomes Wilson's best-known book, *Congressional Government*, which served as his doctoral dissertation and was published in 1885. As a young professor, especially at Bryn Mawr College and Wesleyan University, Wilson devoted much of his energy to developing a theory of the state. This energy manifested itself in essays like "The Modern Democratic State" (1885) and, ultimately, in the book *The State* (1889). As an academic, Wilson also developed a line of thinking on the science of administration. This thinking was launched by his well-known "Study of Administration" in 1886 and continued through his time at Princeton. From 1888 to 1897, Wilson took time off from his home institution to teach an annual five-week lectureship on administration at Johns Hopkins, and his notes from these lectures are a rich source for scholars of Wilson's thoughts on administration. While teaching at Princeton, Wilson also wrote three American histories: *Division and Reunion* (1893), *George Washington* (1896), and the five-volume *History of the American People* (1902). Once he became president of Princeton in 1902, Wilson's scholarly writing came to an end, although he gave several important lectures and addresses. Of these, the series of lectures he delivered at Columbia University in 1907 was among the most interesting, and it became widely known when it was published as his book *Constitutional Government in the United States* in 1908. Wilson, of course, delivered many speeches as a candidate or officeholder, and his 1912 presidential campaign speeches were edited and put into book form in *The New Freedom* (1913).

EXPLANATION OF SOURCES AND TEXTS

Almost all of the selections in this collection were published by Wilson during his lifetime and are therefore in the public domain. In all such cases, the edition of the text that I present here was taken either from its place of original publication or from Wilson's original manuscript, as noted with each selection. Wilson did not formally publish during his lifetime two of the essays in this collection. One of these is "Leaders of Men," which is a lecture that Wilson gave several times in 1889 and 1890. It first appeared in print as an essay in T. H. Vail Motter's 1952 edited collection, *Leaders of Men*. The copyright on that collection has since expired, and the version of the essay presented here is the one found in the Motter book. The other essay in the present volume that Wilson did not formally publish is "Socialism and Democracy," which appeared for the first time in Arthur S. Link's sixty-nine-volume *Papers of Woodrow Wilson*. Permission to reprint that essay in this collection was kindly granted by Princeton University Press.

Wilson's grammar, punctuation, and spelling could be somewhat idiosyncratic, and Wilson particularly liked to anglicize his words. Since the aim of this collection is to present Wilson to the reader in as accurate a manner as possible, I have left almost everything exactly as it was in the original, including any emphasis in Wilson's original text. I have not employed the notation "sic," as I wanted to avoid a frequent disruption of the text. I have intervened editorially in a few cases of extreme need, and in such cases, I have placed brackets around the revisions.

All notes in the text are Wilson's, unless indicated otherwise. While these notes have been reproduced from the original, the numbering of the notes has, in some cases, been reformatted. Wilson occasionally provides internal references to his own works; I have left these in place, even when the referenced works or sections are not included in this collection, so that the student can look them up elsewhere if he so desires. All essays and book chapters are presented in their entirety, with the exception of chapter 2 of *Congressional Government*, from which I have omitted the final part.

ACKNOWLEDGMENTS

Work on this book was made possible through the financial support of the Earhart Foundation, which graciously provided a fellowship research grant during the summer of 2004. I would like to thank, in particular, the foundation's president Ingrid A. Gregg for her assistance and support.

My graduate assistant on this project, Christopher Burkett, provided invaluable service. He was impeccably organized and efficient, and this collection would have been much longer in the making were it not for his efforts.

In constructing a collection such as this, one must also rely heavily on experts in copyrights and special collections. Margaret Aldrich, an intellectual property associate at Princeton University Press, was most patient and helpful, and I thank her and the press for the assistance. Tad Bennicoff was our able contact at Princeton University's Seeley G. Mudd Manuscript Library, and I thank him for his excellent service and acknowledge the library as the source for several of the selections in this volume.

Serena Leigh Krombach, editorial director and senior editor at Lexington Books, encouraged this project from the beginning. I thank her for her support, and I much appreciate the work done on this volume by the entire staff at Lexington.

Finally, I wish to acknowledge the Claremont Institute, and especially its president, Brian T. Kennedy, whose support of me as a research fellow has made so much of my work on Wilson possible over the last several years.

Introduction

It is a common view—or at least it was at one time—that Woodrow Wilson's thought cannot be considered as a coherent whole.[1] This is why, from the point of view of much of the standard scholarship on Wilson, providing a concise account of his political thought is difficult, if not impossible. Many have seen Wilson as a staunch, limited-government, states-rights conservative early in his life who changed (the point of transformation is also a subject of debate) into an ardent Progressive. Others have suggested that Wilson never came around to embracing Progressive thinking. More recently, however, as more of Wilson's works have become accessible, some scholars at least have begun to see a fairly strong continuity in Wilson's thinking on government and politics, from his earliest days of writing and thinking about these matters through the latter stages of his public life. The evidence from Wilson's many books and essays, several of which are excerpted in this collection, support such a view, as I shall explain in this introduction.

Woodrow Wilson is an important figure in American politics and history for many reasons. Most obviously, he served two terms as the twenty-eighth president of the United States, a presidency most known for its stewardship of American involvement in World War I and for Wilson's failed attempt to sign America on to the League of Nations. Wilson also served a partial term as governor of New Jersey before he became president in 1912. But in addition to his political life, Wilson was a prolific scholar and successful academic for more than two decades; he was, in fact, the only professional political scientist ever to become president of the United States. He taught at his alma mater, Princeton University, and became president of that institution in 1902. Before this, Wilson held academic posts at Bryn Mawr College and then Wesleyan University.

While there is much scholarly work and focus on Wilson's presidency, especially the international aspects of it, Wilson is also of great interest because he was a Progressive thinker and because of the important place of Progressivism in the development of American political thought. The essays in this collection were selected with that in mind. In particular, Wilson is of interest to scholars of American political thought because Progressivism—certainly as expounded by Wilson— understood itself as presenting a rationale for moving beyond the political thinking of the American founding. While it is no doubt the case that Wilson often understood his vision as not inconsistent with the democratic spirit of the founding, his intellectual work also makes it very clear that Wilson was engaged in a self-conscious rejection of the theory that had animated the founding era.

A prerequisite for national progress, Wilson believed, was that the founding be understood in its proper historical context. Its principles, in spite of their universalistic claims, were intended to deal with the unique circumstances of that day. And so, Wilson looked instead to what he believed to be the democratic spirit of the founding—one that launched national government as a work in progress, a government that would require continual adjustment to historical circumstances as it tried to fulfill the broad democratic vision of the founders. But this interpretation of the founding ran up against the founders' own self-understanding, as Wilson well knew. This is why much of his scholarship is devoted to a reinterpretation and critique of both the political theory of the founding and of the implementation of that theory in the institutional design of the national government. Wilson understood that the strict limits placed upon the power of the national government by the Constitution, limits that Progressives wanted to see relaxed, if not removed, were grounded in the social contract and natural-rights language of the Declaration of Independence. This meant, for Wilson, that both the Declaration and the Constitution had to be understood anew through a Progressive lens.

Wilson, therefore, sought a reinterpretation of the founding, a reinterpretation grounded in historical contingency. To the founding's ahistorical notion that government is rooted in an understanding of unchanging human nature, Wilson opposed the historical argument that the ends, scope, and role of just government must be defined by the different principles of different epochs and that, therefore, it is impossible to speak of a single form of just government for all ages. This was a self-conscious reinterpretation, as Wilson even suggested that the Declaration ought to be understood by excluding from it the foundational statements on equality and natural rights contained in the first two paragraphs. In a 1911 address, Wilson remarked that "the rhetorical introduction of the Declaration of Independence is the least part of it. . . . If you want to understand the real Declaration of Independence, do not repeat the preface."[2] It was this assertion of historical contingency over the permanent principles of American constitutionalism that animated the main tenets of Wilson's political thought.

Briefly put, those tenets rest on a coupling of historical contingency with a faith in progress. Wilson believed that the human condition improves as history marches forward, and so protections built into government against the danger of problems such as faction became less necessary and increasingly unjust. Ultimately, the problem of faction is solved not by permanently limited government but by history itself. History brings a unity of sentiment and fundamental will to the nation. Whereas *The Federalist* asserts that a diversity of interest will always underlie the extended republic, Wilson contended that history would overcome such particularism with an increasing unity of mind; therefore, the latent causes of faction are not sown in the nature of man, or if they are, this aspect of human nature can be overcome by historical progress. With the unity of national sentiment, political questions will become less contentious and less important. We will cease to concentrate on the question of what should be done and more on the question of how we should do it. This is the principle behind Wilson's suggestion that the modern age is one of administration, where we seek to find the specific means to achieve the ends that we all agree we want. Government in such an age of unity will not be a threat to the individual that has to be checked; rather, the state ought to be an organ of the individuals in society, "beneficent and indispensable,"[3] as Wilson put it. The distinction and tension between the individual and government, a primary feature of early liberalism to which the American founders at least partly subscribed, have been made largely extinct by the progress of history. Instead, the state should become one with the unified will of the people; it must become the organic manifestation of their spirit. The state must therefore be unfettered so that it can implement the will of the people. It makes no sense, Wilson wrote, to limit government in an effort to protect the people from the very manifestation of their own organic will. This need to unfetter the state so that its scope can become whatever the current historical spirit demands means undoing the various institutional limits that early American constitutionalism placed on state power. The state must move beyond the narrow and outdated role assigned to it by the founding generation and must instead take on an institutional form more appropriate to its new mission. Many of the essays collected in this volume form an important part of Wilson's vision for effecting such a change.

WILSON'S HISTORICISM AND ORGANIC CONCEPT OF THE STATE

Perhaps the most obvious influence on Wilson, especially if one pays particular attention to his early writings, is Edmund Burke. On one level, much of Wilson's basic approach to political questions seems a Burkean reaction against social contract theory and the importation of such transhistorical theory into politics. Examination of the corpus of his work shows that Wilson takes this general Burkean inclination in several important directions. Institutionally, Wilson had a strong admiration for the British parliamentary model of government, whose gradual development from a long historical tradition had a significant influence on his view of American constitutionalism. A second important direction was Wilson's Darwinism. While Charles Darwin (through Herbert Spencer) was probably even more influential on several of Wilson's contemporaries, Wilson certainly did sound Darwinian themes in his call for a constant adaptation of politics to the changing historical environment and a reinterpretation of the Constitution according to the "Darwinian principle."[4] Yet the third, and by far most important, direction in which Wilson's thought developed was in its adoption of Hegelianism. Wilson's graduate education at Johns Hopkins seems to have been a decisive influence in this regard, although one can certainly see historicist themes in his earliest writings as well, especially those on religion. Even more than Burke or Darwin, Wilson's thought owes a substantial intellectual debt to G. W. F. Hegel, especially when one considers the historicism and organic-state theory that serve as the backbone for Wilson's political arguments.

Wilson cited Hegel directly in his discussion of the role of philosophy, or abstract thought, in politics. Politics, Wilson contended, is not grounded in anything that transcends the particulars of any given historical epoch. The political principles of any age are instead reflections of its corresponding historical spirit. Wilson explained that "the philosophy of any time is, as Hegel says, 'nothing but the spirit of that time expressed in abstract thought.'"[5] In his textbook on government, *The State*, Wilson developed this reasoning into a comprehensive theory of fundamental political principles.

Wilson began his discussion of the role of government by contending that government cannot be discussed properly by asking what its functions "ought" to be. Such a question would ground government in mere opinion, whereas "sound reasoning concerning government . . . is at all points based upon experience rather than upon theory. . . . What government does must arise from what government is: and what government is must determine what government ought to do."[6] All thought, Wilson explained, is contingent on its historical environment. This contingency means that one cannot talk about different societies in terms of just versus unjust, which would require some abstract principle to serve as the standard for such a judgment. Rather, Wilson discussed various societies in terms of their being more or less historically advanced. In commenting on our progress from the earliest forms of government, Wilson explained that the difference between societies is that some have remained mired in a primitive stage, while others have escaped from such "tutelage of inexorable custom" to adopt the more historically advanced principles of modern times. In fact, Wilson observed, modern practices are usually more advanced than modern political ideas; our principles of government, therefore, need to catch up with historical reality—our political "oughts" need to take their bearing from what actually is.[7]

In order to understand modern government, Wilson rejected looking to some abstract notion of justice and instead examined in detail what government actually had been and how it had evolved. Mirroring Hegel's method in *The Philosophy of History*, Wilson sought to explicate the principles of modern politics by looking at what history has actually given us in the modern state and how such a state came to be. The state is an organic entity, Wilson asserted; it can grow, and it can travel. The earliest form of the state was the primitive family or tribe, which was nomadic. This early society traveled and grew, adapting to new environments and making whatever adjustments were necessary in order to survive. The various major races of the world were "progressive" in this way, and government had its historical foundation in the progress of these races.[8]

Wilson's understanding of the manner in which progress was achieved in human history also mirrored Hegel's argument, insofar as advances were made through a dialectical process. Historical progress came through clashes between opposing customs. Tribes or peoples might develop attachments to different opinions or customs, and the antagonism and ultimate conflict between the competitors gave rise to something more advanced. In order to move history forward, major conflicts were necessary; since custom was normally a matter of religious faith, fighting between competing customs or faiths was frequently severe. The result of this dialectical process is always progress because history only goes in one direction. "Of course," Wilson explained, "in such a competition the better custom would prevail over the worse."[9]

Wilson's assertion that human progress comes at least partly out of a conflict between antagonistic customs also helps us to understand an important problem in politics. Given the origin of government in the family or tribe and one's strong religious attachment to the conventions of one's own tribe, it ought to come as no surprise that we tend to have undue attachments to outdated or historically inferior principles. This observation is integral to Wilson's argument regarding the principles of the American founding. While our undue reverence for the past is not as severe as that of many more ancient societies, Wilson contended that "we have ourselves in a measure canonized our own forefathers of the revolutionary era, worshipping them around fourth of July altars."[10] Such faith-based attachment to the principles of our past presents a problem insofar as it makes it more difficult for us to modify those principles in accordance with the circumstances of the present age.

The Social Contract

Wilson contended that the American attachment to the historically inferior principles of social contract theory presented a serious obstacle to progress. He offered his historical views on American principles as "destructive dissolvents" to the social contract theory of thinkers such as Richard Hooker and John Locke that so influenced the early Americans.[11] While social contract theorists looked to an abstract account of human nature in order to frame the purpose and scope of civil government, Wilson countered that the foundation of government can be uncovered only by looking to the actual history of its development rather than by conjecture or theory. He admitted that our historical knowledge of society's actual beginnings may be limited, but even limited historical knowledge is far superior to "a priori speculations" about the origin of government. Social contract theory rests upon a universal account of human nature, one that can be brought into any particular historical environment as a standard for just government. Yet Wilson reasoned that looking at our contemporary human nature tells us nothing about human nature in past ages, which is why he contended that any theory of government "founded upon our acquaintance with our modern selves" cannot be universal.[12] Social contract theory is best understood as a product of the particular age in which the social contract philosophers promulgated it. The mistake of the social contract theorists, much like the mistake of the American founders, was not in establishing certain principles of government for their own age but in thinking that such historically contingent principles could in fact transcend history and define just government for all ages.

So, Wilson turned away from conjecture about a state of nature and looked instead to history for his understanding of government. *The State* consequently begins with a discussion of the patriarchal family, which Wilson identified as the true original condition of man. In such a condition, there is no concept of individualism. "All that [the individual family members] possess, their lives even and the lives of those dependent upon them, are at the disposal of [the] absolute father-sovereign." Wilson contrasted this factual beginning of society with the radical autonomy posited by social contract theory and concluded that the state-of-nature concept had led to an unfounded emphasis on the individual. The modern state originated in the historical structure of the family, Wilson argued, and is, therefore, a cohesive and fundamental political unit in its own right. The historical reality of the state's origins undermines the claim of "Locke and Locke's co-theorists" and shows how the individual was really an indistinguishable part of a larger community. Even as society developed in history, Wilson claimed, "it grew without any change of this idea."[13]

Democracy Ancient and Modern

Wilson's rejection of social contract theory and the state-of-nature concept on which it is based does not mean that he embraced a return to the ancient political theory that social contract theorists sought to replace. Even though Wilson's grounding of society in the family or tribe echoes certain Aristotelian themes, Wilson was just as critical of ancient thought as he was of early modern thought. Of the latter, he remarked that the "theory simply has no historical foundation"; the former, he wrote, "exaggerates the part played by human choice."[14] Here, Wilson referred to the ancient account of the origin of regimes, an account that emphasized the statesmanship of the lawgiver as fundamental. He explained that the ancient idea of social organization relies too heavily on the exercise of prudence by certain great individuals or on the ability of human choice to affect historical events. Human thought and action are conditioned by their historical environment, and the ancient notion of statesmanship makes the mistake of assuming that great individuals can transcend that environment. Contrary to the ancient notion of prudence, a statesman does not take some abstract principle of justice and apply it as best he can in a particular historical situation; rather, the historical situation itself gives rise to its own principles.

Wilson was also critical of the Aristotelian cycle of regimes, and he wished "to contrast the later facts of political development with this ancient exposition." While the Aristotelian cycle had suggested, according to Wilson, a continuous model of regime change based upon both chance events and the prudent (or imprudent) choices made by individuals, Wilson argued that history, in fact, leads to the permanent victory of modern democratic government. "Democracy seems about universally to prevail," Wilson contended, because the democratic form of government is most consistent with the spirit of modern times. The idea of democracy has triumphed, which is the reason that modern democracy, unlike earlier forms of democracy, is permanent. Wilson wrote that "the cardinal difference between all the ancient forms of government and all the modern" is that "the *democratic idea* has penetrated more or less deeply all the advanced systems of government."[15] In this respect, the earlier, American founding–era liberalism had an important role to play. While founding-era liberalism was imperfect because it emphasized the permanent status of the individual, its victory was an essential step in the eventual triumph of modern democracy. Modern democracy came to fruition through a dialectical process: earlier, more primitive forms of self-government had to rise up and subsequently be overcome in order for history to bear its final fruit. Such reasoning also led Wilson to praise feudalism, not because there was anything inherently good about it but because of its historical utility: "Such a system was . . . fatal to peace and good government, but it cleared the way for the rise of the modern State by utterly destroying the old conception of the State." The founding-era notion of the primacy of individual rights, where the state exists for the individual, was, in turn, an "inevitable" reaction against feudalism and earlier forms of statism. That modern democracy has triumphed over its earlier forms "is thus no accident, but the outcome of great permanent causes."[16]

As Wilson explained in "The Modern Democratic State," the history of the state's development culminates in modern democracy—there is no more advanced form of government. "Democracy is the fullest form of state life: it is the completest possible realization of corporate, cooperate state life for a whole people."[17] This is where, it seems, Wilson's Hegelianism won out over his Darwinism. Instead of an endless adaptation to essentially random changes in environment, Wilson consistently referred to democracy as the intended result of history, the final stage of historical progress. "Democracy is poison to the infant," Wilson wrote, "but tonic to the man." It "is a form of state life which is possible for a nation only in the adult stage of its political development." The idea that democracy is the permanent end of history is an important component of Wilson's rejection of the Aristotelian cycle. When history brings about conditions whereby people act as a whole with a unified will, true democracy has arrived for good. "The cycle of Aristotle," Wilson concluded, "is impossible. For this democracy—this modern democracy—is not the rule of the many, but the rule of the *whole*." The unity of will in modern democracy shows that society has put behind it the Aristotelian problem of the many ruling only for their own interest at the expense of the few. In modern democracy, Wilson explained, "childish fears have been outgrown." The Aristotelian cycle, like all theories of government, was a reflection of, and therefore contingent upon, the historical realities of its own epoch. Aristotle had erected a "philosophy of politics upon generalizations rooted in the changeful fortunes of Hellenic states the old world over." But modern democracy is different; many political thinkers fail to grasp the distinction because they fail to take into account the different historical spirit of contemporary self-government. So, while the history of the twentieth century, after Wilson, might be cause for reevaluation, Wilson contended that modern democracy will not degenerate into tyranny, even though "many theoretical politicians the world over confidently expect modern democracies to throw themselves at the feet of some Caesar."[18]

Unity and the Modern State

It is the unity of the modern democratic state that makes it permanent. Wilson argued that the dialectical process of the state's development, having progressed beyond the "disintegration of feudalism," has led to a unity of will that underlies modern democracy. Wilson characterized modern society as "the Whole," which "has become self-conscious, and by becoming self-directive has set out upon a new course of development."[19] The "common will" underlying modern democratic government distinguishes it from ancient democracy, when the spirit of the times was not ripe for genuine democratic institutions. The real authority behind any government, Wilson explained, is the common will or spirit of the society. Even the despotic governments of past ages can be said to have been based upon the common will of society, insofar as one understands the common will as an implicit expression of the spirit of the age. Wilson also applied this notion of implicit will to the American founding: The founding generation was under the impression that it had consciously chosen its form of government, when in fact the choice had been the consequence of the spirit of the founding era. Wilson conceded that some genuine choice may have been exercised over minor issues— "modifications" on questions of detail—but in general the founders' so-called choice reflected the spirit of the founding epoch.[20]

Wilson explained that government is merely the instrument of society's common will. The will of society evolves in accord with history, and government serves as the "means" by which society implements its organic will in a given era. It is improper to characterize government, therefore, as a necessary evil that poses a potential threat to society. Wilson asserted that government "is no more an evil than is society itself. It is the organic body of society: without it society would be hardly more than a mere abstraction." Government represents the implicit will of society, and it ties the individual to society by using its power to bring individual self-development in line with societal self-development. Government is the means by which "individual self-development may be made at once to serve and to supplement social development." Wilson even conceded his admiration for certain aspects of socialist government, which aims "to bring the individual with his special interests, personal to himself, into complete harmony with society with its general interests." Expressing both Rousseauan and Hegelian themes, Wilson explained that such a harmony between the subjective and the general represents a "revolt from selfish, misguided individualism." The socialists were right, Wilson contended, to criticize the modern industrial organization, which had "magnified that self-interest which is grasping selfishness." The distinction that Wilson made between his own and socialist thought was that the socialists attacked all competition as inevitably leading to an escalation of selfishness, whereas he merely attacked "unfair competition." Wilson's goal was both to maintain individual self-development and to remedy the situation whereby individual self-development was encouraged at the expense of social development. History culminates in the unified will of modern society; government, therefore, must protect society "against the competition that kills" and must reduce "the antagonism between self-development and social development to a minimum."[21]

Individual Liberty and the Power of the State

Because the state is simply the instrument of society's will for development, Wilson wrote that it is both "beneficent" and "indispensable." Its regulatory power is not a potential threat to individual freedom because that power is the organ of society's own will. "If society itself be not an evil, neither surely is government an evil, for government is the indispensable organ of society."[22] As an indispensable and beneficent organ of society, Wilson contended that the state ought to enjoy a wide scope of power. Whereas early American constitutionalism conceived of nature as a consistent limit to state power, Wilson's state does not operate under any permanent limits to its authority. Rather, the state is simultaneously empowered and limited by the common will of society. The extent to which this common will endorses state power is contingent upon the particular stage of society's historical development. The founding generation's strict limits on state power were proper expressions of the spirit of the founding era. But contemporary state power, according to Wilson, needed to reflect the fact that the common will of society had evolved and that the country was operating within a more advanced historical spirit.

From Wilson's perspective, the founders' mistake was assuming that their principles of limited government, although appropriate for their own age, ought instead to serve as permanent limits to state authority in all ages. This mistake arose from the founders' reliance on ahistorical social contract theory for establishing the aims of government, which failed to ground state power in the actual history of its development. Consequently, Wilson reasoned, "government does not stop with the protection of life, liberty, and property, as some have supposed."[23] There is no permanent principle that mandates the protection of private property; it may be regulated by the state to varying degrees, depending upon the particular historical stage of development in which society finds itself. In principle, government ought to be given broad power over an array of issues: Wilson named trade, labor, corporations, public works, sanitation, education, and sumptuary laws, for example. The extent to which government actually does exercise power over such fields is to be determined by society's historically conditioned will. Even political liberties and privileges, Wilson asserted, are not immune from the exercise of state power: if the will of the people in a particular age endorses state action, the call for such action trumps all other considerations. The fundamental point is that the scope of state power is not limited by abstract or transhistorical principles. In this way, Wilson explained, there is no essential difference between modern liberal societies and ancient despotisms: in each, government exercises the power that the spirit of the times allows. As had been the case in ancient societies, "*government does now whatever experience permits or the times demand*; and though it does not do exactly the same things it still does substantially the same kind of things that the ancient state did."[24]

The limits that America's written constitution places on the power and flexibility of the state merely reflect the principles of government particular to the founding epoch. In his later political writings, where he dealt more directly with American constitutional politics, Wilson employed his historical approach and placed the Constitution within a long pattern of historical development. "There was a time when America was blithe with self-confidence," he explained, but now "there are forces at work which she did not dream of in her hopeful youth."[25] The problem was that America had not changed its old forms, or "processes of popular government," and as a result the old constitutional order was standing in the way of progress. In *Constitutional Government*, Wilson urged that the U.S. Constitution must not be interpreted as a rigid set of rules and mechanical limitations on government. Rather, a genuine "constitutional government" is one "whose powers have been adapted to the interests of its people."[26] The interests of the people, as Wilson explained in *The State*, change and evolve as history moves forward, so genuine constitutional government, which is merely the organ of society's will, must adapt accordingly.

Wilson made his constitutional views part of his campaign rhetoric in 1912. In *The New Freedom*, an edited collection of his addresses on the campaign trail, an important theme is Wilson's contrasting of Newtonian and Darwinian understandings of the Constitution. He characterized the constitutionalism of the founders as Newtonian because they had understood a written constitution according to the rules of mechanical movement as placing strict, formulaic limits on the exercise of state power. The founders had constructed the government "with true scientific enthusiasm," and they were "scientists in their way," which was the "best way for their age"—not the best way for the modern age. As Wilson had argued in his earlier writings, a constitution is properly understood organically, not mechanically. The founders failed to perceive that "government is not a machine, but a living thing." It falls under the "theory of organic life. It is accountable to Darwin, not to Newton." Government, like any organism, is "modified by its environment." The old, rigid constitutional structure of limited government, therefore, must be discarded because "no living thing can have its organs offset against each other, as checks, and live." Wilson claimed that Progressives only wanted to "interpret the Constitution according to the Darwinian principle."[27]

In *Constitutional Government*, Wilson emphasized an important point that he had previously developed in *The State*: a significant obstacle to a Progressive constitutionalism comes from the political theory of the Declaration of Independence, which posits that the protection of individual rights, derived from the transhistorical "laws of nature and of nature's God," is the permanent responsibility of just government. The various institutional means devised by the founders to achieve these permanent ends, which constitute what Publius called the "great improvement" to the "science of politics," are also obstacles to progress, especially the separation of powers, bicameralism, and federalism. Whereas the founders had considered these institutional mechanisms to be improved means to attain the timeless ends or "excellencies of republican government," Wilson objected to the very notion of permanent goals for government.[28] This distinction comes across most clearly in Wilson's interpretation of the Declaration. Its meaning, he contended, is that while the idea of liberty is timeless, the ends of government may be changed. Of the Declaration, he wrote,

> We think of it as a highly theoretical document, but except for it assertion that all men are created equal it is not. It is intensely practical, even on the question of liberty. . . . It expressly leaves to each generation of men the determination of what they will do with their lives, *what they will prefer as the form and object of their liberty*, in what they will seek their happiness. . . . In brief, political liberty is the right of those who are governed to adjust the government to their own needs and interests.[29]

The form of liberty is left to the discretion of each generation. As he argued in *The State*, Wilson understood government as a mere instrument for the common will of society; since that common will evolves as history progresses, so, too, must the very nature and role of government.

SEPARATION OF POWERS AS AN OBSTACLE TO PROGRESS

If Wilson's primary critique of American constitutionalism was that it mistakenly aims at protecting individual liberty by restricting the power of government and, consequently, is both undemocratic and inefficient, then the primary institutional manifestation of this problem is the separation of powers. For Wilson, the separation of powers is the source of much of what is wrong with American government. As opposed to a democratic system, which would efficiently translate the current public mind into government action, the separation-of-powers system, as Wilson understood it, was designed to protect the people from themselves by throwing up as many obstacles as possible to the implementation of their will. Such a system only serves to impede genuine democracy, which Wilson wanted to restore by breaking down the walls between the branches, allowing them to work in close coordination for the purpose of constantly adjusting public policy to the current public mind. Wilson's animosity toward the separation of powers was at the heart of his various proposals for a cabinet or parliamentary form of government in the United States and for energetic popular leadership and broad administrative discretion. In general, he saw the separation of powers as fundamentally contrary to his understanding of government as a living, organic extension of the people's will.

Wilson argued that the separation-of-powers system is both inefficient and irresponsible. It is inefficient because it prevents government from solving the problems of modern life in a coordinated way; instead, the various organs of government are busy attacking and struggling against one another. Separation of powers is irresponsible because it makes implementing new public policy difficult, even when the new policy reflects a clear, new direction in public opinion. Unlike parliamentary government, where changes in public opinion can very quickly effect a change in government and a change in policy, the separation-of-powers system prevents just that kind of responsiveness. Wilson elaborated on the problem of irresponsibility in *Congressional Government*:

> It is . . . manifestly a radical defect in our federal system that it parcels out power and confuses responsibility as it does. The main purpose of the Convention of 1787 seems to have been to accomplish this grievous mistake. The "literary theory" of checks and balances is simply a consistent account of what our constitution-makers tried to do; and those checks and balances have proved mischievous just to the extent which they have succeeded in establishing themselves as realities. It is quite safe to say that were it possible to call together again the members of that wonderful Convention to view the work of their hands in the light of the century that has tested it, they would be the first to admit that the only fruit of dividing power had been to make it irresponsible.[30]

Wilson's criticism of the separation of powers from the perspective of responsibility goes back to his earliest political writings in the 1870s. Those writings consistently call for the institution in the United States of some form of cabinet government, where a national legislature is dependent upon majority public opinion, and the executive branch is dependent upon maintaining support in the legislature. The key feature of such a system is that there is no separation between the legislative and executive branches; in fact, the leaders of the legislative branch also serve in the cabinet as leaders of the executive branch. Wilson's writings make it clear that the only remedies to the problems of American government are "certainly none other than those which were rejected by the Constitutional Convention." The most obvious error of the convention was Article I, Section 6, of the Constitution, which prohibits members of Congress from serving simultaneously in the executive branch. In his essay "Cabinet Government in the United States," Wilson explicitly called for the repeal of this section of the Constitution.[31] In a note around this time, he decried "the folly of America in taking away from the national assembly the reverent custom of appointing the great officers of state!"[32] In his marginal notes to several papers in *The Federalist*, Wilson frequently wrote that the best solution to the various problems mentioned by Publius was cabinet government. In particular, in response to those papers in which Publius addresses the personal motivations of public officials, motivations rooted in the self-interest that is fundamental to human nature, Wilson commented that the proper motivations could be supplied by making public officials accountable to public opinion through a cabinet system of government.[33] For Wilson, openness and accountability through a cabinet system will check the potential self-interestedness of officeholders, whereas Publius suggests that channeling self-interest through a separation-of-powers system will lead to a situation where "the private interest of every individual may be a sentinel over the public rights."[34] For Wilson, such a system of ambition counteracting ambition will only prevent unity in government, and without unity, there could be no real coordination and no real leadership.[35]

For Wilson, continuing the separation-of-powers system in modern times is fundamentally wrong because that system is based upon the principles of "older liberalism." This "older liberalism" held that a division of power is necessary to keep the government from tyrannizing over the people. He identified the "theoretical basis" of the division as individualism versus state power, a basis that is no longer applicable in the modern epoch.[36] As Wilson explained in *The State,* the state is not a threat to the individual but is, instead, essential to proper individual self-development. The real marvel for Wilson was that the American system of government had survived at all under the separation of powers. He cited Walter Bagehot's observation that Americans must have an excellent capacity for self-government because it seems they can make any system work, even one as inefficient as the separation of powers. Wilson concurred but warned that even America would fail unless changes were made. And he pointed to the British constitution as a model, particularly because of its cabinet system of interbranch cooperation. During the American founding era, Wilson pointed out, the English constitution had not been in good shape. But unlike its American counterpart, there were no formal restrictions on its growth and development, and so, he saw contemporary English government as a model for modern democracy. As Wilson explained, if the English government "is now superior, it is so because its growth has not been hindered or destroyed by the too tight ligaments of a written fundamental law."[37]

Separating Politics and Administration

Based upon his general objection to the founders' understanding of government and his particular objection to the separation of powers, Wilson put forth a series of institutional proposals designed, in one way or another, to overcome the fixed notion of politics at the heart of limited government. Wilson's institutional substitute for the founders' separation of powers is best understood as the separation of politics and administration. The idea of separating politics and administration broadly defines the different institutional arrangements suggested by Wilson in his scholarship, although the specific institutional means for achieving this separation changed as his thought developed from his earlier to his more mature intellectual works.

For Wilson, the force of history had been bringing about a national unity of public will; the American nation had arrived at a point of fundamental agreement about politics or political justice, or was at least in the final stages of doing so. Consequently, the vital task of government had become administration, which is simply the determination of the specific governmental means needed to achieve the political ends that we all agree we want. The American founders believed that political discord would always remain at the heart of republican government, or that the "latent causes of faction are thus sown in the nature of man,"[38] which led them to limit government in order to guard against majority groups of citizens implementing their own passionate view of political justice at the expense of the rights of other citizens. Wilson's constitutionalism, in contrast, did not need to limit or check government in such a way because national political unity had been achieved.

It is at this point that Wilson's separation of politics and administration brings us to a fundamental paradox in his thought. In his vision of government, it seems that the unified will of the public has a much more direct role to play in politics than the founders had envisioned. Yet, politics, while increasingly democratized in Wilson's thought, also becomes much less authoritative. The emphasis in government shifts to administration. The key to Wilson's separation of politics and administration is to keep the former out of the latter's way. Administration is properly the province of scientific experts in the bureaucracy. The competence of the experts in the specific technological means required to achieve those ends on which we are all agreed gives them the authority to administer or regulate progress unhindered by those within the realm of politics. People or institutions within politics can claim no such expertise.

Wilson's understanding of politics and its separation from administration requires a transformation in the traditional American thinking on legislative and executive power. Wilson proposed such a transformation, which was to unfold according to his vision of arranging the "politics" half of the politics-administration dichotomy. His proposed transformation manifests itself in two distinct forms: the first is the product of Wilson's early political thought, in which he emphasized the importance of Congress and a cabinet form of government responsible to a legislative majority; in his later thought, Wilson became disillusioned with Congress and looked instead to popular leadership under a strong presidency as the key to transforming American institutions.

CONGRESS AS PARLIAMENT

As previously discussed, Wilson's admiration for the British parliamentary system is evident in a number of his writings. In *The State*, Wilson's argument focuses on the gradual development of British democracy and, based upon his reading of Burke, his strong preference for it over the revolutionary and abstract character of the French Revolution. But Wilson also admired the particular manner in which the British parliament conducted its business and the role that it played in the overall British constitutional order. His analysis of the character of parliament as an institution and of the many things that he believed American institutions could learn from it was influenced not only by Burke but also by a long study he made of Bagehot's writings. Wilson learned from Bagehot that parliament is an institution ideally suited for separating politics and administration. Under the parliamentary model, the legislature closely reflects public opinion, while a separate, permanent, apolitical bureaucracy manages the business of day-to-day governing. In Wilson's vision for Congress, expressed most famously in his book *Congressional Government*, the legislature is much more closely tied to public opinion; yet, most authority for the details of governing is shifted away from legislators and into the realm of bureaucracy. The energy of this increasingly democratized Congress needs to be channeled into its "informing function," which Wilson contended is to "be preferred even to its legislative function."[39] Through debate much more open to the public eye, Congress must become more dependent on the will of the people; yet, that public will is really to have no more say over actual governing, since Congress itself is urged to cede much of its responsibility for detailed policy making to professional, unelected administrators.

Wilson also looked for Congress to provide political leadership. Congress was supreme in the American political order; yet, Wilson lamented, there was no real leadership in Congress. There was, therefore, no real leadership of the nation itself. Wilson was particularly critical of the internal organization of the House of Representatives, which he believed served to confound control of the chamber by majority opinion. In his view, the House's structure prevents members from acting upon the policy preferences of their constituents. Wilson championed the plight of new members of the House, whose efforts to seek open debate and consideration of their legislative proposals constantly run afoul of the complicated rules, hierarchy, and standing committee system.[40] The complicated organization of the House inhibits the tight connection that it ought to have with public opinion. The public has little or no understanding of how the institution works. As

Wilson explained, "It is too complex to be understood without an effort. . . . Consequently, very few people do understand it, and its doors are practically shut against the comprehension of the public at large."[41]

Wilson singled out the system of standing committees for special criticism as the primary impediment to accountability. The committee system hides legislation and keeps deliberation out of the public eye, making the members more detached from those whom they represent. The part of the deliberative process that the public can see—the floor debates and voting—is little more than a rubber stamp for the real decision making that has already taken place behind closed doors in committee sessions. Wilson complained that Congress "legislates in committee-rooms; not by the determinations of majorities, but by the resolutions of specially-commissioned minorities; so that it is not far from the truth to say that Congress in session is Congress on public exhibition, whilst Congress in its committee-rooms is Congress at work."[42] Wilson's account of the new member's rude introduction to the committee system is ominous:

> If [the new member] supposes, as he naturally will, that after his bill has been sent up to be read by the clerk he may say a few words in its behalf, and in that belief sets upon his long-considered remarks, he will be knocked down by the rules. . . . The rap of Mr. Speaker's gavel is sharp, immediate, and peremptory. He is curtly informed that no debate is in order; the bill can only be referred to the appropriate Committee. This is, indeed, disheartening; it is his first lesson in committee government, and the master's rod smarts.[43]

The effect of the committee system is that legislation is the product of just a few individuals. These individuals are not powerful because they enjoy public support for their views but because they are successful at brokering power behind the scenes in the standing committees.

Why does Congress operate in such a disorganized, secretive manner? Congress (especially the House), Wilson reasoned, is merely the collection of the narrow, competing interests that Publius contemplates in *Federalist* 10. It is not, Wilson concluded, representative of the broad national will. Even on those rare occasions when Congress does ask for public input, it seeks out only the views of wealthy special interests. Wilson used the example of railroad legislation, in which only railroad executives were invited to testify on the issue of rate regulation.[44] The secretive structure of Congress is therefore also corrupt and must be altered in order to effect an "elevation of public opinion." Instead of being dominated by the hidden influence of special interests, Congress needs to encourage a "public discussion" of the important issues.[45]

In order to achieve a closer connection between public discussion and public policy, Wilson advocated a legislature with a much stronger, but more accountable, party system. Parties in the legislature should be clearly organized under leaders who are easily recognized. In this way, voters can, through their electoral support or rejection of these prominent party leaders and their parties, make known their views on policy matters and bring them to bear in the lawmaking process. Congress will also be wary under such a system. Members will know that they act under the restraint of immediate accountability. They will not feel that they can legislate according to their own subjective will.[46] Wilson hoped that this new party structure would supply Congress with the unity and coordination that it sorely lacked. Without a unified and responsible Congress, Wilson reasoned, there can be no effective representation of the unified national will. There is no greater example of this problem, according to Wilson, than the role of the Speaker of the House. The Speaker is really the only identifiable legislative leader, but he is not accountable to the nation or to any unified public voice. Instead, the Speaker is a mere power broker whose power is limited by that of the standing committees and their chairmen.[47] Congressional leaders like the Speaker should be those most visible to the people and most accountable to them. Congressional leaders ought to be national party leaders, and in turn, these congressional and party leaders ought also to constitute the president's cabinet. In this way, Wilson's aim of breaking down the separation of powers could be realized and the old system replaced by direct coordination between the legislative and executive branches.

PRESIDENTIAL LEADERSHIP

As Wilson's thought matured, he became more convinced that Congress would never be able to fulfill the new institutional role that he was contemplating for it. The impediments to national leadership in Congress, which Wilson had noted in his early writings, later convinced him that Congress would never sufficiently embody the unity of national will needed to lead the politics side of the politics-administration dichotomy. This realization led Wilson to expound a second and somewhat different form of institutional political science, one that emphasized the popular leadership of the president. Strong presidential leadership did not represent, however, a fundamental change in Wilson's understanding of the ends of constitutional government. Rather, the shift to the presidency signaled a discovery of new institutional means to bring politics into a more direct connection with majority opinion. Wilson wrote that "the House seems to have missed . . . the right to be [the nation's] principal spokesman in affairs." Because the House "has greatly weakened itself as an organ of public opinion," the president's connection to the people must be developed and strengthened.[48]

As had his arguments concerning Congress, Wilson's new institutional vision for the presidency required the president to look beyond his constitutionally defined powers and duties. Instead, Wilson urged that the president should concentrate on his role as the embodiment of the nation's popular will, the role Wilson had initially envisioned for Congress. In modern times, it is more important for the president to be leader of the whole nation than it is for him to be the chief officer of the executive branch. Wilson contrasted the president's duties as "legal executive" with his "political powers," advocating an emphasis on the latter as a means of using popular opinion to transcend the rigid separation-of-powers structure of the old "Newtonian" constitutional framework.[49] As opposed to remaining confined to the constitutionally defined powers and duties of his own branch, the president's role as popular leader means that he must, as the embodiment of the national will, move Congress and the other parts of government to act in a coordinated way.

The president's new role in Wilson's institutional plan is based upon the president's connection to public opinion. It is the duty of each president to adapt himself to the needs and interests of the day. This is why Wilson remarked that each presidency in American history had been unique. Each presidency represents a different stage in the evolution of the American political order. Wilson said that "both men and circumstances" created the unique characteristics of each presidency.[50] The president is uniquely situated to adapt himself to changes in the public mood (something Congress ultimately could not do because of its secrecy and disorganization) because he is the only official with a true national mandate through a nationwide election. Just as Wilson had praised the British parliament for its connection to popular majorities, he said that the president "is at once the choice of the party and of the nation." The president "is the only party nominee for whom the whole nation votes. . . . No one else represents the people as a whole, exercising a national choice." The president is the "spokesman for the real sentiment and purpose of the country."[51]

Wilson emphasized the person of the president, not his office: it is the man himself and his personality that come to embody the national will. "Governments are what the politicians make them," Wilson wrote, "and it is easier to write of the President than of the presidency."[52] This is why a president's expertise in public affairs is not as important as his having a forceful personality and other qualities of popular leadership. Wilson wrote that America needs "a man who will be and who will seem to the country in some sort an embodiment of the character and purpose it wishes its government to have—a man who understands his own day and the needs of the country."[53]

As an embodiment of the public will, the president can transcend the government and coordinate its activities. Wilson defined a constitutional government as one that can adapt itself to the changing interests of its people, and this adaptation can best be accomplished through the coordination provided by the president's leadership. Congress could not lead the whole of government because it had become too bogged down by competing narrow interests and by stubbornly confining itself to the details of legislating. Wilson explained that "there can be no successful government without leadership or without the intimate, almost instinctive, coordination of the organs of life and action."[54] This is why it is wrong to limit the president with the traditional checks of the Constitution. The president is "the unifying force in our complex system" and must not be relegated to managing only one branch of it.[55] Just as a parliament serves as the embodiment of the public will that guides the whole government, and just as Wilson had initially wanted the U.S. Congress to serve as the public's superintendent over the entire scope of political affairs, the president must lead America's politics in a direction that adapts itself to the changing sentiments and interests of the public mind.

If the president is to provide the kind of coordination and leadership that Wilson envisioned, if he is to overcome a rigid separation-of-powers structure that seeks to confine public officials to their respective branches, the president will need to employ some extraconstitutional tools. Wilson believed, therefore, a reinvigorated party system and an aggressive style of popular rhetoric to be the key means of national leadership.

The Party System as Leadership Tool

Wilson reasoned that the party system is essential to enabling the presidential leader to coordinate the whole of government and move it in a clear direction. Yet, for Wilson, a strong and responsible party system did not mean a reinvigoration of the manner in which parties had been strong in the nineteenth century. The nineteenth-century party system served to guard against the potential excesses of democracy. It maintained a distance between presidential candidates and the people, thus reducing the risk of demagoguery by discouraging candidates from resorting to the popular arts. By retaining significant control over the nomination process, party leaders constitute a powerful check on the presidency. For Wilson, to be sure, parties needed to be prominent, strong, and disciplined in the governing process—not as masters over the leader, however, but as his effective instruments, or tools, of leadership. Parties needed to serve the president, not the other way around.

The legal system of the founders had served to isolate the various officials of government in their respective departments, and so, Wilson reasoned, such a formal system could only have been "solidified and drawn" into a coherent whole "by the external authority of party."[56] Precisely because parties were outside the formal system of government, they were not affected by the forced fragmentation of the founders' constitutionalism. As Wilson wrote, "There must, therefore, be an exterior organization, voluntarily formed and independent of the law, whose object it shall be to bind [the branches] together in some sort of harmony and cooperation. That exterior organization is the political party."[57] Looking back upon American history in *Constitutional Government*, Wilson remarked that without parties, "it would hardly have been possible for the voters of the country to be united in truly national judgments upon national questions," and he commented that "it would be hard to exaggerate the importance of the nationalizing influence of our great political parties."[58] The division of authority between municipal, state, and federal levels, and the variety of elections required at each level, would make it impossible for the nation to come together as a whole without the unify-ing force of parties. Parties excel, Wilson explained, at a unified mastery of de-tail and personnel, or, as he described it, in "their control of the little tides that eventually flood the great channels of national action."[59] Because of their ability to overcome both federalism and separation of powers, Wilson advocated the in-volvement of strong and disciplined parties in governing. For this reason, unlike some other Progressives (Herbert Croly and Theodore Roosevelt, in particular), Wilson was not a proponent of removing local politics from the realm of parti-sanship or even national party affiliation.[60]

Yet, while Wilson wanted strong parties to play a prominent role in governing, his concept of presidential leadership led to an important paradox: parties were to be strong in governing but to play a much subordinated role in candidate selec-tion. The problem with parties, as Wilson saw it, was not their strength or the prominence of their role in governing; instead, it was that parties were not nearly responsible enough to the public will. The president as party leader would there-fore become critical, since he could use his position as the embodiment of popu-lar will to direct parties as instruments of his popular leadership. Wilson conse-quently criticized party machines and nominating conventions and advocated more strongly the use of the primary for candidate selection. This modification to the selection system (obviously more central to his theory than to his practice) was Wilson's way of bringing the two key elements of governing—the informal party system and the formal institutional system—together in a manner more re-sponsible to the public. America was unique, Wilson observed, in that the party system was a "distinct authority outside the formal government," leading to a uniquely American distinction between the "politician" (the party manager) and the "statesman" (the public official).[61] For Wilson, the next step for the party and selection system was to bring the politician and the statesman together into the single person of the leader. In this way, the corruption of unaccountable party managers could be eliminated and the strength and discipline of the party system put into the service of a responsible leader. The president, with his formal elec-toral connection to the national will, was the natural choice both to coordinate the government and to manage the party.

The problem such an arrangement raises is that the leader is expected to exert party discipline in governing, while the party itself has a much diminished con-trol over candidate selection. One could argue that the twentieth century wit-nessed an erosion of the party strength that Wilson seems to have admired at least in part because parties lost any real control over the candidate-selection process. This perhaps explains why Wilson emphasized the personal and charismatic traits of the president as popular leader. And so, the second extraconstitutional tool of presidential leadership, aggressive popular rhetoric, was probably the more im-portant means by which Wilson believed national leaders could coordinate and move the political apparatus.

Popular Rhetoric as Leadership Tool

In addition to a transformed party system, Wilson believed that the president could use popular rhetoric to achieve more direct contact with public opinion and as a means of moving both the government and the people themselves in the direction that he believed history to be traveling. In this way, the democratic nature of rhetoric, Wilson believed, can also facilitate an elite form of political leadership.

Even though many of Wilson's political writings complain that the institutional scheme of the founders puts governing at too great a distance from public opinion, and even though Wilson's proposals for Congress and especially the presidency call for those institutions to come into much more direct contact with the public will, Wilson's actual argument on presidential power and rhetoric does not allow for as much popular control of governing as might first be believed. While the political institutions become democratized in a certain way, this democratization tends to put power in the hands of governing elites who have advanced knowledge of the spirit of the age and the course of history. Wilson's famous chapter on the presidency in *Constitutional Government* certainly emphasizes the president's connection to the people. Yet, Wilson's president seems to serve not merely (or even primarily) as a follower of the public's will but as its potential shaper and leader.

The ideal leader can take his own vision of society's direction and use popular rhetoric to draw the people to it and move them accordingly. It is for this very purpose that the democratic nature of Wilson's presidency is essential. A more democratized presidency is more amenable to the tools of popular rhetoric; it is one where the leader can use his mastery of popular rhetoric to mold public opinion. Wilson wrote that "a president whom [the country] trusts can not only lead it, but form it to his own views." Such a president leads by "giving direction to opinion."[62] As Wilson had explained in *The State*, government is the means by which society keeps up with the evolution of its own implicit will; government must adapt to the changes in public will brought about by the force of history. In his essay "Leaders of Men," Wilson suggested that a good leader is not so much concerned with simply figuring out what the public will is and using government to implement it. Rather, the leader is a particularly keen interpreter of the spirit of the times and may therefore know the direction in which history is pulling the public will better than the public itself.[63] The purpose of the leader's skillful popular rhetoric, at least partly, is to convince the public that he in fact has the most advanced vision of history's course and that his vision represents the future course of the people's own will. For Wilson, the presidency must be made more democratic precisely so that the president's rhetorical skill can be employed to move the masses more efficiently in the direction that the leaders believe history is traveling.[64]

Wilson's argument on elite leadership is also evident in his discussion of the proper historical conditions for genuine democracy. In "The Modern Democratic State," Wilson wrote that the improved education of modern times has brought about an essential condition for the advent of democracy, namely, an education where the elites are better equipped to lead and the people are better equipped to follow that elite leadership:

> Where all minds are awake some minds will be wide awake. And such are the conditions of common counsel: a few minds to originate and suggest, many minds to weigh and appreciate; some to draw up resolutions, many to consider them. . . . Not everybody can lead: but everybody can have a voice in deciding results.[65]

Universal education helps to make the people capable of considering leadership suggestions. But modern education not only aids in facilitating political leadership; it is also essential to developing an elite class of scientific experts who will serve as the nation's administrators. While political leaders are responsible for moving the public will in the direction of history, the educated administrative apparatus must manage the daily details of progress.

APOLITICAL ADMINISTRATION

Even in his earliest writings, Wilson sounded the call for a class of educated experts able to rise above the corruption and narrowness of politics. Wilson saw a political system mired in special-interest conflict, and he concluded that the country needed a young, apolitical class in order to right itself. Wilson wrote that "it would not be the part either of wisdom or of good will to encourage young men to do service in the partisan contentions of politics."[66] Instead, Wilson contended that this young, educated, apolitical class must focus its energies on "national administration." He elaborated,

> The greatest issue of the time seems an issue of life and death. If the national administration can be reformed it can endure; if it cannot be, it must end. Robust as its constitution has proved to be, the federal government cannot long continue to live in the poisonous atmosphere of fraud and malfeasance. If the civil service cannot by gentle means be purged of the vicious diseases which fifty years of the partisan spoils system have fixed upon it, heroic remedies must be resorted to.

The focus of the newly educated, nonpartisan class must be to bring "a new spirit," "not a new party," to "the present treatment and future settlement of this and others of the pressing questions of public administration." Wilson again expressed the theme that modern education is integral to training this new class of apolitical experts. In particular, the elite universities should take it as their primary mission to train those who will objectively administer the state. "An intelligent nation cannot be led or ruled save by thoroughly-trained and completely-educated men," Wilson explained. "Only comprehensive information and entire mastery of principles and details can qualify for command." Wilson trumpeted the power of expertise, of "special knowledge, and its importance to those who would lead."[67]

Expertise is necessary for national administration because, as Wilson argued in "The Study of Administration," the "business" of governing has become increasingly complex. The politics-administration dichotomy allows a professional class of experts, instead of a multiplicity of politicians with narrow, competing, and subjective interests, to handle this complex business of the modern state. Wilson praised the civil service movement because it sought to professionalize government, making it more efficient in terms of both personnel and organization. The new personnel would be more efficient administrators because they would be divorced from the realm of politics.[68]

The important point for Wilson is the idea that administrative principles and constitutional or political principles are quite distinct. Wilson referred to "the patriotism" and "the disinterested ambition" of the new professional class, which would enable it to adjust government objectively to the modern spirit. The attempt to bring administration within the constitutional order, to rest administrative authority on the more fundamental constitutional authority, posed a significant challenge to efficient adaptation. Wilson reasoned that understanding the clear distinction between politics and administration, or between constitutional law and regulation, "might deliver us from the too great detail of legislative enactment; give us administrative elasticity and discretion; free us from the idea that checks and balances are to be carried down through all stages of organization."[69]

Wilson relied heavily on European sources for his study of administration, precisely because his approach to administration was a novelty to American constitutionalism, especially the notion that there are legitimate state powers beyond those granted by the Constitution to the political branches of government. As he explained,

> The functions of government are in a very real sense independent of legislation, and even constitutions, because [they are] as old as government and inherent in its very nature. The bulk and complex minuteness of our positive law, which covers almost every case that can arise in Administration, obscures for us the fact that Administration cannot wait upon legislation, but must be given leave, or take it, to proceed without specific warrant in giving effect to the characteristic life of the State.[70]

Wilson suggested that the question of how far the law circumscribes the scope of administrative discretion was an unsettled question in America, and he urged that administration be properly understood and given as wide a sphere as possible. This wide sphere for administration means that it must cross over the traditional separation-of-powers boundaries; indeed, Wilson contrasted the theory of separation of powers to what he called the "actual division of powers," where there are many "legislative and judicial acts of the administration."[71]

The wide berth that Wilson wanted to give to administrative decision making helps to clarify who actually governs under Wilson's system. While Wilson advocated connecting politics much more directly with public opinion, his writings show that the public is not to be brought more directly into the realm of administrative decision making. "The problem," Wilson explained, "is to make public opinion efficient without suffering it to be meddlesome." Public opinion is a "clumsy nuisance" when it comes to the "oversight of the daily details and in the choice of the daily means of government." So, while public opinion ought to be brought more directly into politics, politics must confine itself to general superintendence, to the role of expressing the unified will of the nation. "Let administrative study," Wilson wrote, "find the best means for giving public criticism this control and for shutting it out from all other interference."[72]

Wilson placed administrative power on an entirely different plane from constitutional power, and it is this sharp distinction between constitutional politics and administrative discretion that differentiates Wilson from those earlier American thinkers who had also placed great importance on national administration, particularly Alexander Hamilton. While the connection between Hamilton's and Wilson's administrative thought is occasionally made, it is essential to remember that Wilson saw his argument on administration as something almost completely foreign precisely because the American tradition had failed to perceive the sharp contrast between constitutional and administrative power. Wilson explained that administration "stands apart even from the debatable ground for constitutional study. . . . Administrative questions are not political questions." This is why Wilson had to admit the difficulty of placing administrative discretion of the sort he had in mind within the traditional constitutional order: "One cannot easily make clear to every one just where administration resides in the various departments."[73] Indeed, Hamilton did write in *Federalist* 68 that "the true test of a good government is its aptitude and tendency to produce good administration," but he made this statement only after clarifying that it would be a "heresy" to agree with the poet who said, "For forms of government let fools contest—that which is best administered is best."[74] One cannot consider the quality of administration, in other words, as unaffected by regime type, and thus, Hamilton and Wilson really meant different things when they used the word "administration." Hamilton conceived of it as part of the republican executive, accountable to the reason of the people through the forms of the Constitution. Wilson made a great effort to explain that his vision of administration was much different because he believed that the quality of administration had been degraded by those (like Hamilton) who had conceived of it too narrowly, that is, within the confines of the constitutional executive. Wilson's entire claim to charting new territory in his famous "Study of Administration" rests on this difference in the traditional understanding of administration. The problem with the Hamiltonian understanding, from a Wilsonian perspective, is that it cannot conceive of administrative powers that are somehow bestowed upon the state outside of the formal granting of power to the political branches by the Constitution.

This contrast between Wilson's administrative thought and Hamilton's helps to clarify Wilson's political thought as a whole and is a useful way of concluding this brief introduction to it. The Progressives themselves, along with many who have written about the Progressive era, frequently use the terms "Hamiltonian" and "Jeffersonian" to distinguish between various elements of the movement. These terms can be of some use in understanding the different camps within the Progressive movement; yet, they can also be misleading. While Hamilton and Jefferson disagreed passionately about the means of government, they were much more akin to each other on the foundational principles of government than either of them is to Wilson. The Hamiltonian-Jeffersonian dichotomy poses the danger, therefore, of hiding the far more fundamental, principled difference between Wilson's Progressive liberalism, which is grounded in historicism, and founding-era liberalism, which is grounded in transhistorical natural-rights theory and of which Hamilton and Jefferson were both primary adherents. Wilson himself was quite conscious of this difference and put it at the heart of his most candid and important writings on the principles of government.

NOTES

1. The purpose of this introduction is to provide a brief overview of the main themes of Wilson's political thought. That such an endeavor will inevitably simplify the many complexities involved goes without saying; I would encourage readers interested in a more in-depth treatment of the issues raised here to see my book, *Woodrow Wilson and the Roots of Modern Liberalism* (Lanham, MD: Rowman & Littlefield, 2005), as well as the other treatments of Wilson's political thought listed in the selected bibliography to this collection. I also avoid citing in this introduction the various articles and books on Wilson's thought in the secondary literature since my aim here is to familiarize readers with the primary texts in Wilson's corpus. Several portions of this introduction are drawn from a modified version of my essay, "Woodrow Wilson, the Organic State, and American Republicanism," in *History of American Political Thought*, ed. Bryan-Paul Frost and Jeffrey Sikkenga, 549–68 (Lanham, MD: Lexington Books, 2003). To a lesser extent, I also rely upon portions of my book, mentioned above.

2. Woodrow Wilson, "An Address to the Jefferson Club in Los Angeles," May 12, 1911, in *The Papers of Woodrow Wilson* (hereafter cited as *PWW*), ed. Arthur S. Link (Princeton, NJ: Princeton University Press, 1966–1993), 23:33–34. Emphasis in all citations of Wilson will be in the original unless otherwise specified. I have, in all cases, provided citations to the standard sources. In those cases where the work cited is also excerpted in this collection, I direct readers to the appropriate page number from this collection, *Essential Political Writings*.

3. Wilson, *The State* (Boston: D.C. Heath, 1889), 658–59. See also *Essential Political Writings*, 62–63.

4. Wilson, *The New Freedom* (New York: Doubleday, Page & Company, 1913), 48. See also *Essential Political Writings*, 121.

5. Wilson, "The Study of Administration," November 1, 1886, in *PWW* 5:361. See also *Essential Political Writings*, 232.

6. *The State*, 637–38.

7. *The State*, 21. See also *Essential Political Writings*, 43.

8. *The State*, 9, 17. See also *Essential Political Writings*, 35–36, 41–42.

9. *The State*, 24–25. See also *Essential Political Writings*, 46.

10. *The State*, 19–20. See also *Essential Political Writings*, 43.

11. *The State*, 11. See also *Essential Political Writings*, 38.

12. *The State*, 1–2. See also *Essential Political Writings*, 31.

13. *The State*, 7, 17–18. See also *Essential Political Writings*, 35, 41.

14. *The State*, 13–14. See also *Essential Political Writings*, 40.

15. *The State*, 600, 603–5. See also *Essential Political Writings*, 54–55, 56, 58.

16. *The State*, 607–9. See also *Essential Political Writings*, 59–60.

17. Wilson, "The Modern Democratic State," December 1, 1885, in *PWW* 5:92.

18. "Modern Democratic State," in *PWW* 5:71–4, 76, 80–1.

19. *The State*, 609. See also *Essential Political Writings*, 61.

20. *The State*, 596–97. See also *Essential Political Writings*, 52.

21. *The State*, 658–61. See also *Essential Political Writings*, 63.

22. *The State*, 658–59. See also *Essential Political Writings*, 63.

23. *The State*, 647.

24. *The State*, 651–55.

25. *New Freedom*, 28. See also *Essential Political Writings*, 115.

26. Wilson, *Constitutional Government in the United States* (New York: Columbia University Press, 1911), 2.

27. *New Freedom*, 46–48. See also *Essential Political Writings*, 121.

28. Publius, *The Federalist Papers*, ed. Charles R. Kesler and Clinton Rossiter (New York: Mentor, 1999), 9:40–41.

29. *Constitutional Government*, 4. Emphasis added.

30. Wilson, *Congressional Government* (1885; repr., Gloucester, MA: Peter Smith, 1973), 187.

31. Wilson, "Cabinet Government in the United States," August 1879, in *PWW* 1:497. See also *Essential Political Writings*, 130–31.

32. Wilson, "Marginal Notes on John Richard Green," July 27, 1878, in *PWW* 1:387.

33. Wilson, "Marginal Notes on *The Federalist on the New Constitution*," February/March 1880, in *PWW* 1:598–601.

34. *Federalist*, 51:290.

35. Wilson, "Leaderless Government," August 5, 1897, in *PWW* 10:299.

36. Wilson, "Notes for Lectures at the Johns Hopkins," January 26, 1891, in *PWW* 7:134.

37. *Congressional Government*, 202–3. See also *Essential Political Writings*, 164.

38. *Federalist*, 10:47.

39. *Congressional Government*, 198. See also *Essential Political Writings*, 161.

40. *Congressional Government*, 60–61. See also *Essential Political Writings*, 142–43.

41. *Congressional Government*, 57. See also *Essential Political Writings*, 141.

42. *Congressional Government*, 69. See also *Essential Political Writings*, 149.

43. *Congressional Government*, 61–62. See also *Essential Political Writings*, 144.

44. *Congressional Government*, 72. See also *Essential Political Writings*, 151–52.

45. *Congressional Government*, 72–73. See also *Essential Political Writings*, 152.

46. *Congressional Government*, 79–80. See also *Essential Political Writings*, 156–57.

47. *Congressional Government*, 58. See also *Essential Political Writings*, 142.

48. *Constitutional Government*, 109.

49. *Constitutional Government*, 66–67. See also *Essential Political Writings*, 182.

50. *Constitutional Government*, 59. See also *Essential Political Writings*, 178.

51. *Constitutional Government*, 67–68. See also *Essential Political Writings*, 182–83.

52. *Constitutional Government*, 54. See also *Essential Political Writings*, 175.

53. *Constitutional Government*, 65. See also *Essential Political Writings*, 181.

54. *Constitutional Government*, 57. See also *Essential Political Writings*, 176–77.

55. *Constitutional Government*, 59–60. See also *Essential Political Writings*, 178.

56. *Constitutional Government*, 204. See also *Essential Political Writings*, 193.

57. *Constitutional Government*, 207. See also *Essential Political Writings*, 194–95.

58. *Constitutional Government*, 217. See also *Essential Political Writings*, 200.

59. *Constitutional Government*, 207. See also *Essential Political Writings*, 195.

60. See *Constitutional Government*, 209. See also *Essential Political Writings*, 195–96.

61. *Constitutional Government*, 212. See also *Essential Political Writings*, 197.

62. *Constitutional Government*, 66, 68. See also *Essential Political Writings*, 182–83.

63. Wilson, "Leaders of Men," June 17, 1890, in *PWW* 6:659. See also *Essential Political Writings*, 221–22.

64. "Leaders of Men," in *PWW* 6:649–50. See also *Essential Political Writings*, 213–14.

65. "Modern Democratic State," in *PWW* 5:91.

66. Wilson, "What Can Be Done for Constitutional Liberty," March 21, 1881, in *PWW* 2:33.

67. "What Can Be Done," in *PWW* 2:34–36.

68. "Study of Administration," in *PWW* 5:370. See also *Essential Political Writings*, 240.

69. "Notes for Lectures," in *PWW* 7:122.

70. "Notes for Lectures," in *PWW* 7:121.

71. "Notes for Lectures," in *PWW* 7:134–38.

72. "Study of Administration," in *PWW* 5:374–75. See also *Essential Political Writings*, 243.

73. "Study of Administration," in *PWW* 5:371. See also *Essential Political Writings*, 241.

74. *Federalist*, 68:382.

Part I
Progress and the Organic State

The State *

Chapters 1, 2, 13, and 16

CHAPTER 1. THE PROBABLE ORIGIN OF GOVERNMENT.

1. **Nature of the Question.**—The probable origin of government is a question of fact, to be settled, not by conjecture, but by history. Its answer is to be sought amidst such traces as remain to us of the history of primitive societies. Facts have come down to us from that early time in fragments, many of them having been revealed only by inference, and having been built together by the sagacious ingenuity of scholars much as complete skeletons have been reared by inspired naturalists in the light of the meagre suggestions of only a fossil joint or two. As those fragments of primitive animals have been kept for us sealed up in the earth's rocks, so fragments of primitive institutions have been preserved, embedded in the rocks of surviving law or custom, mixed up with the rubbish of accumulated tradition, crystallized in the organization of still savage tribes, or kept curiously in the museum of fact and rumor swept together by some ancient historian. Limited and perplexing as such means of reconstructing history may be, they repay patient comparison and analysis as richly as do the materials of the archæologist and the philologian. The facts as to the origin and early history of government are at least as available as the facts concerning the growth and kinship of languages or the genesis and development of the arts and sciences. At any rate, such light as we can get from the knowledge of the infancy of society thus meagerly afforded us is better than that which might be derived from any *a priori* speculations founded upon our acquaintance with our modern selves, or from any fancies, how learnedly

---

* Chapters excerpted from *The State* (Boston: D.C. Heath & Co., 1889), 1–16, 17–29, 593–609, 656–68. Where Wilson directs the reader to "sections" or "secs.," these are internal references to other parts of *The State*, unless stated otherwise. (Editor's note).

31

soever constructed, that we could weave as to the way in which history might plausibly be read backwards.

2. **Races to be studied: the Aryans.**—For purposes of widest comparison in tracing the development of government it would of course be desirable to include in a study of early society not only those Aryan and Semitic races which have played the chief parts in the history of the world, but also every primitive tribe, whether Hottentot or Iroquois, Finn or Turk, of whose institutions and development we know anything at all. Such a world-wide survey would be necessary to any induction which should claim to trace government in all its forms to a common archetype. But, practically, no such sweeping together of incongruous savage usage and tradition is needed to construct a safe text from which to study the governments that have grown and come to full flower in the political world to which we belong. In order to trace the lineage of the European and American governments which have constituted the order of social life for those stronger and nobler races which have made the most notable progress in civilization, it is essential to know the political history of the Greeks, the Latins, the Teutons, and the Celts principally, if not only, and the original political habits and ideas of the Aryan and Semitic races alone. The existing governments of Europe and America furnish the dominating types of to-day. To know other systems that are defeated or dead would aid only indirectly towards an understanding of those which are alive and triumphant, as the survived fittest.

3. **Semitic and Turanian Instance.**—Even Semitic institutions, indeed, must occupy only a secondary place in such inquiries. The main stocks of modern European forms of government are Aryan. The institutional history of Semitic or Turanian peoples is not so much part of the history of those governments as analogous to it in many of the earlier stages of development. Aryan, Semitic, and Turanian races alike seem to have passed at one period or another through similar forms of social organization. Each, consequently, furnishes illustrations in its history, and in those social customs and combinations which have most successfully survived the wreck of change, of probable early forms and possible successive stages of political life among the others. Aryan practice may often be freed from doubt by Semitic or Turanian instance; but it is Aryan practice we principally wish to know.

4. **Government rested First upon Kinship.**—What is known of the central nations of history clearly reveals the fact that social organization, and consequently government (which is the visible form of social organization), originated in *kinship*. The original bond of union and the original sanction for magisterial authority were one and the same thing, namely, real or feigned blood relationship. In other words, families were the primitive

states. The original State was a Family. Historically the State of to-day may be regarded as in an important sense only an enlarged Family: 'State' is 'Family' writ large.

5. **Early History of the Family; was it originally Patriarchal?**—The origin of government is, therefore, intimately connected with the early history of the family. But the conclusions to be drawn from what is known of the beginnings of the family unfortunately furnish matter for much modern difference of opinion. This difference of opinion may be definitely summed up in the two following contrasted views :—

(1) That the *patriarchal* family, to which the early history of the greater races runs back, and with which that history seems to begin, was the family in its original estate,—the original, the true archaic family.

The patriarchal family is that in which descent is traced to a common male ancestor, through a direct male line, and in which the authority of rule vests in the eldest living male ascendant.

(2) That the patriarchal family, which is acknowledged to be found in one stage or another of the development of almost every race, was a developed and comparatively late form of the family, and not its first form, having been evolved through various stages and varieties of polyandry (plurality of husbands) and of polygamy (plurality of wives) out of a possibly original state of promiscuity and utter confusion in the relations of the sexes and of consequent confusion in blood-relationship and in the government of offspring.

In brief, it is held on the one hand that the patriarchal family was the original family; and on the other, that it was not the original but a derived form, others of a less distinct organization preceding it.

6. **The Evidence: India.**—As has been intimated, the evidence upon which the first-named view is based is drawn chiefly from the history of what I have called the central races of the world,—those Aryan races, namely, which now dominate the continents of Europe and America, and which, besides fringing Africa with their intrusive settlements, have long since returned upon the East and reconquered much of their original home territory in Asia. In India the English have begun of late years to realize more fully than before that they are in the midst of fellow-Aryans whose stayed civilization and long-crystallized institutions have kept them back very near to their earliest social habits. In the caste system of India much of the most ancient law of the race, many of its most rudimentary conceptions of social relationships, have stuck fast, caught in a crust of immemorial observance. Many of the corners of India, besides, contain rude village-communities whose isolation, weakness, or inertia have delayed them still nearer the starting-point of social life. Among these belated Aryans all the plainer signs point to the patriarchal family as the family of their origin.

7. **Slavonic Communities, Ancient Irish Law, and Old Teutonic Customs.** — In Russia, in Dalmatia, and in Croatia there still survive Slavonic village-communities of a very primitive type which give equally unequivocal testimony of the patriarchal organization as the original order of their social life. Ancient Irish law says the same thing of the archaic forms of social organization among the Aryan Celts: that the patriarchal family was the first political unit of the race. And to these the antique Teutonic community, still to be seen through all the changes of history in England and on the continent, adds the testimony of many customs of land tenure and of communal solidarity founded upon a clear tradition of kinship derived from a common ancestor.

8. **Greek and Roman Families.** — Besides these comparatively modern evidences of survived law and custom, we have, as clearer evidence still, the undoubted social beginnings of Greek and Roman politics. They too originated, if history is to be taken at its most plainly written word, in the patriarchal family. Roman law, that prolific mother of modern legal idea and practice, has this descent from the time when the father of the family ruled as the king and high priest of his little state impressed upon every feature of it. Greek institutions speak hardly less distinctly of a similar descent. These great classic Aryan stocks, at any rate, cannot be conclusively shown to have known any earlier form of social practice than that of the patriarchal family.

9. **A Doubt.** — Still, even Aryan institutions bear some obscure traces — traces of a possible early confusion in blood-relationships — which suggest a polity not patriarchal; and those who regard the patriarchal family as a comparatively late development point to these traces with the suggestion that they are possibly significant of the universal applicability of their own view as to the archaic types of society. Even where such traces are most distinct, however, in legend and custom, they are by no means so distinct as to necessitate a doubt as to the substantial correctness of the patriarchal theory. They are all susceptible of explanations which would sustain, or at least not impair, that theory.

10. **The Non-Aryan Family.** — All the really substantial evidence of the absence from early society of anything like definite forms of the family, based upon clear kinship such as is presupposed in the patriarchal theory, is drawn from what, from our present point of view, we may call the outlying races, — the non-Aryan races. Many of these races have remained stationary, evidently for centuries, in what, comparing their condition with our own, we call a savage state, in which there is good reason to believe that very early systems of social order have been perpetuated. In such cases evidences abound of the reckoning of kinship through mothers only, as if in matter-of-course doubt as to paternity; of consanguinity signified throughout the wide circle of a tribe, not by real or supposed common descent from a human ancestor, but by

means of the fiction of common descent from some bird or beast, from which the tribe takes its name, as if for lack of any better means of determining common blood; of marriages of brothers with sisters, and of groups of men with groups of women, or of groups of men with some one woman. In the case of some of these tribes, moreover, among whom polygamy or even monogamy now exists, together with a patriarchal discipline, it is thought to be possible to trace clear indications of an evolution of these more civilized forms of family organization from earlier practices of loose multiple marriages or even still earlier promiscuity in the sexual relation.

It is thus that color of probability is given to the view that the patriarchal family, in these cases almost certainly, has in all cases possibly been developed from such originals.

11. **Aryan Tradition.**—These proofs, however, reach the Aryan races only by doubtful inference, through rare and obscure signs. No belief is more deeply fixed in the traditions of these stronger races than the belief of direct common descent, through males, from a common male ancestor, human or divine; and nothing could be more numerous or distinct than the traces inhering in the very heart of their polity of an original patriarchal organization of the family as the archetype of their political order.

12. **From the Patriarchal Family to the State.**—The patriarchal family being taken, then, as the original political unit of these races, we have a sufficiently clear picture of the infancy of government. First there is the family ruled by the father as king and priest. There is no majority for the sons so long as their father lives. They may marry and have children, but they can have no entirely separate and independent authority during their father's life save such as he suffers them to exercise. All that they possess, their lives even and the lives of those dependent upon them, are at the disposal of this absolute father-sovereign. The family broadens in time into the 'House,' the *gens*, and over this too the chiefest kinsman rules. There are common religious rites and observances which the *gens* regards as symbolic of its unity as a composite family; and heads of houses exercise high representative and probably certain imperative magisterial functions by virtue of their position. Houses at length unite into tribes; and the chieftain is still hedged about by the sanctity of common kinship with the tribesmen whom he rules. He is, in theory at least, the chief kinsman, the kinsman in authority. Finally, tribes unite, and the ancient state emerges, with its king, the father and priest of his people.

13. **Prepossessions to be put away.**—In looking back to these first stages of political development, it is necessary to put away from the mind certain prepossessions which are both proper and legitimate to modern conceptions of government, but which could have found no place in primitive thought on the

subject. It is not possible nowadays to understand the early history of institutions without thus first divesting the mind of many conceptions most natural and apparently most necessary to it. The centuries which separate us from the infancy of society separate us also, by the whole length of the history of human thought, from the ideas into which the fathers of the race were born; and nothing but a most credulous movement of the imagination can enable the student of to-day to throw himself back into those conceptions of social connection and authority in which government took its rise.

14. **The State and the Land.**—How is it possible, for instance, for the modern mind to conceive distinctly a *travelling* political organization, a state without territorial boundaries or the need of them, composed of persons, but associated with no fixed or certain habitat? And yet such were the early states,— nomadic groups, now and again hunting, fishing, or tending their herds by this or that particular river or upon this or that familiar mountain slope or inland seashore, but never regarding themselves or regarded by their neighbors as finally identified with any definite territory. Historians have pointed out the abundant evidences of these facts that are to be found in the history of Europe no further back than the fifth century of our own era. The Franks came pouring into the Roman empire just because they had had no idea theretofore of being confined to any particular Frank-*land*. They left no France behind them at the sources of the Rhine; and their kings quitted those earlier seats of their race, not as kings of France, but as kings of the Franks. There were kings of the Franks when the territory now called Germany, as well as that now known as France, was in the possession of that imperious race: and they became kings of France only when, some centuries later, they had settled down to the unaccustomed habit of confining themselves to a single land. Drawn by the processes of feudalization (secs. 243, 253, 268, 269), sovereignty then found at last a local habitation and a new name.

15. The same was true of the other Germanic nations. They also had chiefs who were *their* chiefs, not the chiefs of their lands. There were kings of the English for many a year, even for several centuries after A.D. 449, before there was such a thing as a king of England. John, indeed, was the first officially to assume the latter title. From the first, it is true, social organization has everywhere tended to connect itself more and more intimately with the land from which each social group has drawn its sustenance. When the migratory life was over, especially, and the settled occupations of agriculture had brought men to a stand upon the land which they were leaning to till, political life, like all the other communal activities, came to be associated more and more directly with the land on which each community lived. But such a connection between lordship and land was a slowly developed notion, not a notion twin-born with the notion of government.

16. Modern definitions of a state always limit sovereignty to some definite land. "The State," says Bluntschli, "is the politically organized people (*Volkperson*) *of a particular land*"; and all other authoritative writers similarly set distinct physical boundaries to the state. Such an idea would not have been intelligible to the first builders of government. They could not have understood why they might not move their whole people, 'bag and baggage,' to other lands, or why, for the matter of that, they might not keep them moving their tents and possession unrestingly from place to place in perpetual migration, without in the least disturbing the integrity or even the administration of their infant 'State.' Each organized group of men had other means of knowing their unity than mere neighborhood to one another; other means of distinguishing themselves from similar groups of men than distance or the intervention of mountain or stream. The original governments were knit together by bonds closer than those of geography, more real than the bonds of mere contiguity. They were bound together by real or assumed kinship. They had a corporate existence which they regarded as inhering in their blood and as expressed in all their daily relations with each other. They lived together because of these relations; they were not related because they lived together.

17. **Contract versus Status.**—Scarcely less necessary to modern thought than the idea of territoriality as connected with the existence of a state, is the idea of contract as determining the relations of individuals. And yet this idea, too, must be put away if we would understand primitive society. In that society men were *born* into the station and the part they were to have throughout life, as they still are among the peoples who preserve their earliest conceptions of social order. This is known as the law of *status*. It is not a matter of choice or of voluntary arrangement in what relations men shall stand towards each other as individuals. He who is born a slave, let him remain a slave; the artisan, an artisan; the priest, a priest,—is the command of the law of status. Excellency cannot avail to raise any man above his parentage; aptitude may operate only within the sphere of each man's birth-right. No man may lose 'caste' without losing respectability also and forfeiting the protection of the law. Or, to go back to a less developed society, no son, however gifted, may lawfully break away from the authority of his father, however cruel or incapable that father may be; or make any alliance which will in the least degree draw him away from the family alliance and duty into which he was born. There is no thought of contract. Every man's career is determined for him before his birth. His blood makes his life. To break away from one's birth station, under such a system, is to make breach not only of social, but also of religious duty, and to bring upon oneself the curses of men and gods. Primitive society rested, not upon contract, but upon status. Status had to be broken through by some conscious or unconscious revolution before so much as the idea of contract could arise; and when that idea did arise, change and variety

were assured. Change of the existing social order was the last thing of which the primitive state dreamed; and those races which allowed the rule of status to harden about their lives still stand where they stood a thousand years ago. "The leaving of men to have their careers determined by their efficiencies," says Mr. Spencer, "we may call the principle of change in social organization."

18. Theories concerning the Origin of the State: the Contract Theory.— Such views of primitive society furnish us with destructive dissolvents of certain theories once of almost universal vogue as to the origin of government. The most famous, and for our present purposes most important, of these theories is that which ascribes the origin of government to a 'social compact' among primitive men.

The most notable names connected with this theory as used to account for the existence of political society are the names of Hooker, Hobbes, Locke, and Rousseau. It is to be found developed in Hooker's *Ecclesiastical Polity*, Hobbes' *Leviathan*, Locke's *Civil Government*, and Rousseau's *The Social Contract*.

This theory begins always with the assumption that there exists, outside of and above the laws of men, a Law of Nature.[1] Hobbes conceived this Law to include "justice," "equity," "modesty," "mercy"; "in sum, 'doing to others as we would be done to.'" All its chief commentators considered it the abstract standard to which human law should conform. Into this Law primitive men were born. It was binding upon their individual consciences; but those consciences were overwhelmed by individual pride, ambition, desire, and passion, which were strong enough to abrogate Nature's Law. That Law, besides, did not bind men *together*. Its dictates, if obeyed, would indeed enable them to live tolerably with one another; but its dictates were not obeyed; and, even if they had been, would have furnished no permanent frame of civil government, inasmuch as it did not sanction magistracies, the setting of some men to be judges of the duty and conduct of other men, but left each conscience to command absolutely its possessor. In the language of the 'judicious Hooker,' the laws of Nature "do bind men absolutely, even as they are men, although they have never any settled fellowship, never any solemn agreement, amongst themselves what to do or not to do; but forasmuch as we are not by ourselves sufficient to furnish ourselves with competent store of things needful for such a life as our Nature doth desire, a life fit for the dignity of man, therefore to supply these defects and imperfections which are in us living single and solely by ourselves, we are naturally induced to seek communion and fellowship with others. This was the cause of men uniting themselves at first in politic societies."[2] In other words, the belligerent, non-social

---

[1] For the natural history of this conception of a Law of Nature, see [Henry Sumner] Maine, *Ancient Law*, Chap. III. Also *post*, secs. 208, 209.

[2] [Richard Hooker, *Of the Laws of*] *Ecclesiastical Polity*, Book I., sec. 10.

parts of man's nature were originally too strong for this Law of Nature, and the 'state of nature,' in which that Law, and only that Law, offered restraint to the selfish passions, became practically a *state of war*, and consequently intolerable. It was brought to an end in the only way in which such a condition of affairs could be brought to an end without mutual extermination, namely, by common consent, by men's "agreeing together mutually to enter into one community and make one body politic." (Locke.) This agreement meant submission to some one common authority, which should judge between man and man; the surrender on the part of each man of all rights antagonistic to the rights of others; forbearance and co-operation. Locke confidently affirmed "that all men are naturally in that state (a state, *i.e.*, of nature), and remain so till, by their own consents, they make themselves members of some politic society." It was only as the result of deliberate choice, in the presence of the possible alternative of continuing in this state of nature, that commonwealths, *i.e.*, regularly constituted governments, came into being.

19. **Traditions of an Original Law-giver.**—Ancient tradition had another way of accounting for the origin of laws and institutions. The thought of almost every nation of antiquity went back to some single law-giver in whose hands their government had taken its essential and characteristic form, if not its beginning. There was a Moses in the background of many a history besides that of the Jews. In the East there was Menu; Crete had her Minos; Athens her Solon; Sparta her Lycurgus; Rome her Numa; England her Alfred. These names do not indeed in every instance stand so far back as the beginning of all government; but they do carry the mind back in almost every case to the birth of *national* systems, and suggest the overshadowing influence of individual statesmen as the creative power in framing the greater combinations of politics. They bring the conception of conscious choice into the history of institutions. They look upon systems as *made*, rather than as developed.

20. **Theory of the Divine Origin of the State.**—Not altogether unlike these ancient conceptions of law-givers towering above other men in wisdom and authority, dominating political construction, and possibly inspired by divine suggestion, is that more modern idea which attributes human government to the immediate institution of God himself,—to the direct mandate of the Creator. This theory has taken either the definite form of regarding human rulers as the direct vicegerents of God, or the vague form of regarding government as in some way given man as part of his original make-up.

21. **The Theories and the Facts.**—Modern research into the early history of mankind has made it possible to reconstruct, in outline, much of the thought

and practice of primitive society, and has thus revealed facts which render it impossible for us to accept any of these views as adequately explaining what they pretend to explain. The defects of the social compact theory are too plain to need more than brief mention. That theory simply has no historical foundation. *Status* was the basis of primitive society: the individual counted for nothing; society—the family, the tribe—counted for everything. Government came, so to say, before the individual. There was, consequently, no place for contract, and yet this theory makes contract the first fact of social life. Such a contract as it imagines could not have stood unless supported by that reverence for 'law' which is an altogether modern principle of action. The times in which government originated knew absolutely nothing of law as we conceive law. The only bond was kinship,—the common blood of the community; the only individuality was the individuality of the community as a whole. Man was merged in society. Without kinship there was no duty and no union. It was not by compounding rights, but by assuming kinship, that groups widened into states—not by contract, but by adoption. Not deliberate and reasoned respect for law, but habitual and instinctive respect for authority, held men together; and authority did not rest upon mutual agreement, but upon mutual subordination.

22. Of the theories of the origination of government in individual law-giving or in divine dictate, it is sufficient to say that the one exaggerates the part played by human choice, and the other the part played by man's implanted instincts, in the formation and shaping of political society.

23. **The Truth in the Theories.**—Upon each of these theories, nevertheless, there evidently lies the shadow of a truth. Although government did not originate in a deliberate contract, and although no system of law or of social order was ever made 'out of hand' by any one man, government was not all a mere spontaneous growth. Deliberate choice has always played a part in its development. It was not, on the one hand, given to man ready-made by God, nor was it, on the other hand, a human contrivance. In its origin it was spontaneous, natural, twin-born with man and the family; Aristotle was simply stating a fact when he said, "Man is by nature a political animal." But, once having arisen, government was affected, and profoundly affected, by man's choice; only that choice entered, not to originate, but to modify government.

24. **Conclusion.**—Viewed in the light of "the observed and recorded experience of mankind," "the ground and origin of society is not a compact; that never existed in any known case, and never was a condition of obligation either in primitive or developed societies, either between subjects and sovereign, or between the equal members of a sovereign body. The true ground is the acceptance of conditions which came into existence by the sociability inherent

in man, and were developed by man's spontaneous search after convenience. The statement that while the constitution of man is the work of nature, that of the state is the work of art, is as misleading as the opposite statement that governments are not made, but grow. The truth lies between them, in such propositions as that institutions owe their existence and development to deliberate human effort, working in accordance with circumstances naturally fixed both in human character and in the external field of its activity."[3]

CHAPTER 2. THE PROBABLE EARLY DEVELOPMENT OF GOVERNMENT.

25. **The Beginnings of Government.**—Government must have had substantially the same early history amongst all progressive races. It must have begun in clearly defined family discipline. Such discipline would scarcely be possible among races in which consanguinity was subject to profound confusion and in which family discipline therefore had no clear basis of authority on which to rest. In every case, it would seem, the origination of what we would deem government must have awaited the development of some such definite family as that in which the father was known, and known as ruler. Whether or not, therefore, the patriarchal family was the first form of the family, it must have furnished the first adequate form of government.

26. **The Family the Primal Unit.**—The family, then, was the primal unit of political society, and the seed-bed of all larger growths of government. The individuals that were drawn together to constitute the earliest communities were not individual men, as Locke and Locke's co-theorists would lead us to believe, but individual families, and the organization of these families, whether singly or in groups, furnished the ideas in which political society took its root. We have already seen what the nature of that organization was. The members of each family were bound together by kinship. The father's authority bore the single sanction of his being the fountain-head of the common blood-relationship. No other bond was known, or was then conceivable, but this single bond of kinship. A man out of the circle of kinship was outside the boundaries of possible friendship, was as of course an alien and an enemy.

27. **Persistence of the Idea of Kinship.**—When society grew, it grew without any change of this idea. Kinship was still, actually or theoretically, its only amalgam. The commonwealth was conceived of as being only a larger kindred. When by natural increase a family multiplied its branches and widened into a *gens*, and there was no grandfather, great-grandfather, or other patriarch

---

[3] John Morley, *Rousseau* [(New York: Scribner, Armstrong, & Co., 1873)], vol. II, pp. 183–84.

living to keep it together in actual domestic oneness, it would still not separate. The extinct authority of the actual ancestor could be replaced by the less comprehensive but little less revered authority of some selected elder of the 'house,' the oldest living ascendant, or the most capable. Here would be the materials for a complete body politic held together by the old fibre of actual kinship.

28. **Fictitious Kinship: Adoption.**—Organization upon the basis of a fictitious kinship was hardly less naturally contrived in primitive society. There was the ready, and immemorial, fiction of *adoption*, which to the thought of that time seemed scarcely a fiction at all. The adopted man was no less real a member of the family than was he who was natural-born. His admittance to the sacred, the exclusive religious mysteries of the family, at which no stranger was ever suffered even to be present, and his acceptance of the family gods as his own gods, was not less efficacious in making him one with the household and the kin than if he had opened his veins to receive their blood. And so, too, houses could grow by the adoption of families, through the grafting of the alien branches into this same sacred stock of the esoteric religion of the kindred. Whether naturally, therefore, or thus artificially, houses widened into tribes, and tribes into commonwealths without loss of that kinship in the absence of which, to the thinking of early men, there could be no communion, and therefore no community, at all.

29. **Kinship and Religion.**—In this development kinship and religion operated as the two chief formative influences. Religion seems in most instances to have been at first only the expression of kinship. The central and most sacred worship of each group of men, whether family or tribe, was the worship of *ancestors*. At the family or communal altar the worshipper came into the presence of the shades of the great dead of his family or race. To them he did homage; from them he craved protection and guidance. The adopted man, therefore, received into this hallowed communion with the gods of the family, was accepting its fathers as his own, was taking upon himself the most solemn duties and acquiring the most sacred privileges of kinship. So, too, of the family adopted into the *gens*, or the *gens* received into the tribe. The new group accepted the ancestry by accepting the worship of the adopting house or community.

Religion was thus quite inseparably linked with kinship. It may be said to have been the thought of which kinship was the embodiment. It was the sign and seal of the common blood, the expression of its oneness, its sanctity, its obligations. He who had entered into the bonds of this religion had, therefore, entered into the heart of kinship and taken of its life-blood. His blood-relationship was thus rendered no fiction at all to the thought of that day, but a solemn verity, to which every religious ceremonial bore impressive witness.

30. **The Bonds of Religion and Precedent.**—The results of such a system of life and thought were most momentous. It is commonplace now to remark upon English regard for precedent, and upon the interesting development of 'common' and 'case' law. But not even an Englishman or an American can easily conceive of any such reverential regard for precedent as must have resulted from a canonization of ancestors. We have ourselves in a measure canonized our own forefathers of the revolutionary era, worshipping them around fourth of July altars, to the great benefit both of our patriotism and of our political morality. But the men of '76, we are all willing to acknowledge, were at their greatest only men. The ancestor of the primitive man became, on the contrary, a god, and a god of undying power. His spirit lived on to bless or to curse. His favor had to be propitiated, his anger appeased. And herein was a terribly effective sanction for precedent. It was no light matter to depart from the practices of these potent ancestors. To do so was to run in the face of the deities. It was to outrage all religious feeling, to break away from all the duties of spiritual kinship. Precedent was under such circumstances imperative. Precedent of course soon aggregated into custom,—such custom as it is now scarcely possible to conceive of,—a supreme, uniform, imperious, infrangible rule of life which brought within its inexorable commands every detail of daily conduct.

31. **The Reign of Custom.**—This reign of customary law was long and decisive. Its tendency was to stiffen social life into a formula. It left almost no room at all for the play of individuality. The family was a despotism, society a routine. There was for each man a rigorous drill of conformity to the custom of his tribe and house. Superstition strengthened every cord and knot of the network of observance which bound men to the practices of their fathers and their neighbors. That tyranny of social convention which men of independent or erratic impulse nowadays find so irksome—that 'tyranny of one's next door neighbor' against which there are now and again found men bold enough to rebel—had its ideal archetype in this rigid uniformity of custom which held ancient society in hard crystallization.

32. **Fixity of System the Rule, Change the Exception.**—Such was the discipline that moulded the infancy of political society: within the family, the supreme will of the father; outside the family, the changeless standards of public opinion. The tendency, of course, was for custom to become fixed in a crust too solid ever to be broken through. In the majority of cases, indeed, this tendency was fulfilled. Many races have never come out of this tutelage of inexorable custom. Many others have advanced only so far beyond it as those caste systems in which the law of *status* and the supremacy of immemorial custom have worked out their logical result in an unchanging balance of hereditary classes. The majority of mankind have remained stationary in

one or another of the earliest stages of political development, their laws now constituting as it were ancient records out of which the learned may rewrite the early history of those other races whom primitive custom did not stagnate, but whose systems both of government and of thought still retain many traces (illegible without illumination from the facts of modern savage life) of a similar infancy. Stagnation has been the rule, progress the exception. The greater part of the world illustrates in its laws and institutions what the rest of the world has escaped; this rest of the world illustrates what favorable change was capable of making out of the primitive practices with which the greater part of the world has remained *per force* content.

33. **Changes of System outrun Changes of Idea.**—The original likeness of the progressive races to those which have stood still is witnessed by that persistency of idea of which I have already spoken. Progress has brought nations out of the primitive practices vastly more rapidly than it has brought them out of the primitive ideas of political society. Practical reform has now and again attained a speed that has never been possible to thought. Instances of this truth so abound in the daily history of the most progressive nations of the world of to-day that it ought not to be difficult for us to realize its validity in the world of the first days of society. Our own guilds and unions and orders, merely voluntary and conventional organizations as they are, retain in their still vivid sense of the *brotherhood* of their members at least a reminiscence of the ideas of that early time when kinship was the only conceivable basis of association between man and man, when "each assemblage of men seems to have been conceived as a Family."[4] In England political change has made the great strides of the last two centuries without making the Crown any less the central object of the theoretical or lawyerly conception of the English constitution. Every day witnesses important extensions and even alterations of the law in our courts under the semblance of a simple application of old rules (secs. 201, 1187, 1188). Circumstances alter principles as well as cases; but it is only the cases which are supposed to be altered. The principles remain, in form, the same. Men still carry their brides on wedding journeys, although the necessity for doing so ceased with the practice, once universal, of stealing a bride. 'Good blood' still continues to work wonders, though achievement has come to be the only real patent of nobility in the modern world. In a thousand ways we are more advanced than we *think* we are.

34. **How did Change enter?**—The great question, then, is, How did change enter at all that great nursery of custom in which all nations once wore short clothes, and in which so many nations still occupy themselves with the superstitions and the small play of childhood? How did it come about

---

[4] [Henry Sumner] Maine, Early History of Institutions, p. 232.

that some men became progressive, while most did not? This is a question by no means easy to answer, but there are probabilities which may throw some light upon it.

35. **Differences of Custom.**—In the first place, it is not probable that all the groups of men in that early time had the same customs. Custom was doubtless as flexible and malleable in its infancy as it was inflexible and changeless in its old age. In proportion as group separated from group in the restless days of the nomadic life, custom would become differentiated from custom. Then, after first being the cause, isolation would become the natural result of differences of life and belief. A family or tribe which had taken itself apart and built up a practice and opinion peculiar to itself would thereby have made itself irrevocably a stranger to its one-time kinsmen of other tribes. When its life did touch their life, it would touch to clash, and not to harmonize or unite. There would be a Trojan war. The Greeks had themselves come from these very Ægean coasts of Asia Minor, and these Trojans were doubtless their forgotten and now alien kinsmen. Greeks, Romans, Celts, had probably once been a single people; but how unlike did they become!

36. **Antagonism between Customs.**—We need not specially spur our imaginations to realize how repugnant, how naturally antagonistic, to each other families or tribes or races would be rendered by differences of custom. "We all know that there is nothing that human beings (especially when in a low state of culture) are so little disposed to tolerate as divergencies of custom," says Mr. Hamerton, who is so sure of the fact that he does not stop to illustrate it. How 'odd,' if not 'ridiculous,' the ways of life and the forms of belief often seem to us in a foreign country,—how instinctively we pronounce them inferior to our own! The Chinaman manages his rice much more skilfully with his 'chop-sticks' than we manage ours with our forks; and yet how 'queer,' how 'absurd' chopsticks are! And so also in the weightier matters of social and religious practice.

37. **Competition of Customs.**—To the view of the primitive man all customs, great or small, were matters of religion. His whole life was an affair of religion. For every detail of conduct he was accountable to his gods and to the religious sentiment of his own people. To tolerate any practices different from those which were sanctioned by the immemorial usage of the tribe was to tolerate impiety. It was a matter of the deepest moment, therefore, with each tribal group to keep itself uncontaminated by alien custom, to stamp such custom out wherever or whenever it could be discovered. That was a time of war, and war meant a competition of customs. The conqueror crushed out the practices of the conquered and compelled them into conformity with his own.

38. **The Better prevail.**—Of course in such a competition the better custom would prevail over the worse.[5] The patriarchal family, with its strict discipline of the young men of the tribe, would unquestionably be "the best campaigning family,"—would supply the best internal organization for war. Hence, probably, the national aspect of the world to-day: peoples of patriarchal tradition occupying in unquestioned ascendency the choicest districts of the earth; all others thrust out into the heats or colds of the less-favored continents, or crowded into the forgotten corners and valley-closets of the world. So, too, with the more invigorating and sustaining religions. Those tribes which were least intimidated by petty phantoms of superstition, least hampered by the chains of empty but imperative religious ceremonial, by the engrossing observance of times and seasons, having greater confidence in their gods, would have greater confidence in themselves, would be freer to win fortune by their own hands, instead of passively seeking it in the signs of the heavens or in the aspects of nearer nature; and so would be the surer conquerors of the earth. Religion and the family organization were for these early groups of kindred men the two indexes of character. In them was contained inferiority or superiority. The most serviceable customs won the day.

39. **Isolation, Stagnation.**—Absolute isolation for any of these early groups would of course have meant stagnation; just as surely as contact with other groups meant war. The world, accordingly, abounds in stagnated nationalities; for it is full of instances of isolation. The great caste nations are examples. It is, of course, only by a figure of speech that we can speak of vast peoples like those of China and India as isolated, though it is scarcely a figure of speech to say that they are stagnated. Still in a very real sense even these populous nations were isolated. We may say, from what we discern of the movements of the nations from their original seats in Asia, that the races of China and India were the 'back-water' from the great streams of migration. Those great streams turned towards Europe and left these outlying waters to subside at their leisure. In subsiding there was no little commotion amongst them. There were doubtless as many inter-tribal wars in the early history of China before the amalgamation of the vast kingdom as there have been in the history of India. That same competition of custom with custom which took place elsewhere, also took place there. But the tribes which pressed into China were probably from the first much of a kind, with differing but not too widely contrasted customs which made it possible for them to assume at a now very remote period a uniformity of religion and of social organization never known amongst the peoples that had gone to the West; so that, before the history that the rest of the world remembers had begun, China's wall had

---

[5] For the best development of the whole idea of this paragraph and others in this connection, see [Walter] Bagehot, *Physics and Politics*, chap. II.

shut her in to a safe stagnation of monotonous uniformity. The great Indian castes were similarly set apart in their vast peninsula by the gigantic mountains which piled themselves between them and the rest of the continent. The later conquests which China and India suffered at the hands of Oriental invaders resulted in mere overlordships, which changed the destination of taxes, but did not touch the forms of local custom.

40. **Movement and Change in the West.**—It is easy to imagine a rapid death-rate, or at least an incessant transformation, amongst the customs of those races which migrated and competed in the West. There was not only the contact with each other which precipitated war and settled the question of predominance between custom and custom; there was also the slow but potent leaven of shifting scene and changing circumstance. The movement of the peoples was not the march of a host. It was only the slow progress of advancing races, its stages often centuries long, its delays fruitful of new habits and new aspirations. We have, doubtless, a type of what took place in those early days in the transformation of the Greeks after they had come down to the sea from the interior of Asia Minor. We can dimly see them beginning a new life there on those fertile coasts. Slowly they acquired familiarity with their new neighbor, the ocean. They learned its moods. They imagined new gods as breathing in its mild or storming in its tempestuous winds. They at length trusted themselves to its mercy in boats. The handling of boats made them sailors; and, lured from island to island across that inviting sea, they reached those later homes of their race with which their name was to be ever afterwards associated. And they reached this new country changed men, their hearts strengthened for bolder adventure, their hands quick with a readier skill, their minds open to greater enthusiasms and enriched with warmer imaginings, their whole nature profoundly affected by contact with Father Ægeus.

41. **Migration and Conquest.**—And so, to a greater or less extent, it must have been with other races in their movements towards their final seats. Not only the changes of circumstance and the exigencies of new conditions of life, but also the conquests necessarily incident to those days of migration, must have worked great, though slow, alterations in national character. We know the Latins to have been of the same stock with the Greeks; but by the time the Latins have reached Italy they are already radically different in habit, belief, and capacity from the Greeks, who have, by other routes, reached and settled Magna Græcia. Conquest changes not only the conquered, but also the conquerors. Insensibly, it may be, but deeply, they are affected by the character of the subdued or absorbed races. Norman does not merge with Saxon without getting Saxon blood into his own veins, and Saxon thoughts into his head; neither had Saxon overcome Celt without being himself more or less

taken captive by Celtic superstition. And these are but historical instances of what must have been more or less characteristic of similar events in 'prehistoric' times.

42. **Inter-tribal Imitation.**—There must, too, have been among the less successful or only partially successful races a powerful tendency towards *imitation* constantly at work,—imitation of the institutions of their more successful neighbors and rivals. Just as we see, in the histories of the Old Testament, frequent instances of peoples defeated by Jewish arms incontinently forsaking their own divinities and humbly commending themselves to the God of Israel, so must many another race, defeated or foiled in unrecorded wars, have forced themselves to learn the customs in order that they might equal the tactics of rival races.

43. **Individual Initiative and Imitation.**—And this impulse towards imitation, powerful as between group and group, would of course, in times of movement and conquest, be even more potent as amongst individual men. Such times would be rich with opportunity for those who had energy and enterprise. Many a great career could be carved out of the events of days of steady achievement. Men would, as pioneers in a new country or as leaders in war, be more or less freed from the narrow restrictions of hard and fast custom. They could be unconventional. Their individual gifts could have play. Each success would not only establish their right to be themselves, but would also raise up after them hosts of imitators. New types would find acceptance in the national life; and so a new leaven would be introduced. Individual initiative would at last be permitted a voice, even as against immemorial custom.

44. **Institutional Changes: Choice of Rulers.**—It is easy to see how, under the bracing influences of race competition, such forces of change would operate to initiate and hasten a progress towards the perfecting of institutions and the final abolition of slavery to habit. And it is no less plain to see how such forces of change would affect the constitution of government. It is evident that, as has been said (sec. 38), the patriarchal family did furnish the best campaigning materials, and that those races whose primitive organization was of this type did rapidly come to possess the "most-competed-for" parts of the earth. They did come to be the chief, the central races of history. But race aggregations, through conquest or adoption, must have worked considerable changes in the political bearings of the patriarchal principle. The direct line of male descent from the reputed common progenitor of the race could hardly continue indefinitely to be observed in filling the chieftainship of the race. A distinct element of choice—of election—must have crept in at a very early period. The individual initiative of which I have spoken, contributed very powerfully to effect this change. The oldest male of the hitherto

reigning family was no longer chosen as of course, but the wisest or the bravest. It was even open to the national choice to go upon occasion altogether outside this succession and choose a leader of force and resource from some other family.

45. **Hereditary replaced by Political Magistracy.**—Of course mere growth had much to do with these transformations. As tribes grew into nations, by all the processes of natural and artificial increase, all distinctness of mutual blood-relationship faded away. Direct common lines of descent became hopelessly obscured. Cross-kinships fell into inextricable confusion. Family government and race government became necessarily divorced,—differentiated. The state continued to be conceived as a Family; but the headship of this vast and complex family ceased to be natural and became *political*. So soon as hereditary title was broken in upon, the family no longer dominated the state; the state at last dominated the family. It often fell out that a son, absolutely subject to his father in the family, was by election made master of his father outside the family, in the state. Political had at least begun to grow away from domestic authority.

46. **Summary.**—It will be possible to set forth the nature of these changes more distinctly when discussing Greek and Roman institutions at length in the next chapter. Enough has been said here to make plain the approaches to those systems of government with which we are familiar in the modern world. We can understand how custom crystallized about the primitive man; how in the case of the majority of mankind it preserved itself against all essential change; how with the favored minority of the race it was broken by war, altered by imperative circumstance, modified by imitation, and infringed by individual initiative; how change resulted in progress; and how, at last, kinsmen became fellow-citizens.

CHAPTER 13. NATURE AND FORMS OF GOVERNMENT.

1154. **Government Rests upon Authority and Force.**—The essential characteristic of all government, whatever its form, is authority. There must in every instance be, on the one hand, governors, and, on the other, those who are governed. And the authority of governors, directly or indirectly, rests in all cases ultimately on *force*. Government, in its last analysis, is organized force. Not necessarily or invariably organized armed force, but the will of one man, of many men, or of a community prepared by organization to realize its own purposes with reference to the common affairs of the community. Organized, that is, to rule, to dominate. The machinery of government necessary to such an organization consists of instrumentalities fitted to enforce in the conduct of the common affairs of a community the will of the sovereign man, the sovereign minority, or the sovereign majority.

1155. **Not necessarily upon Obvious Force.**—This analysis of government, as consisting of authority resting on force, is not, however, to be interpreted too literally, too narrowly. The force behind authority must not be looked for as if it were always to be seen or were always being exercised. That there is authority lodged with ruler or magistrate is in every case evident enough; but that that authority rests upon force is not always a fact upon the surface, and is therefore in one sense not always practically significant. In the case of any particular government, the force upon which the authority of its officers rests may never once, for generations together, take the shape of armed force. Happily there are in our own day many governments, and those among the most prominent, which seldom coerce their subjects, seeming in their tranquil noiseless operations to run themselves. They in a sense operate without the exercise of force. But there is force behind them none the less because it never shows itself. The strongest birds flap their wings the least. There are just as powerful engines in the screw-propeller, for all she glides so noiselessly, as in the side-wheeler that churns and splashes way through the water. The better governments of our day—those which rest, not upon the armed strength of governors, but upon the free consent of the governed—are without open demonstration of force in their operations. They are founded upon constitutions and laws whose source and sanction are the will of the majority. The force which they embody is not the force of a dominant dynasty nor of a prevalent minority, but the force of an agreeing majority. And the overwhelming nature of this force is evident in the fact that the minority very seldom challenge its exercise. It is latent just because it is understood to be omnipotent. There is force behind the authority of the elected magistrate, no less than behind that of the usurping despot, a much greater force behind the President of the United States, than behind the Czar of Russia. The difference lies in the *display* of coercive power. Physical force is the prop of both, though in the one it is the last, while in the other it is the first resort.

1156. **The Governing Force in Ancient and in Modern Society**.—These elements of authority and force in government are thus quite plain to be seen in modern society, even when the constitution of that society is democratic; but they are not so easily discoverable upon a first view in primitive society. It is common nowadays when referring to the affairs of the most progressive nations to speak of 'government by public opinion,' 'government by the popular voice'; and such phrases possibly describe sufficiently well all full-grown democratic systems. But no one intends such expressions to conceal the fact that the majority, which utters 'public opinion,' does not prevail because the minority are convinced, but because they are outnumbered and have against them not the 'popular voice' only, but the 'popular power' as well—that it is the potential might rather than the wisdom of the majority which gives it its right to rule. When once majorities have learned to have opinions and to organize themselves for enforcing them, they rule by virtue of power no less than do despots with standing armies or concerting minorities dominating unorganized majorities. But, though it was clearly opinion which ruled in primitive societies, this conception of the might of majorities hardly seems to fit our ideas of primitive systems of government. What shall we say of them in connection with our present analysis of government? They were neither democracies in which the will of majorities chose the ways of government, nor despotisms, in which the will of an individual controlled, nor oligarchies, in which the purposes of a minority prevailed. Where shall we place the force which lay behind the authority exercised under them? Was the power of the father in the patriarchal family power of arm, mere domineering strength of will? What was the force that sustained the authority of the tribal chieftain or of that chief of chiefs, the king? That authority was not independent of the consent of those over whom it was exercised; and yet it was not formulated by that consent. That consent may be said to have been involuntary, *inbred*. It was born of the habit of the race. It was congenital. It consisted of a custom and tradition, moreover, which bound the chief no less than it bound his subjects. He might no more transgress the unwritten law of the race than might the humblest of his fellow-tribesmen. He was governed scarcely less than they were. All were under bondage to strictly prescribed ways of life. Where then lay the force which sanctioned the authority of chief and sub-chief and father in this society? Not in the will of the ruler: that was bound by the prescriptions of custom. Not in the popular choice: over that too the law of custom reigned.

1157. **The Force of the Common Will in Ancient Society.**—The real residence of force in such societies as these can be most easily discovered if we look at them under other circumstances. Nations still under the dominion of customary law have within historical times been conquered by alien conquerors; but in no such case did the will of the conqueror have free scope in regulating the affairs of the conquered. Seldom did it have any scope at all. The alien throne was maintained by force of arms, and taxes were mercilessly wrung from the subject populations; but never did the despot venture to change the customs of the conquered land. Its native laws he no more dared to touch than would a prince of the dynasty which he had displaced. He dared not play with the forces latent in the prejudices, the fanaticism of his subjects. He knew that those forces were volcanic, and that no prop of armed men could save his throne from overthrow and destruction should they once break forth. He really had no authority to govern, but only a power to despoil,—for the idea of government is inseparable from the conception of *legal regulation*. If, therefore, in the light of such cases, we conceive the throne of such a society as occupied by some native prince whose authority rested upon the laws of his country, it is plain to see that the real force upon which authority rests under a government so constituted is after all the force of public opinion, in a sense hardly less vividly real than if we spoke of a modern democracy. The law inheres in the common will: and it is that law upon which the authority of the prince is founded. He rules according to the common will: for that will is, that immemorial custom be inviolably observed. The force latent in that common will both backs and limits his authority.

1158. **Public Opinion, Ancient and Modern.**—The fact that the public opinion of such societies made no choice of laws or constitutions need not confuse for us the analogy between that public opinion and our own. Our own approval of the government under which we live, though doubtless conscious and in a way voluntary, is largely hereditary—is largely an inbred and inculcated approbation. There is a large amount of mere *drift* in it. Conformity to what is established is much the easiest habit in opinion. Our constructive choice even in our own governments, under which there is no divine canon against change, is limited to *modifications*. The generation that saw our federal system established may have imagined themselves out-of-hand creators, originators, of government; but we of this generation have taken what was given us, and are not controlled by laws altogether of our own making. Our constitutional life was made for us long ago. We are like primitive men in the public opinion which preserves, though unlike them in the public opinion which alters our institutions. Their stationary common thought contained the generic forces of government no less than does our own progressive public thought.

1159. **The True Nature of Government.**—What, then, in the last analysis, is the nature of government? If it rests upon authority and force, but upon authority which depends upon the acquiescence of the general will and upon force suppressed, latent, withheld except under extraordinary circumstances, what principle lies behind these phenomena, at the heart of government? The answer is hidden in the nature of Society itself. Society is in no sense artificial; it is as truly natural and organic as the individual man himself. As Aristotle said, man is by nature a social animal; his social function is as normal with him as is his individual function. Since the family was formed, he has not been without politics, without political association. Society, therefore, is compounded of the common habit, an evolution of experience, an interlaced growth of tenacious relationships, a compact, living, organic whole, structural, not mechanical.

1160. **Society an Organism, Government an Organ.**—Government is merely the executive organ of society, the organ through which its habit acts, through which its will becomes operative, through which it adapts itself to its environment and works out for itself a more effective life. There is clear reason, therefore, why the disciplinary action of society upon the individual is exceptional; clear reason also why the power of the despot must recognize certain ultimate limits and bounds; and clear reason why sudden or violent changes of government lead to equally violent and often fatal reaction and revolution. It is only the exceptional individual who is not held fast in his obedience to the common habit of social duty and comity. The despot's power, like the potter's, is limited by the characteristics of the materials in which he works, of the society which he manipulates; and change which roughly breaks with the common thought will lack the sympathy of that thought, will provoke its opposition, and will inevitably be crushed by that opposition. Society, like other organisms, can be changed only by evolution, and revolution is the antipode of evolution. The public order is preserved because order inheres in the character of society.

1161. **The Forms of Government: Their Significance.**—The forms of government do not affect the essence of government: the bayonets of the tyrant, the quick concert and superior force of an organized minority, the latent force of a self-governed majority,—all these depend upon the organic character and development of the community. "The obedience of the subject to the sovereign has its root not in contract but in force,—the force of the sovereign to punish disobedience;"[6] but that force must be backed by the general habit (secs. 1200–1206). The forms of government are, however, in every way most important to be observed, for the very reason that they express the character of government, and indicate its history. They exhibit the stages of political development, and make clear the necessary constituents and ordinary purposes of government, historically considered. They illustrate, too, the sanctions upon which it rests.

1162. **Aristotle's Analysis of the Forms of Government.**—It has been common for writers on politics in speaking of the several forms of government to rewrite Aristotle, and it is not easy to depart from the practice. For, although Aristotle's enumeration was not quite exhaustive, and although his descriptions will not quite fit modern types of government, his enumeration still serves as a most excellent frame on which to hang an exposition of the forms of government, and his descriptions at least furnish points of contrast between ancient and modern governments by observing which we can the more clearly understand the latter.

---

[6] John Morley, *Rousseau*, vol. II, p. 184.

1163. Aristotle considered Monarchy, Aristocracy, and Democracy (Ochlocracy) the three standard forms of government. The first he defined as the rule of One, the second as the rule of the Few, the third as the rule of the Many.[7] Off against these standard and, so to say, *healthful* forms he set their degenerate shapes. Tyranny he conceived to be the degenerate shape of Monarchy, Oligarchy the degenerate shape of Aristocracy, and Anarchy (or mob-rule) the degenerate shape of Democracy. His observation of the political world about him led him to believe that there was in every case a strong, an inevitable tendency for the pure forms to sink into the degenerate.

1164. **The Cycle of Degeneracy and Revolution.**—He outlined a cycle of degeneracies and revolutions through which, as he conceived, every State of long life was apt to pass. His idea was this. The natural first form of government for every state would be the rule of a monarch, of the single strong man with sovereign power given him because of his strength. This monarch would usually hand on his kingdom to his children. They might confidently be expected to forget those pledges and those views of the public good which had bound and guided him. Their sovereignty would sink into tyranny. At length their tyranny would meet its decisive check at some Runnymede. There would be revolt; and the princely leaders of revolt, taking government into their own hands, would set up an Aristocracy. But aristocracies, though often public-spirited and just in their youth, always decline, in their later years, into a dotage of selfish oligarchy. Oligarchy is even more hateful to civil liberty, is even a graver hindrance to healthful civil life than tyranny. A class bent upon subserving only their own interests can devise injustice in greater variety than can a single despot: and their insolence is always quick to goad the many to hot revolution. To this revolution succeeds Democracy. But Democracy too has its old age of degeneracy—an old age in which it loses its early respect for law, its first amiability of mutual concession. It breaks out into license and Anarchy, and none but a Cæsar can bring it back to reason and order. The cycle is completed. The throne is set up again, and a new series of deteriorations and revolutions begins.

1165. **Modern Contrasts to the Aristotelian Forms of Government.**—The confirmations of this view furnished by the history of Europe since the time of Aristotle have been striking and numerous enough to render it still oftentimes convenient as a scheme by which to observe the course of political history even in our own days. But it is still more instructive to con-

---

[7] Not of the absolute majority, as we shall see presently when contrasting ancient and modern democracy (secs. 1170, 1173).

trast the later facts of political development with this ancient exposition of the laws of politics. Observe, then, the differences between modern and ancient types of government, and the likelihood that the historian of the future, if not of the present and the immediate past, will have to record more divergencies from the cycle of Aristotle than correspondences with it.

1166. **The Modern Absolute Monarchy.**—Taking the Russian government of to-day as a type of the vast absolute Monarchies which have grown up in Europe since the death of Aristotle, it is evident that the modern monarch, if he be indeed monarch, has a much deeper and wider reach of power than had the ancient monarch. The monarch of our day is a Legislator; the ancient monarch was not. Ancient society may be said hardly to have known what legislation was. Custom was for it the law of public as well as of private life: and custom could not be enacted. At any rate ancient monarchies were not legislative. The despot issued edicts—imperative commands covering particular cases or affecting particular individuals: the Roman emperors were among the first to promulgate 'constitutions,'—general rules of law to be applied universally. The modern despot can do more even than that. He can regulate by his command public affairs not only but private as well—can even upset local custom and bring all his subjects under uniform legislative control. Nor is he in the least bound to observe his own laws. A word—and that his own word—will set them aside: a word will abolish, a word restore, them. He is absolute over his subjects not only—ancient despots were that—but over all laws also—which no ancient despot was.

1167. Of course these statements are meant to be taken with certain important limitations. The modern despot as well as the ancient is hound by the habit of his people. He may change laws, hut he may not change life as easily; and the national traditions and national character, the rural and commercial habit of his kingdom, bind him very absolutely. The limitation is not often felt by the monarch, simply because he has himself been bred in the atmosphere of the national life and unconsciously conforms to it (secs. 1200–1206).

1168. **The Modern Monarchy usually 'Limited.'**—But the present government of Russia is abnormal in the Europe of to-day, as abnormal as that of the Turk—a belated example of those crude forms of politics which the rest of Europe has outgrown. Turning to the other monarchies of to-day, it is at once plain that they present the strongest contrast possible to any absolute monarchy ancient or modern. Almost without exception in Europe, they are 'limited' by the resolutions of a popular parliament. The people have a distinct and often an imperative voice in the conduct of public affairs.

1169. **Is Monarchy now succeeded by Aristocracy?**—And what is to be said of Aristotle's cycle in connection with modern monarchies? Does any one suppose it possible that when the despotism of the Czar falls it will be succeeded by an aristocracy; or that when the modified authority of the emperors of Austria and Germany or the king of Italy still further exchanges substance for shadow, a limited class will succeed to the reality of power? Is there any longer any place between Monarchy and Democracy for Aristocracy? Has it not been crowded out?

1170. **English and Ancient Aristocracy contrasted.**—Indeed, since the extension of the franchise in England to the working classes, no example of a real Aristocracy is left in the modern world. At the beginning of this century the government of England, called a 'limited monarchy,' was in reality an Aristocracy. Parliament and the entire administration of the kingdom were in the hands of the classes having wealth or nobility. The members of the House of Lords and the crown together controlled a majority of the seats in the House of Commons. England was 'represented' by her upper classes almost exclusively. That Aristocracy has been set aside by the Reform Bills of 1832, 1867, and 1885; but it is worth while looking back to it, in order to contrast a modern type of Aristocracy with those ancient aristocracies which were present to the mind of Aristotle. An ancient Aristocracy *constituted* the state; the English aristocracy merely controlled the state. Under the widest citizenship known even to ancient democracy less than half the adult male subjects of the state shared the franchise. The ancient Democracy itself was a government by a minority. The ancient Aristocracy was a government by a still narrower minority; and this narrow minority monopolized office and power not only, but citizenship as well. There were no citizens but they. They were the State. Every one else existed for the state, only they were part of it. In England the case was very different. There the franchise was not confined to the aristocrats; it was only controlled by them. Nor did the aristocrats of England consider themselves the whole of the State. They were quite conscious—and quite content—that they had the State virtually in their possession; but they looked upon themselves as holding it in trust for the people of Great Britain. Their legislation was, in fact, class legislation, after a very narrow sort; but they did not think that it was. They regarded their rule as eminently advantageous to the kingdom; and they unquestionably had, or tried to have, the real interests of the kingdom at heart. They led the state, but did not constitute it.

1171. **Present and Future Prevalence of Democracy.**—If Aristocracy seems about to disappear, Democracy seems about universally to prevail. Ever since the rise of popular education in the last century and its vast development since have assured a thinking weight to the masses of the people everywhere, the advance of democratic opinion and the spread of democratic institutions have been most marked and most significant. They have destroyed almost all pure forms of Monarchy and Aristocracy by introducing into them imperative forces of popular thought and the concrete institutions of popular representation; and they promise to reduce politics to a single pure form by excluding all other governing forces and institutions but those of a wide suffrage and a democratic representation,—by reducing all forms of government to Democracy.

1172. **Differences of Form between Ancient and Modern Democracies.**—The differences of form to be observed between ancient and modern Democracies are wide and important. Ancient Democracies were 'immediate'; ours are 'mediate,' that is to say, *representative*. Every citizen of the Athenian State—to take that as a type—had a right to appear and vote in proper person in the popular assembly, and in those committees of that assembly which acted as criminal courts; the modern voter votes for a representative who is to sit for him in the popular chamber—he himself has not even the right of entrance there. This idea of representation—even the idea of a vote by proxy—was hardly known to the ancients; among us it is all-pervading. Even the elected magistrate of an ancient Democracy was not looked upon as a representative of his fellow-citizens. *He was the State*, so far as his functions went, and so long as his term of office lasted. He could break through all law or custom, if he dared. It was only when his term had expired and he was again a private citizen that he could be called to account. There was no impeachment while in office. To our thought all elected to office—whether Presidents, ministers, or legislators—are representatives. The limitations as to the size of the state involved in the absence from ancient conception of the principle of representation is obvious. A State in which all citizens were also legislators must of necessity be small. The modern representative state has no such limitation. It may cover a continent.

1173. **Nature of Democracy, Ancient and Modern.**—The differences of nature to be observed between ancient and modern Democracies are no less wide and important. The ancient Democracy was a class government. As already pointed out, it was only a broader Aristocracy. Its franchise was at widest an exclusive privilege, extending only to a minority. There were slaves under its heel; there were even freedmen who could never hope to enter its citizenship. Class subordination was of the essence of its constitution. From the modern Democratic State, on the other hand, both slavery and class subordination are excluded as inconsistent with its theory, not only, but, more than that, as antagonistic to its very being. Its citizenship is as wide as its native population; its suffrage as wide as its qualified citizenship,—it knows no non-citizen class. And there is still another difference between the Democracy of Aristotle and the Democracy of de Tocqueville and Bentham. The citizens of the former lived for the State; the citizen of the latter lives for himself, and the State is for him. The modern Democratic State exists for the sake of the individual; the individual, in Greek conception, lived for the State. The ancient State recognized no personal rights—all rights were State rights; the modern State recognizes no State rights which are independent of personal rights.

1174. **Growth of the Democratic Idea**.—In making the last statement embrace 'the ancient State' irrespective of kind and 'the modern State,' of whatever form, I have pointed out what I conceive to be the cardinal difference between all the ancient forms of government and all the modern. It is a difference which I have already stated in another way. The *democratic idea* has penetrated more or less deeply all the advanced systems of government, and has penetrated them in consequence of that change of thought which has given to the individual an importance quite independent of his membership of a State. I can here only indicate the historical steps of that change of thought; I cannot go at any length into its causes.

1175. **Subordination of the Individual in the Ancient State**.—We have seen that, in the history of political society, if we have read that history aright, the rights of government—the magistracies and subordinations of kinship—antedate what we now call the rights of the individual. A man was at first nobody in himself; he was only the kinsman of somebody else. The father himself, or the chief, commanded only because of priority in kinship: to that all rights of all men were relative. Society was the unit; the individual the fraction. Man existed for society. He was all his life long in tutelage; only society was old enough to take charge of itself. The state was the only Individual.

1176. **Individualism of Christianity and Teutonic Institutions**.—There was no essential change in this idea for centuries. Through all the developments of government down to the time of the rise of the Roman Empire the State continued, in the conception of the western nations at least, to eclipse the individual. Private rights had no standing as against the State. Subsequently many influences combined to break in upon this immemorial conception. Chief among these influences were Christianity and the institutions of the German conquerors of the fifth century. Christianity gave each man a magistracy over himself by insisting upon his personal, individual responsibility to God. For right living, at any rate, each man was to have only his own conscience as a guide. In these deepest matters there must be for the Christian an individuality which no claim of his State upon him could rightfully be suffered to infringe. The German nations brought into the Romanized and partially Christianized world of the fifth century an individuality of another sort,—the idea of allegiance to individuals (sec. 228). Perhaps their idea that each man had a money-value which must be paid by any one who might slay him also contributed to the process of making men units instead of state-fractions; but their idea of personal allegiance played the more prominent part in the transformation of society which resulted from their western conquests. The Roman knew no allegiance save allegiance to his State. He swore fealty to his *imperator* as to a representative of that State, not as to an individual. The Teuton, on the other hand, bound himself to his leader by a bond of personal service which the Roman either could not understand or understood only to despise. There were, therefore, individuals in the German State: great chiefs or warriors with a following (*comitatus*) of devoted volunteers ready to die for them in frays not directed by the state, but of their own provoking (secs. 226–228). There was with all German tribes freedom of individual movement and combination within the ranks,—a wide play of individual initiative. When the German settled down as master amongst the Romanized populations of western and southern Europe, his thought was led captive by the conceptions of the Roman law, as all subsequent thought that has known it has been, and his habits were much modified by those of his new subjects; but this strong element of individualism was not destroyed by the contact. It lived to constitute one of the chief features of the Feudal System.

1177. **The Transitional Feudal System.**—The Feudal System was made up of elaborate gradations of personal allegiance. The only State possible under that system was a disintegrate state embracing not a unified people, but a nation atomized into its individual elements. A king there might be, but he was lord, not of his people, but of his barons. He was himself baron also, and as such had many a direct subject pledged to serve him; but as king the barons were his only direct subjects; and the barons were heedful of their allegiance to him only when he could make it to their interest to be so, or their peril not to be. They were the kings of the people, who owed direct allegiance to them alone, and to the king only through them. Kingdoms were only greater baronies, baronies lesser kingdoms. One small part of the people served one baron, another part served another baron. As a whole they served no one master. They were not a whole: they were jarring, disconnected segments of a nation. Every man had his own lord, and antagonized every one who had not the same lord as he (secs. 238–243).

1178. **Rise of the Modern State.**—Such a system was, of course, fatal to peace and good government, but it cleared the way for the rise of the modern

State by utterly destroying the old conception of the State. The State of the ancients had been an entity in itself—an entity to which the entity of the individual was altogether subordinate. The Feudal State was merely an aggregation of individuals,—a loose bundle of separated series of men knowing no common aim or action. It not only had no actual unity: it had no thought of unity. National unity came at last,—in France, for instance, by the subjugation of the barons by the king (sec. 253); in England by the joint effort of people and barons against the throne,—but when it came it was the ancient unity with a difference. Men were no longer State fractions; they had become State integers. The State *seemed* less like a natural organism and more like a deliberately organized association. Personal allegiance to kings had everywhere taken the place of native membership of a body politic. Men were now subjects, not citizens.

1179. **Renaissance and Reformation.**—Presently came the thirteenth century with its wonders of personal adventure and individual enterprise in discovery, piracy, and trade. Following hard upon these, the Renaissance woke men to a philosophical study of their surroundings—and above all of their long-time unquestioned systems of thought. Then arose Luther to reiterate the almost forgotten truths of the individuality of men's consciences, the right of individual judgment. Ere long the new thoughts had penetrated to the masses of the people. Reformers had begun to cast aside their scholastic weapons and come down to the common folk about them, talking their own vulgar tongue and craving their acquiescence in the new doctrines of deliverance from mental and spiritual bondage to Pope or Schoolman. National literatures were born. Thought had broken away from its exclusion in cloisters and universities and had gone out to challenge the people to a use of their own minds. By using their minds, the people gradually put away the childish things of their days of ignorance, and began to claim a part in affairs. Finally, systematized popular education has completed the story. Nations are growing up into manhood. Peoples are becoming old enough to govern themselves.

1180. **The Modern Force of Majorities.**—It is thus no accident, but the outcome of great permanent causes, that there is no more to be found among the civilized races of Europe any satisfactory example of Aristotle's Monarchies and Aristocracies. The force of modern governments is not now often the force of minorities. It is getting to be more and more the force of majorities. The sanction of every rule not founded upon sheer military despotism is the consent of a thinking people. Military despotisms are now seen to be necessarily ephemeral. Only monarchs who are revered as seeking to serve their subjects are any longer safe upon their thrones. Monarchies exist only by democratic consent.

1181. **New Character of Society.**—And, more than that, the result has been to give to society a new integration. The common habit is now operative again, not in acquiescence and submission merely, but in initiative and progress as well. Society is not the organism it once was,—its members are given freer play, fuller opportunity for origination; but its organic character is again prominent. It is the Whole which has emerged from the disintegration of feudalism and the specialization of absolute monarchy. The Whole, too, has become self-conscious, and by becoming self-directive has set out upon a new course of development.

CHAPTER 16. THE OBJECTS OF GOVERNMENT.

1265. **Character of the Subject.**—Political interest and controversy centre nowhere more acutely than in the question, What are the proper objects of government? This is one of those difficult questions upon which it is possible for many sharply opposed views to be held apparently with almost equal weight of reason. Its central difficulty is this, that it is a question which can be answered, if answered at all, only by the aid of a broad and careful wisdom whose conclusions are based upon the widest possible inductions from the facts of political experience in all its phases. Such wisdom is of course quite beyond the capacity of most thinkers and actors in the field of politics; and the consequence has been that this question, perhaps more than any other in the whole scope of political science, has provoked great wars of doctrine.

1266. **The Extreme Views Held.**—What part shall government play in the affairs of society?—that is the question which has been the gauge of controversial battle. Stated in another way, it is the very question which I postponed when discussing the functions of government (sec. 1231), '*What*,' namely, '*ought the functions of government to be?*' On the one hand there are extremists who cry constantly to government, 'Hands off,' '*laissez faire*,' '*laissez passer*'*!* who look upon every act of government which is not merely an act of police with jealousy, who regard government as necessary, but as a necessary evil, and who would have government hold back from everything which could by any possibility be accomplished by individual initiative and endeavor. On the other hand, there are those who, with equal extremeness of view in the opposite direction, would have society lean fondly upon government for guidance and assistance in every affair of life, who, captivated by some glimpse of public power and beneficence caught in the pages of ancient or mediæval historian or by some dream of co-operative endeavor cunningly imagined by the great fathers of Socialism, believe that the state can be made a wise foster-mother to every member of the family politic.

Between these two extremes, again, there are all grades, all shades and colors, all degrees of enmity or of partiality to state action.

1267. **Historical Foundation for Opposite Views.**—Enmity to exaggerated state action, even a keen desire to keep that action down to its lowest possible terms, is easily furnished with impressive justification. It must unreservedly be admitted that history abounds with warnings of no uncertain sound against indulging the state with a too great liberty of interference with the life and work of its citizens. Much as there is that is attractive in the political life of the city states of Greece and Rome, in which the public power was suffered to be omnipotent,—their splendid public spirit, their incomparable organic wholeness, their fine play of rival talents, serving both the common thought and the common action, their variety, their conception of public virtue, there is also much to blame,—their too wanton invasion of that privacy of the individual life in which alone family virtue can dwell secure, their callous tyranny over minorities in matters which might have been left to individual choice, their sacrifice of personal independence for the sake of public solidarity, their hasty average judgments, their too confident trust in the public voice. They, it is true, could not have had the individual liberty which we cherish without breaking violently with their own history, with the necessary order of their development; but neither can we, on the other hand, imitate them without an equally violent departure from our own normal development and a reversion to the now too primitive methods of their pocket republics.

1268. Unquestionable as it is, too, that mediæval history affords many seductive examples of an absence of grinding, heartless competition and a strength of mutual interdependence, confidence, and helpfulness between class and class such as the modern economist may be pardoned for wishing to see revived; and true though it be that the history of Prussia under some of the greater Hohenzollern gives at least colorable justification to the opinion that state interference may under many circumstances be full of benefit for the industrial upbuilding of a state, it must, on the other hand, be remembered that neither the feudal system, nor the mediæval guild system, nor the paternalism of Frederic the Great can be rehabilitated now that the nineteenth century has wrought its revolutions in industry, in church, and in state; and that, even if these great systems of the past could be revived, we would be sorely puzzled to reinstate their blessings without restoring at the same time their acknowledged evils. No student of history can wisely censure those who protest against state paternalism.

1269. **The State a Beneficent and Indispensable Organ of Society.**—It by no means follows, however, that because the state may unwisely interfere in the life of the individual, it must be pronounced in itself and by nature a necessary evil. It is no more an evil than is society itself. It is the organic body of society: without it society would be hardly more than a mere abstraction. If the name had not been restricted to a single, narrow, extreme, and radically mistaken class of thinkers, we ought all to regard ourselves and to act as *socialists*, believers in the wholesomeness and beneficence of the body politic. If the history of society proves anything, it proves the absolute naturalness of government, its rootage in the nature of man, its origin in kinship, and its identification with all that makes man superior to the brute creation. Individually man is but poorly equipped to dominate other animals: his lordship comes by combination, his strength is concerted strength, his sovereignty is the sovereignty of union. Outside of society man's mind can avail him little as an instrument of supremacy, and government is the visible form of society: if society itself be not an evil, neither surely is government an evil, for government is the indispensable organ of society.

1270. Every means, therefore, by which society may be perfected through the instrumentality of government, every means by which individual rights can be fitly adjusted and harmonized with public duties, by which individual self-development may be made at once to serve and to supplement social development, ought certainly to be diligently sought, and, when found, sedulously fostered by every friend of society. Such is the socialism to which every true lover of his kind ought to adhere with the full grip of every noble affection that is in him.

1271. **Socialism and the Modern Industrial Organization.**—It is possible indeed, to understand, and even in a measure to sympathize with, the enthusiasm of those special classes of agitators whom we have dubbed with the too great name of 'Socialists.' The schemes of social reform and regeneration which they support with so much ardor, however mistaken they may be,—and surely most of them are mistaken enough to provoke the laughter of children,—have the right end in view: they seek to bring the individual with his special interests, personal to himself, into complete harmony with society with its general interests, common to all. Their method is always some sort of co-operation, meant to perfect mutual helpfulness. They speak, too, a revolt from selfish, misguided individualism; and certainly modern individualism has much about it that is hateful, too hateful to last. The modern industrial organization has so distorted competition as to put it into the power of some to tyrannize over many, as to enable the rich and the strong to combine against the poor and the weak. It has given a woeful material meaning to that spiritual law that "to him that hath shall be given, and from him that hath not shall be taken away even the little that he seemeth to have."[8] It has magnified that self-interest which is grasping selfishness and has thrust out love and compassion not only, but free competition in part, as well. Surely it would be better, exclaims the Socialist, altogether to stamp out competition by making all men equally subject to the public order, to an imperative law of social co-operation! But the Socialist mistakes: it is not competition that kills, but unfair competition, the pretence and form of it where the substance and reality of it cannot exist.

1272. **A Middle Ground**.—But there is a middle ground. The schemes which Socialists have proposed society assuredly cannot accept, and no scheme which involves the complete control of the individual by government can be devised which differs from theirs very much for the better. A truer doctrine must be found, which gives wide freedom to the individual for his self-development and yet guards that freedom against the competition that kills, and reduces the antagonism between self-development and social development to a minimum. And such a doctrine can be formulated, surely, without too great vagueness.

1273. **The Objects of Society the Objects of Government**.—Government, as I have said, is the organ of society, its only potent and universal instrument: its objects must be the objects of society. What, then, are the objects of society? What *is* society? It is an organic association of individuals for mutual aid. Mutual aid to what? To self-development. The hope of society lies in an infinite individual variety, in the freest possible play of individual forces: only in that can it find that wealth of resource which constitutes civilization, with all its appliances for satisfying human wants and mitigating human sufferings, all its incitements to thought and spurs to action. It should be the end of government *to accomplish the objects of organized society*: there must be constant adjustments of governmental assistance to the needs of a changing social and industrial organization. Not license of interference on the part of government, only strength and adaptation of regulation. The regulation that I mean is not interference: it is the equalization of conditions, so far as possible, in all branches of endeavor; and the equalization of conditions is the very opposite of interference.

1274. Every rule of development is a rule of adaptation, a rule for meeting 'the circumstances of the case'; but the circumstances of the case, it must be remembered, are not, so far as government is concerned, the circumstances of any individual case, but the circumstances of society's case, the general

---

[8] F[rancis] A. Walker's *Political Economy* (Advanced Course) [New York: Henry Holt & Co., 1883], sec. 346.

conditions of social organization. The case for society stands thus: the individual must be assured the best means, the best and fullest opportunities, for complete self-development: in no other way can society itself gain variety and strength. But one of the most indispensable conditions of opportunity for self-development government alone, society's controlling organ, can supply. All combination which necessarily creates monopoly, which necessarily puts and keeps indispensable means of industrial or social development in the hands of a few, and those few, not the few selected by society itself but the few selected by arbitrary fortune, must be under either the direct or the indirect control of society. To society alone can the power of dominating combination belong: and society cannot suffer any of its members to enjoy such a power for their own private gain independently of its own strict regulation or oversight.

1275. **Natural Monopolies.**—It is quite possible to distinguish natural monopolies from other classes of undertakings; their distinctive marks are thus enumerated by Mr. T. H. Farrer in his excellent little volume on *The State in its relation to Trade* which forms one of the well-known English Citizen series:[9]

"1. What they supply is a necessary," a necessary, that is, to life, like water, or a necessary to industrial action, like railroad transportation.

"2. They occupy peculiarly favored spots or lines of land." Here again the best illustration is afforded by railroads or by telegraph lines, by water-works, etc.

"3. The article or convenience they supply is used at the place and in connection with the plant or machinery by which it is supplied;" that is to say, at the favored spots or along the favored lines of land.

"4. This article or convenience can in general be largely, if not indefinitely increased, without proportionate increase in plant and capital;" that is to say, the initial outlay having been made, the favored spot or line of land having been occupied, every subsequent increase of business will increase profits because it will not proportionately, or anything like proportionately, increase the outlay for services or machinery needed. Those who are outside of the established business, therefore, are upon an equality of competition neither as regards available spots or lines of land nor as regards opportunities to secure business in a competition of rates.

"5. Certain and harmonious arrangement, which can only be attained by unity, are paramount considerations." Wide and systematic organization is necessary.

---

[9] [Thomas H. Farrer, *The State and Its Relation to Trade* (London: 1883),] p. 71. Mr. Farrer is Permanent Secretary of the English Board of Trade (sec. 694).

1276. Such enterprises invariably give to a limited number of persons the opportunity to command certain necessaries of life, of comfort, or of industrial success against their fellow countrymen and for their own advantage. Once established in any field, there can be no real competition between them and those who would afterwards enter that field. No agency should be suffered to have such control except a public agency which may be compelled by public opinion to act without selfish narrowness, upon perfectly equal conditions as towards all, or some agency upon which the government may keep a strong hold of regulation.

1277. **Control not necessarily Administration.**—Society can by no means afford to allow the use for private gain and without regulation of undertakings necessary to its own healthful and efficient operation and yet of a sort to exclude equality in competition. Experience has proved that the self-interest of those who have controlled such undertakings for private gain is not coincident with the public interest: even enlightened self-interest may often discover means of illicit pecuniary advantage in unjust discriminations between individuals in the use of such instrumentalities. But the proposition that the government should control such dominating organizations of capital may by no means be wrested to mean by any necessary implication that the government should itself administer those instrumentalities of economic action which cannot be used except as monopolies. In such cases, as Mr. Farrer says, "there are two great alternatives. (1) Ownership and management by private enterprise and capital under regulation by the state. (2) Ownership and management by Government, central or local." Government regulation may in most cases suffice. Indeed, such are the difficulties in the way of establishing and maintaining careful business management on the part of government, that control ought to be preferred to direct administration in as many cases as possible,—in every case in which control without administration can be made effectual.

1278. **Equalization of Competition.**—There are some things outside the field of natural monopolies in which individual action cannot secure equalization of the conditions of competition; and in these also, as in the regulation of monopolies, the practice of governments, of our own as well as of others, has been decisively on the side of governmental regulation. By forbidding child labor, by supervising the sanitary conditions of factories, by limiting the employment of women in occupations hurtful to their health, by instituting official tests of the purity or the quality of goods sold, by limiting hours of labor in certain trades, by a hundred and one limitations of the power of unscrupulous or heartless men to out-do the scrupulous and merciful in trade or industry, government has assisted equity. Those who would act in moderation and good conscience in cases where moderation and good conscience, to be indulged, require an increased outlay of money, in better ventilated buildings, in greater care as to the quality of goods, etc., cannot act upon their principles so long as more grinding conditions for labor or more unscrupulous use of the opportunities of trade secure to the unconscientious an unquestionable and sometimes even a permanent advantage; they have only the choice of denying their consciences or retiring from business. In scores of such cases government has intervened and will intervene; but by way, not of interference, by way, rather, of making competition equal between those who would rightfully conduct enterprise and those who basely conduct it. It is in this way that society protects itself against permanent injury and deterioration, and secures healthful equality of opportunity for self-development.

1279. **Society greater than Government.**—Society, it must always be remembered, is vastly bigger and more important than its instrument, Government. Government should serve Society, by no means rule or dominate it. Government should not be made an end in itself; it is a means only,—a means to be freely adapted to advance the best interests of the social organism. The State exists for the sake of Society, not Society for the sake of the State.

1280. **Natural Limits to State Action.**—And that there are natural and imperative limits to state action no one who seriously studies the structure of society can doubt. The limit of state functions is the limit of *necessary co-operation* on the part of Society as a whole, the limit beyond which such combination ceases to be imperative for the public good and becomes merely convenient for industrial or social enterprise. Co-operation is necessary in the sense here intended when it is indispensable to the equalization of the conditions of endeavor, indispensable to the maintenance of uniform rules of individual rights and relationships, indispensable because to omit it would inevitably be to hamper or degrade some for the advancement of others in the scale of wealth and social standing.

1281. There are relations in which men invariably have need of each other, in which universal co-operation is the indispensable condition of even tolerable existence. Only some universal authority can make opportunities equal as between man and man. The divisions of labor and the combinations of commerce may for the most part be left to contract, to free individual arrangement, but the equalization of the conditions which affect all alike may no more be left to individual initiative than may the organization of government itself. Churches, clubs, corporations, fraternities, guilds, partnerships, unions have for their ends one or another special enterprise for the development of man's spiritual or material well-being: they are all more or less advisable. But the family and the state have as their end a general enterprise for the betterment and equalization of the conditions of individual development: they are indispensable.

1282. The point at which public combination ceases to be imperative is of course not susceptible of clear indication in general terms; but it is not on that account indistinct. The bounds of family association are not indistinct because they are marked only by the immaturity of the young and by the parental and filial affections,—things not all of which are defined in the law. The rule that the state should do nothing which is equally possible under equitable conditions to optional associations is a sufficiently clear line of distinction between governments and corporations. Those who regard the state as an optional, conventional union simply, a mere partnership, open wide the doors to the worst forms of socialism. Unless the state has a nature which is quite clearly defined by that invariable, universal, immutable mutual interdependence which runs beyond the family relations and cannot be satisfied by family ties, we have absolutely no criterion by which we can limit, except arbitrarily, the activities of the state. The criterion supplied by the native necessity of state relations, on the other hand, banishes such license of state action.

1283. The state, for instance, ought not to supervise private morals because they belong to the sphere of separate individual responsibility, not to the sphere of mutual dependence. Thought and conscience are private. Opinion is optional. The state may intervene only where common action, uniform law are indispensable. Whatever is merely convenient is optional, and therefore not an affair for the state. Churches are spiritually convenient; joint-stock companies are capitalistically convenient; but when the state constitutes itself a church or a mere business association it institutes a monopoly no better than others. It should do nothing which is not in any case both indispensable to social or industrial life and necessarily monopolistic.

1284. **The Family and the State.**—It is the proper object of the family to mould the individual, to form him in the period of immaturity in the practice of morality and obedience. This period of subordination over, he is called out into an independent, self-directive activity. The ties of family affection still bind him, but they bind him with silken, not with iron bonds. He has left his 'minority' and reached his 'majority.' It is the proper object of the state to give leave to his individuality, in order that that individuality may add its quota of variety to the sum of national activity. Family discipline is variable, selective, formative: it must lead the individual. But the state must not lead. It must create conditions, but not mould individuals. Its discipline must be invariable, uniform, impersonal. Family methods rest upon individual inequality, state methods upon individual equality. Family order rests upon tutelage, state order upon franchise, upon privilege.

1285. **The State and Education.**—In one field the state would seem at first sight to usurp the family function, the field, namely, of education. But such is not in reality the case. Education is the proper office of the state for two reasons, both of which come within the principles we have been discussing. Popular education is necessary for the preservation of those conditions of freedom, political and social, which are indispensable to free individual development. And, in the second place, no instrumentality less universal in its power and authority than government can secure popular education. In brief, in order to secure popular education the action of society as a whole is necessary; and popular education is indispensable to that equalization of the conditions of personal development which we have taken to be the proper object of society. Without popular education, moreover, no government that rests upon popular action can long endure: the people must be schooled in the knowledge, and if possible in the virtues, upon which the maintenance and success of free institutions depend. No free government can last in health if it lose hold of the traditions of its history, and in the public schools these traditions may be and should be sedulously preserved, carefully replanted in the thought and consciousness of each successive generation.

1286. **Historical Conditions of Governmental Action.**—Whatever view be taken in each particular case of the rightfulness or advisability of state regulation and control, one rule there is which may not be departed from under any circumstances, and that is the rule of historical continuity. In politics nothing radically novel may safely be attempted. No result of value can ever be reached in politics except through slow and gradual development, the careful adaptations and nice modifications of growth. Nothing may be done by leaps. More than that, each people, each nation, must live upon the lines of its own experience. Nations are no more capable of borrowing experience than individuals are. The histories of other peoples may furnish us with light, but they cannot furnish us with conditions of action. Every nation must constantly keep in touch with its past: it cannot run towards its ends around sharp corners.

1287. **Summary.**—This, then, is the sum of the whole matter: the end of government is the facilitation of the objects of society. The rule of governmental action is necessary co-operation; the method of political development is conservative adaptation, shaping old habits into new ones, modifying old means to accomplish new ends.

"Christ's Army" *

One of the favorite figures with sacred writers in their references to the inhabitants of this world is that of representing mankind as divided into two great armies. The field of battle is the world. From the abodes of righteousness advances the host of God's people under the leadership of Christ. Immediately behind the great Captain of Salvation come the veteran regiments of the soldiers of the cross with steady tread, their feet shod with the preparation of the Gospel of Peace, girt about with truth, their breast-plates of righteousness glittering beneath the bright rays of their Master's love, each one grasping the sword of the Spirit. Later come the younger troops all eager for the fray. From the opposite side of the field, advancing from the tents of wickedness, come the hosts of sin led by the Prince of Lies himself, riding upon death's horse. Behind him a mighty army marshalled by fiends under the dark banners of iniquity. The object of the warfare on the part of the first is to gain glory for their Great Leader as well as the best good of the conquered by persuading them to leave the ranks of the evil one and enlist under their great Redeemer; that of the other to entice as many as will listen to them to go with them by the alluring paths of worldliness to everlasting destruction. The foes meet upon the great battle field of every-day life. With one sweeping charge the Christian band falls upon the overwhelming numbers of the Prince of Darkness and are met with a cloud of fiery darts from the hands of the Evil One. The battle waxes fierce. Some of the Christian leaders faithfully and eagerly press onward, rallying their broken ranks more vigorously upon every repulse. Others stand with folded arms, only now and then languidly issuing an order or encouraging their followers, and ever incurring the displeasure of their gracious Master by failing to carry out his orders or properly marshall and encourage his forces. The followers of the former, fight manfully, with only here

* "Christ's Army," Wilmington North Carolina *The Presbyterian*, August 23, 1876. (Editor's note).

and there a laggard or coward; those of the latter partake of the spirit of their leaders and do little towards gaining the battle. The hosts of sin, ever and anon charging, break through the weak portions of the opposing battalions, and then again quail before the uplifted swords of the Spirit. Here, the plumes streaming from the glistening helmets of salvation are seen among the retreating brigades of sin; there, Satan leads his followers to victory over the dead bodies of many a soldier of the Cross. Thus the battle of life progresses and the army of Saints ever gains ground under divine generalship; now slowly, now rapidly, driving before them with irresistible force the broken ranks of the enemy.

Surely in this great contest there is a part for every one, and each one will be made to render a strict account of his conduct on the day of battle. Will any one hesitate as to the part he shall take in this conflict? Will any one dare to enlist under the banners of the Prince of Lies, under whose dark folds he only marches to the darkness of hell? For there is no middle course, no neutrality. Each and every one must enlist either with the followers of Christ or those of Satan. How much more glorious to fight for the divine Prince of Peace, under whose glorious standards, whose shining folds are inscribed with *Love to God*, he will advance to sure victory and an everlasting reward! All professing Christians are, no doubt, more or less enthused by such thoughts as these, and hope that they can feel themselves soldiers in Christ's great army; but they do not *know* that they are such. Why should they not know? If they would be assured of the fact that their names are in the great Roll Book, let them fight for Christ. Ah! but how do this? As you would fight for any other cause. You know your enemies. They are evil thoughts, evil desires, evil associations. To avoid evil thoughts altogether is, of course, impossible. But whenever one of these subtle warriors of evil attacks you, do not fear to test your breastplate; wield with power the sword of the Spirit and with skill the shield of faith. Overcome evil desires, those powerful and ever present enemies, by constant watchfulness and with the strong weapon of prayer, and by cultivating those heavenly desires which are sure to root out the evil ones. Avoid evil associations, evil companions. No one can make a good soldier who keeps company with the emissaries and friends of the enemy. These companions can be avoided by avoiding the places where they are to be found and seeking the more congenial and pleasant company of the good and upright, whose companionship will strengthen you in the struggle by making you feel that you are not alone in it. In every minor thing watch yourself and let no fiery dart enter your soul. One who thus faithfully does his duty and purifies himself in the smallest things has little to fear from the foe, and, if he withal leads others by his example and precept to do likewise, and fears not to warn the enemies of the Cross to turn from the error of their ways, he may rest assured that his name is enrolled among the soldiers of the Cross.

Twiwood.

"Christian Progress"*

Addison, in his thoughtful essay on the immateriality of the soul, has made use of this beautiful figure: "The soul considered with its Creator, is like one of those mathematical lines that may draw nearer to another to all eternity without a possibility of touching it: and can there be a thought so transporting as to consider ourselves in these perpetual approaches to Him, who is not only the standard of perfection but of happiness." In this essay, which forms one of the most pleasing numbers of the *Spectator*, this genial writer seems to view the soul in its relations to its creator, rather in a philosophical light than in the light of revelation, and in its more specially religious bearings. He takes a pleasing glance at the possibilities and noble resources of the soul, and views it as something which was meant for, and is capable of almost infinite development in power and virtue. To a thoughtful reader, however, he suggests many a thought pregnant with deep meaning. He suggests that approximation to the divine character which is possible to every Christian who moulds his life after the perfect pattern with which our Lord has furnished us. But he does not seem to realize the difficulty which attends soul-progress. Turning to our Bibles we can study this subject by the aid of the light of inspired teachings. The Bible everywhere represents the Christian life as a progress,—a progress of the soul. But, although it always speaks of the Christian's journey as a pleasant one, since it is the only road in which true happiness can be found, it never describes it as a path strewn with flowers, but rather as one attended with and obstructed by many difficulties. In order to advance, the Christian must needs strain every muscle. This strain, though necessary at all times, is not, of necessity irksome, as God's all-powerful arm is ever around us, and the darkness which surrounds us is seldom so dense as to shut out the radiance of the

* "Christian Progress," Wilmington North Carolina *The Presbyterian*, December 20, 1876. (Editor's note).

Almighty's loving smiles. We can conceive of no more constant or eager striver after perfection than the apostle Paul, and yet even he said: "Brethren, I count not myself to have apprehended: but this one thing I do, forgetting those things which are behind, and reaching unto those things which are before, I press toward the mark for the prize of the high calling of God in Christ Jesus." All through his epistles he expresses this same distrust of himself, and gives vent to fears, lest his carnal mind should gain the mastery. In one place he says: "But I keep under my body, and bring it into subjection: lest that by any means, when I have preached to others, I myself should be a castaway." If this mighty soul, whose chief and only aim was to "walk worthy of the high vocation wherewith he was called," was troubled by such fears as these, what should be the feeling of the listless, half-souled follower of Christ! As the followers of this mighty Prince of Light we are ever under the stern necessity of fighting for our own safety, as well as the general advance of Christian doctrine. He who pretends to fight under the great banner of Love, should rejoice that there is no armor for his back, that to retreat is death, and should thus go forward with an eagerness and will which no slight cause can turn from their object.

Twiwood.

Part II
Political Liberty and the Scope and Ends of Government

"Socialism and Democracy"*

Is it possible that in practical America we are becoming sentimentalists? To judge by much of our periodical literature, one would think so. All resolution about great affairs seems now "sicklied o'er with a pale cast of thought." Our magazine writers smile sadly at the old-time optimism of their country; are themselves full of forebodings; expend much force and enthusiasm and strong (as well as weak) English style in disclosing social evils and economic bugbears; are moved by a fine sympathy for the unfortunate and a fine anger against those who bring wrong upon their fellows: but where amidst all these themes for the conscience is there a theme for the courage of the reader? Where are the brave plans of reform which should follow such prologues?

No man with a heart can withhold sympathy from the laborer whose strength is wasted and whose hope is thwarted in the service of the heartless and close-fisted; but, then, no man with a head ought to speak that sympathy in the public prints unless he have some manly, thought-out ways of betterment to propose. One wearies easily, it must be confessed, of woful-warnings; one sighs often for a little tonic of actual thinking grounded in sane, clear-sighted perception of what is possible to be done. Sentiment is not despicable — it may be elevating and noble, it may be inspiring, and in some mental fields it is self-sufficing — but when uttered concerning great social and political questions it needs the addition of practical, initiative sense to keep it sweet and to prevent its becoming insipid.

I point these remarks particularly at current discussions of socialism, and principally of 'state socialism,' which is almost the only form of socialism seriously discussed among us, out-side the Anti-Poverty Society. Is there not a plentiful

*"Socialism and Democracy," reproduced from the essay published in *The Papers of Woodrow Wilson*, edited by Arthur S. Link, Vol. 5 (Princeton University Press, 1968, 1996), 559–62. Reprinted with the permission of Princeton University Press. (Editor's note).

lack of nerve and purpose in what we read and hear nowadays on this momentous topic. One might be excused for taking and keeping the impression that there can be no great need for haste in the settlement of the questions mooted in connexion with it, inasmuch as the debating of them has not yet passed beyond its rhetorical and pulpit stage. It is easy to make socialism, as theoretically developed by the greater and saner socialistic writers, intelligible not only, but even attractive, as a conception; it is easy also to render it a thing of fear to timorous minds, and to make many signs of the times bear menace of it; the only hard task is to give it validity and strength as a program in practical politics. Yet the whole interest of socialism for those whose thinking extends beyond the covers of books and the paragraphs of periodicals lies in what it will mean in practice. It is a question of practical politics, or else it is only a thesis for engaging discourse.

Even mere discoursers, one would think, would be attracted to treat of the practical means of realizing for society the principles of socialism, for much the most interesting and striking features of it emerge only when its actual applications to concrete affairs are examined. These actual applications of it are the part of it which is much the most worth talking about—even for those whose only object is to talk effectively.

Roundly described, socialism is a proposition that every community, by means of whatever forms of organization may be most effective for the purpose, see to it for itself that each one of its members finds the employment for which he is best suited and is rewarded according to his diligence and merit, all proper surroundings of moral influence being secured to him by the public authority. 'State socialism' is willing to act through state authority as it is at present organized. It proposes that all idea of a limitation of public authority by individual rights be put out of view, and that the State consider itself bound to stop only at what is unwise or futile in its universal superintendence alike of individual and of public interests. The thesis of the state socialist is, that no line can be drawn between private and public affairs which the State may not cross at will; that omnipotence of legislation is the first postulate of all just political theory.

Applied in a democratic state, such doctrine sounds radical, but not revolutionary. It is only an acceptance of the extremest logical conclusions deducible from democratic principles long ago received as respectable. For it is very clear that in fundamental theory socialism and democracy are almost if not quite one and the same. They both rest at bottom upon the absolute right of the community to determine its own destiny and that of its members. Men as communities are supreme over men as individuals. Limits of wisdom and convenience to the public control there may be: limits of principle there are, upon strict analysis, none.

It is of capital importance to note this substantial correspondence of fundamental conception as between socialism and democracy: a whole system of practical politics may be erected upon it without further foundation. The germinal conceptions of democracy are as free from all thought of a limitation of the public authority as are the corresponding conceptions of socialism; the individual rights which the democracy of our own century has actually observed, were suggested to it by a political Philosophy radically individualistic, but not necessarily democratic. Democracy is bound by no principle of its own nature to say itself nay as to the exercise of any power. Here, then, lies the point. The difference between democracy and socialism is not an essential difference, but only a practical difference—is a difference of *organization* and *policy*, not a difference of primary motive. Democracy has not undertaken the tasks which socialists clamour to have undertaken; but it refrains from them, not for lack of adequate principles or suitable motives, but for lack of adequate organization and suitable hardihood: because it cannot see its way clear to accomplishing them with credit. Moreover it may be said that democrats of to-day hold off from such undertakings because they are of to-day, and not of the days, which history very well remembers, when government had the temerity to try everything. The best thought of modern time having recognized a difference between social and political questions, democratic government, like all other governments, seeks to confine itself to those political concerns which have, in the eyes of the judicious, approved themselves appropriate to the sphere and capacity of public authority.

The socialist does not disregard the obvious lessons of history concerning overwrought government: at least he thinks he does not. He denies that he is urging the resumption of tasks which have been repeatedly shown to be impossible. He points to the incontrovertible fact that the economic and social conditions of life in our century are not only superficially but radically different from those of any other time whatever. Many affairs of life which were once easily to be handled by individuals have now become so entangled amongst the complexities of international trade relations, so confused by the multiplicity of news-voices, or so hoisted into the winds of speculation that only powerful combinations of wealth and influence can compass them. Corporations grow on every hand, and on every hand not only swallow and overawe individuals but also compete with governments. The contest is no longer between government and individuals; it is now between government and dangerous combinations and individuals. Here is a monstrously changed aspect of the social world. In face of such circumstances, must not government lay aside all timid scruple and boldly make itself an agency for social reform as well as for political control?

'Yes,' says the democrat, 'perhaps it must. You know it is my principle, no less than yours, that every man shall have an equal chance with every other man: if I saw my way to it as a practical politician, I should be willing to go farther and superintend every man's use of his chance. But the means? The question with me is not whether the community has power to act as it may please in these matters, but how it can act with practical advantage—a question of *policy*.'

A question of policy primarily, but also a question of organization, that is to say of *administration*.

"A Calendar of Great Americans"*

Before a calendar of great Americans can be made out, a valid canon of Americanism must first be established. Not every great man born and bred in America was a great "American." Some of the notable men born among us were simply great Englishmen; others had in all the habits of their thought and life the strong flavor of a peculiar region, and were great New Englanders or great Southerners; other, masters in the fields of science or of pure thought, showed nothing either distinctively national or characteristically provincial, and were simply great men; while a few displayed odd cross-strains of blood or breeding. The great Englishmen bred in America, like Hamilton and Madison; the great provincials, like John Adams and Calhoun; the authors of such thought as might have been native to any clime, like Asa Gray and Emerson; and the men of mixed breed, like Jefferson and Benton,—must be excluded from our present list. We must pick out men who have created or exemplified a distinctively American standard and type of greatness.

To make such a selection is not to create an artificial standard of greatness, or to claim that greatness is in any case hallowed or exalted merely because it is American. It is simply to recognize a peculiar stamp of character, a special make-up of mind and faculties, as the specific product of our national life, not displacing or eclipsing talents of a different kind, but supplementing them, and so adding to the world's variety. There is an American type of man, and those who have exhibited this type with a certain unmistakable distinction and perfection have been great "Americans." It has required the utmost variety of character and energy to establish a great nation, with a polity at once free and firm, upon this continent,

*"A Calendar of Great Americans," New York *Forum* XVI (February 1894): 715–27. (Editor's note).

81

and no sound type of manliness could have been dispensed with in the effort. We could no more have done without our great Englishmen, to keep the past steadily in mind and make every change conservative of principle, than we could have done without the men whose whole impulse was forward, whose whole genius was for origination, natural masters of the art of subduing a wilderness.

Certainly one of the greatest figures in our history is the figure of Alexander Hamilton. American historians, though compelled always to admire him, often in spite of themselves, have been inclined, like the mass of men in his own day, to look at him askance. They hint, when they do not plainly say, that he was not "American." He rejected, if he did not despise, democratic principles; advocated a government as strong, almost, as a monarchy; and defended the government which was actually set up, like the skilled advocate he was, only because it was the strongest that could be had under the circumstances. He believed in authority, and he had no faith in the aggregate wisdom of masses of men. He had, it is true, that deep and passionate love of liberty, and that steadfast purpose in the maintenance of it, that mark the best Englishmen everywhere; but his ideas of government stuck fast in the old-world polities, and his statesmanship was of Europe rather than of America. And yet the genius and the stead-fast spirit of this man were absolutely indispensable to us. No one less masterful, no one less resolute than he to drill the minority, if necessary, to have their way against the majority, could have done the great work of organization by which he established the national credit, and with the national credit the national government itself. A pliant, popular, optimistic man would have failed utterly in the task. A great radical mind in his place would have brought disaster upon us: only a great conservative genius could have succeeded. It is safe to say that, without men of Hamilton's cast of mind, building the past into the future with a deep passion for order and old wisdom, our national life would have miscarried at the very first. This tried English talent for conservation gave to our fibre at the very outset the stiffness of maturity.

James Madison, too, we may be said to have inherited. His invaluable gifts of counsel were of the sort so happily imparted to us with our English blood at the first planting of the States which formed the Union. A grave and prudent man, and yet brave withal when new counsel was to be taken, he stands at the beginning of our national history, even in his young manhood, as he faced and led the constitutional convention, a type of the slow and thoughtful English genius for affairs. He held old and tested convictions of the uses of liberty; he was competently read in the history of government; processes of revolution were in his thought no more than processes of adaptation: exigencies were to be met by modification, not by experiment. His reasonable spirit runs through all the proceedings of the great convention that gave us the Constitution, and that noble instrument seems the product of character like his. For all it is so American in its content, it is in its method a thoroughly English production, so full is it of old principles, so conservative of experience, so care fully compounded of compromises, of concessions made and accepted. Such men are of a stock so fine as to need no titles to make it noble, and yet so old and so distinguished as actually to bear the chief titles of English liberty. Madison came of the long line of English constitutional statesmen.

There is a type of genius which closely approaches this in character, but which is, nevertheless, distinctively American. It is to be seen in John Marshall and in Daniel Webster. In these men a new set of ideas find expression, ideas which all the world has received as American. Webster was not an English but an American constitutional statesman. For the English statesman constitutional issues are issues of policy rather than issues of law. He constantly handles questions of change: his constitution is always a-making. He must at every turn construct, and he is deemed conservative if only his rule be consistency and continuity with the past. He will search diligently for precedent, but he is content if the precedent contain only a germ of the policy he proposes. His standards are set him, not by law, but by opinion: his constitution is an ideal of cautious and orderly change. Its fixed element is the conception of political liberty: a conception which, though steeped in history, must ever be added to and altered by social change. The American constitutional statesman, on the contrary, constructs policies like a lawyer. The standard with which he must square his conduct is set him by a document upon whose definite sentences the whole structure of the government directly rests. That document, moreover, is the concrete embodiment of a peculiar theory of government. That theory is, that definitive laws, selected by a power outside the government, are the structural iron of the entire fabric of politics, and that nothing which cannot be constructed upon this stiff framework is a safe or legitimate part of policy. Law is, in his conception, creative of States, and they live only by such permissions as they can extract from it. The functions of the judge and the functions of the man of affairs have, therefore, been very closely related in our history, and John Marshall, scarcely less than Daniel Webster, was a constitutional statesman. With all Madison's conservative temper and wide-eyed prudence in counsel, the subject-matter of thought for both of these men was not English liberty or the experience of men everywhere in self-government, but the meaning stored up in the explicit sentences of a written fundamental law. They taught men the new—the American—art of extracting life out of the letter, not of statutes merely (that art was not new), but of statute-built institutions and documented governments: the art of saturating politics with law without grossly discoloring law with politics. Other nations have had written constitutions, but no other nation has ever filled a written constitution with this singularly compounded content, of a sound legal conscience and a strong national purpose. It would have been easy to deal with our Constitution like subtle dialecticians; but Webster and Marshall did much more and much better than that. They viewed the fundamental law as a great organic product, a vehicle of life as well as a charter of authority; in disclosing its life they did not damage its tissue; and in thus expanding the law without impairing its structure or authority they made great contributions alike to statesmanship and to jurisprudence. Our notable literature of decision and commentary in the field of constitutional law is America's distinctive contribution to the history and the science of law. John Marshall wrought out much of its substance; Webster diffused its great body of principles throughout national policy, mediating between the law and affairs. The figures of the two men must hold the eye of the world as the figures of two great national representatives, as the figures of two great Americans.

The representative national greatness and function of these men appear more clearly still when they are contrasted with men like John Adams and John C. Calhoun, whose greatness was not national. John Adams represented one element of our national character, and represented it nobly, with a singular dignity and greatness. He was an eminent Puritan statesman, and the Puritan ingredient has colored all our national life. We have gotten strength and persistency and some part of our steady moral purpose from it. But in the quick growth and exuberant expansion of the nation it has been only one element among many. The Puritan blood has mixed with many another strain. The stiff Puritan character has been mellowed by many a transfusion of gentler and more hopeful elements. So soon as the Adams fashion of man became more narrow, intense, acidulous, intractable, according to the tendencies of its nature, in the person of John Quincy Adams, it lost the sympathy, lost even the tolerance, of the country, and the national choice took its reckless leap from a Puritan President to Andrew Jackson, a man cast in the rough original pattern of American life at the heart of the continent. John Adams had not himself been a very acceptable President. He had none of the national optimism, and could not understand those who did have it. He had none of the characteristic adaptability of the delocalized American, and was just a bit ridiculous in his stiffness at the Court of St. James, for all he was so honorable and so imposing. His type—be it said without disrespect—was provincial. Unmistakably a great man, his greatness was of the commonwealth, not of the empire.

Calhoun, too, was a great provincial. Although a giant, he had no heart to use his great strength for national purposes. In his youth, it is true, he did catch some of the generous ardor for national enterprise which filled the air in his day; and all his life through, with a truly pathetic earnestness, he retained his affection for his first ideal. But when the rights and interests of his section were made to appear incompatible with a liberal and boldly constructive interpretation of the Constitution, he fell out of national counsels and devoted all the strength of his extraordinary mind to holding the nation's thought and power back within the strait limits of a literal construction of the law. In powers of reasoning his mind deserves to rank with Webster's and Marshall's: he handled questions of law like a master, as they did. He had, moreover, a keen insight into the essential principles and character of liberty. His thought moved eloquently along some of the oldest and safest lines of English thought in the field of government. He made substantive contributions to the permanent philosophy of politics. His reasoning has been discredited, not so much because it was not theoretically sound within its limits, as because its practical outcome was a negation which embarrassed the whole movement of national affairs. He would have held the nation still, in an old equipoise, at one time normal enough, but impossible to maintain. Webster and Marshall gave leave to the energy of change inherent in all the national life, making law a rule, but not an interdict; a living guide, but not a blind and rigid discipline: but Calhoun sought to fix law as a barrier across the path of policy, commanding the life of the nation to stand still. The strength displayed in the effort, the intellectual power and address, abundantly entitle him to be called great; but his purpose was not national. It regarded but a section of the country, and marked him—again be it said with all respect—a great provincial.

Jefferson was not a thorough American because of the strain of French philosophy that permeated and weakened all his thought. Benton was altogether American so far as the natural strain of his blood was concerned, but he had encumbered his natural parts arid inclinations with a mass of undigested and shapeless learning. Bred in the West, where everything was new, he had filled his head with the thought of books (evidently very poor books) which exhibited the ideals of communities in which everything was old. He thought of the Roman Senate when he sat in the Senate of the United States. He paraded classical figures whenever he spoke, upon a stage where both their costume and their action seemed grotesque. A pedantic frontiersman, he was a living and a pompous antinomy. Meant by nature to be an American, he spoiled the plan by applying a most unsuitable gloss of shallow and irrelevant learning. Jefferson was of course an almost immeasurably greater man than Benton, but he was un-American in somewhat the same way. He brought a foreign product of thought to a market where no natural or wholesome demand for it could exist. There were not two incompatible parts to him, as in Benton's case: he was a philosophical radical by nature as well as by acquirement; his reading and his temperament went suitably together. The man is homogeneous throughout. The American shows in him very plainly, too, notwithstanding the strong and inherent dash of what was foreign in his make-up. He was a natural leader and manager of men, not because he was imperative or masterful, but because of a native shrewdness, tact, and sagacity, an inborn art and aptness for combination, such as no Frenchman ever displayed in the management of common men. Jefferson had just a touch of rusticity about him, besides; and it was not pretence on his part or merely a love of power that made him democratic. His indiscriminate hospitality, his almost passionate love for the simple equality of country life, his steady devotion to what he deemed to be the cause of the people, all mark him a genuine democrat, a nature native to America. It is his speculative philosophy that is exotic, and that runs like a false and artificial note through all his thought. It was un-American in being abstract, sentimental, rationalistic, rather than practical. That he held it sincerely need not be doubted; but the more sincerely he accepted it so much the more thoroughly was he un-American. His writings lack hard and practical sense. Liberty, among us, is not a sentiment, in deed, but a product of experience; its derivation is not rationalistic, but practical. It is a hard-headed spirit of independence, not the conclusion of a syllogism. The very aerated quality of Jefferson's principles gives them an air of insincerity, which attaches to them rather because they do not suit the climate of the country and the practical aspect of affairs than because they do not suit the character of Jefferson's mind and the atmosphere of abstract philosophy. It is because both they and the philosophical system of which they form a part do seem suitable to his mind and character, that we must pronounce him, though a great man, not a great American.

It is by the frank consideration of such concrete cases that we can construct, both negatively and affirmatively, our canons of Americanism. The American spirit is something more than the old, the immemorial Saxon spirit of liberty from which it sprang. It has been bred by the conditions attending the great task which we have all the century been carrying forward: the task, at once material and ideal, of subduing a wilderness and covering all the wide stretches of a vast continent with a single free and stable polity. It is, accordingly, above all things, a hopeful and confident spirit. It is progressive, optimistically progressive, and ambitious of objects of national scope and advantage. It is unpedantic, unprovincial, unspeculative, unfastidious; regardful of law, but as using it, not as being used by it or dominated by any formalism whatever; in a sense unrefined, because full of rude force; but prompted by large and generous motives, and often as tolerant as it is resolute. No one man, unless it be Lincoln, has ever proved big or various enough to embody this active and full-hearted spirit in all its qualities; and the men who have been too narrow or too speculative or too pedantic to represent it have, nevertheless, added to the strong and stirring variety of our national life, making it fuller and richer in motive and energy; but its several aspects are none the less noteworthy as they separately appear in different men.

One of the first men to exhibit this American spirit with an unmistakable touch of greatness and distinction was Benjamin Franklin. It was characteristic of America that this self-made man should become a philosopher, a founder of philosophical societies, an authoritative man of science; that his philosophy of life should be so homely and so practical in its maxims, and uttered with so shrewd a wit; that one region should be his birth place and another his home; that he should favor effective political union among the colonies from the first, and should play a sage and active part in the establishment of national independence and the planning of national organization; and that he should represent his countrymen abroad. They could have had no spokesman who represented more sides of their character. Franklin was a sort of multiple American. He was versatile without lacking solidity; he was a practical statesman without ceasing to be a sagacious philosopher. He came of the people, and was democratic; but he had raised himself out of the general mass of unnamed men, and so stood for the democratic law, not of equality, but of self-selection in endeavor. One can feel sure that Franklin would have succeeded in any part of the national life that it might have fallen to his lot to take part in. He will stand the final and characteristic test of Americanism: he would unquestionably have made a successful frontiersman, capable at once of wielding the axe and of administering justice from the fallen trunk.

Washington hardly seems an American, as most of his biographers depict him. He is too colorless, too cold, too prudent. He seems more like a wise and dispassionate Mr. Alworthy, advising a nation as he would a parish, than like a man building states and marshalling a nation in a wilderness. But the real Washington was as thoroughly an American as Jackson or Lincoln. What we take for lack of passion in him was but the reserve and self-mastery natural to a man of his class and breeding in Virginia. He was no parlor politician, either. He had seen the frontier, and far beyond it where the French forts lay. He knew the rough life of the country as few other men could. His thoughts did not live at Mount Vernon. He knew difficulty as intimately and faced it always with as quiet a mastery as William the Silent. This calm, straightforward, high-spirited man, making charts of the western country, noting the natural land and water routes into the heart of the continent, marking how the French power lay, conceiving the policy which should dispossess it, and the engineering achievements which should make the utmost resources of the land our own; counselling Braddock how to enter the forest, but not deserting him because he would not take advice; planning step by step, by patient correspondence with influential men everywhere, the meetings, conferences, common resolves which were finally to bring the great constitutional convention together; planning, too, always for the country as well as for Virginia; and presiding at last over the establishment and organization of the government of the Union: he certainly—the most suitable instrument of the national life at every moment of crisis—is a great American. Those noble words which he uttered amidst the first doubtings of the constitutional convention might serve as a motto for the best efforts of liberty wherever free men strive: "Let us raise a standard to which the wise and honest can repair; the event is in the hand of God."

In Henry Clay we have an American of a most authentic pattern. There was no man of his generation who represented more of America than he did. The singular, almost irresistible attraction he had for men of every class and every temperament came, not from the arts of the politician, but from the instant sympathy established between him and every fellow countryman of his. He does not seem to have exercised the same fascination upon foreigners. They felt toward him as some New Englanders did: he seemed to them plausible merely, too indiscriminately open and cordial to be sincere,—a bit of a charlatan. No man who really takes the trouble to understand Henry Clay, or who has quick enough parts to sympathize with him, can deem him false. It is the odd combination of two different elements in him that makes him seem irregular and inconstant. His nature was of the West, blown through with quick winds of ardor and aggression, a bit reckless and defiant; but his art was of the East, ready with soft and placating phrases, reminiscent of old and reverenced ideals, thoughtful of compromise and accommodation. He had all the address of the trained and sophisticated politician, bred in an old and sensitive society; but his purposes ran free of cautious restraints, and his real ideals were those of the somewhat bumptious Americanism which was pushing the frontier forward in the West, which believed itself capable of doing anything it might put its hand to, despised conventional restraints, and followed a vague but resplendent "manifest destiny" with lusty hurrahs. His purposes were sincere, even if often crude and uninstructed; it was only because the subtle arts of politics seemed inconsistent with the direct dash and bold spirit of the man that they sat upon him like an insincerity. He thoroughly, and by mere unconscious sympathy, represented the double America of his day, made up of a West which hurried and gave bold strokes, and of an East which held back, fearing the pace, thoughtful and mindful of the instructive past. The one part had to be served without offending the other: and that was Clay's mediatorial function.

Andrew Jackson was altogether of the West. Of his sincerity nobody has ever had any real doubt; and his Americanism is now at any rate equally unimpeachable. He was like Clay with the social imagination of the orator, and the art and sophistication of the eastern politician, left out. He came into our national politics like a cyclone from off the Western prairies. Americans of the present day perceptibly shudder at the very recollection of Jackson. He seems to them a great Vandal, playing fast and loose alike with institutions and with tested and established policy, debauching politics like a modern spoilsman. But whether we would accept him as a type of ourselves or not, the men of his own day accepted him with enthusiasm. He did not need to be explained to them. They crowded to his stand like men free at last, after long and tedious restraint, to make their own choice, follow their own man. There can be no mistaking the spontaneity of the thoroughgoing support he received. He was the new type of energy and self-confidence bred by life outside the States that had been colonies. It was a terrible energy, threatening sheer destruction to many a carefully wrought arrangement handed on to us from the past; it was a perilous self-confidence, founded in sheer strength rather than in wisdom. The government did not pass through the throes of that signal awakening of the new national spirit without serious rack and damage. But it was no disease. It was only an incautious, abounding, madcap strength that proved so dangerous in its readiness for every rash endeavor. It was necessary that the West should be let into the play: it was even necessary that she should assert her right to the leading role. It was done without good taste, but that does not condemn it. We have no doubt refined and schooled the hoyden influences of that crude time, and they are vastly safer now than then, when they first came bounding in; but they mightily stirred and enriched our blood from the first. Now that we have thoroughly suffered this Jackson change, and it is over, we are ready to recognize it as quite as radically American as anything in all our history.

Lincoln, nevertheless, rather than Jackson, was the supreme American of our history. In Clay, East and West were mixed without being fused or harmonized: he seems like two men. In Jackson there was not even a mixture; he was all of a piece, and altogether unacceptable to some parts of the country,—a frontier statesman. But in Lincoln the elements were combined and harmonized. The most singular thing about the wonderful career of the man is the way in which he steadily grew into a national stature. He began an amorphous, unlicked cub, bred in the rudest of human lairs; but, as he grew, everything formed, informed, transformed him. The process was slow but unbroken. He was not fit to be President until he actually became President. He was fit then because, learning everything as he went, he had found out how much there was to learn, and had still an infinite capacity for learning. The quiet voices of sentiment and the murmurs of resolution that went whispering through the land, his ear always caught, when others could hear nothing but their own words. He never ceased to be a common man: that was his source of strength. But he was a common man with genius, a genius for things American, for insight into the common thought, for mastery of the fundamental things of politics that inhere in human nature and cast hardly more than their shadows on constitutions, for the practical niceties of affairs, for judging men and assessing arguments. Jackson had no social imagination: no unfamiliar community made any impression on him. His whole fibre stiffened young, and nothing afterward could modify or even deeply affect it. But Lincoln was always a-making; he would have died unfinished if the terrible storms of the war had not stung him to learn in those four years what no other twenty could have taught him. And, as he stands there in his complete manhood, at the most perilous helm in Christendom, what a marvellous composite figure he is! The whole country is summed up in him: the rude Western strength, tempered with shrewdness and a broad and humane wit; the Eastern conservatism, regardful of law and devoted to fixed standards of duty. He even understood the South, as no other Northern man of his generation did. He respected, because he comprehended, though he could not hold, its view of the Constitution; he appreciated the inexorable compulsions of its past in respect of slavery; he would have secured it once more, and speedily if possible, in its right to self-government, when the fight was fought out. To the Eastern politicians he seemed like an accident; but to history he must seem like a providence.

Grant was Lincoln's suitable instrument, a great American general, the appropriate product of West Point. A Western man, he had no thought of commonwealths politically separate, and was instinctively for the Union; a man of the common people, he deemed himself always an instrument, never a master, and did his work, though ruthlessly, without malice: a sturdy, hard-willed taciturn man, a sort of Lincoln the Silent in thought and spirit. He does not appeal to the imagination very deeply; there is a sort of common greatness about him, great gifts combined singularly with a great mediocrity; but such peculiarities seem to make him all the more American,—national in spirit, thoroughgoing in method, masterful in purpose.

And yet it is no contradiction to say that Robert E. Lee also was a great American. He fought on the opposite side, but he fought in the same spirit, and for a principle which is in a sense scarcely less American than the principle of Union. He represented the idea of the inherent—the essential—separateness of self-government. This was not the principle of secession: that principle involved the separate right of the several self-governing units of the federal system to judge of national questions themselves independently, and as a check upon the federal government,—to adjudge the very objects of the Union. Lee did not believe in secession, but he did believe in the local rootage of all government. This is at bottom, no doubt, an English idea; but it has had a characteristic American development. It is the reverse side of the shield which bears upon it the devices of the Union, a side too much overlooked and obscured since the war. It conceives the individual State a community united by the most intimate associations, the first home and foster-mother of every man born into the citizenship of the nation. Lee considered himself a member of one of these great families; he could not conceive of the nation apart from the State: above all, he could not live in the nation divorced from his neighbors. His own community must decide his political destiny and duty.

This was also the spirit of Patrick Henry and of Sam Houston,—men much alike in the cardinal principle of their natures. Patrick Henry resisted the formation of the Union only because he feared to disturb the local rootage of self-government, to disperse power so widely that neighbors could not control it. It was not a disloyal or a separatist spirit, but only a jealous spirit of liberty. Sam Houston, too, deemed the character a community should give itself so great a matter that the community, once made, ought itself to judge of the national associations most conducive to its liberty and progress. Without liberty of this intensive character there could have been no vital national liberty; and Sam Houston, Patrick Henry, and Robert E. Lee are none the less great Americans because they represented only one cardinal principle of the national life. Self-government has its intrinsic antinomies as well as its harmonies.

Among men of letters Lowell is doubtless most typically American, though Curtis must find an eligible place in the list. Lowell was self-conscious, though the truest greatness is not; he was a trifle too "smart," besides, and there is no "smartness" in great literature. But both the self-consciousness and the smartness must be admitted to be American; and Lowell was so versatile, so urbane, of so large a spirit, and so admirable in the scope of his sympathies, that he must certainly go on the calendar.

There need be no fear that we shall be obliged to stop with Lowell in literature, or with any of the men who have been named in the field of achievement. We shall not in the future have to take one type of Americanism at a time. The frontier is gone: it has reached the Pacific. The country grows rapidly homogeneous. With the same pace it grows various, and multiform in all its life. The man of the simple or local type cannot any longer deal in the great manner with any national problem. The great men of our future must be of the composite type of greatness: sound-hearted, hopeful, confident of the validity of liberty, tenacious of the deeper principles of American institutions, but with the old rashness schooled and sobered, and instinct tempered by instruction. They must be wise with an adult, not with an adolescent wisdom. Some day we shall be of one mind, our ideals fixed, our purposes harmonized, our nationality complete and consentaneous: then will come our great literature and our greatest men.

Woodrow Wilson.

"An Address on Thomas Jefferson"*

Mr. Chairman, ladies, and gentlemen of the Democratic Club. I often wonder why you draw modest academic persons out of their seclusion to speak to you on public occasions. I suppose it is because you feel so much immersed in affairs and know so much about them that you occasionally want to hear someone talk who doesn't known anything about them, for the refreshment of that removed and impartial point of view which you are sure to get from such persons. And yet I suppose that academic men are no more removed from the present scene than Jefferson himself; and therefore you give me as my toast a person as remote as I am from public affairs.

It is a singular thing to reflect upon that a body of active men like yourselves should gather about the shrine of a ghost. It is interesting to reflect that the man is dead and gone whom we meet here to celebrate to-night, and that it is only by the recollection of the historian that we are reminded of his career and of his principles; and yet it is one of the reassuring circumstances of human affairs that men of this sort do not die, that they rule us by their spirits from their urns; that there is something, as has already been so eloquently said, that is immortal in their principles.

I must confess that looking back to the life of Jefferson he seems to me a rather dim figure. He was not a man who appeared on occasions like this, for example. He was not a man who undertook to make public addresses or often let his voice be heard among his fellow citizens. He preferred the closet. He preferred the written paper. He preferred that quiet utterance of the statesman which comes through

---

* "An Address on Thomas Jefferson," reproduced from an account entitled "Address of Dr. Woodrow Wilson," published in National Democratic Club, *Annual Dinner on Jefferson Day April the Sixteenth One Thousand Nine Hundred and Six, At the Waldorf-Astoria*, 18–27. The original account includes indications where applause or laughter came from the audience; such references have been deleted here. (Editor's note).

the printed word. We think of him, not as a man who mixed with the people, but rather as a man withdrawn, aristocratic, exclusive, who nevertheless gave to a nation the law of popular action.

A great many persons look upon him as a literary man who had an uncanny gift for making party programmes and organizing party victories, a sort of secret, Machiavelian, Italian hand in politics; and yet if you look back to the real Thomas Jefferson you will find him a typical American. Did you never reflect that Albermarle County, Virginia, when he was born in it, was a frontier, and that this man whom you think of as the quintessence of a civilized community was a frontiersman? He was born at the front of American life. His was that wide view of American affairs which revealed itself also to Washington when he threaded the western forests, and met the French at their outposts upon the waters of the Ohio. He lived among the plain, the plainest people of his time and drank directly at the sources of Democratic feeling. It is true that he consorted with philosophers on the other side of the water. It is true that he found himself a very suitable companion for them. But while in his abstract thinking, he was a child of his age, in his action he was a child of his country. That is the apparent contradiction in the man, that while he preached the abstract tenets of a speculative political philosophy, he nevertheless took leave to act like a wise American politician.

There seemed to be a touch of charlatanry about him, but in fact there was none. What he undertook to do was to push certain definite principles forward. When he wrote they assumed an abstract aspect. When he acted there was no abstraction about them. He did not believe that the Constitution of the U.S. warranted the purchase of the Louisiana Territory; but he advocated its purchase, saying in a letter that he was very well aware it made waste paper of the Constitution. He preferred to make waste paper of the Constitution rather than make a waste of America, devastated by wars between European powers and the power to which by plain destiny it really belonged. He had two principles and only two. He believed in the right of the individual to opportunity, and in the right of people to a free development and he knew that anything which checked either the one or the other of these checked the growth of America. He had the good sense to make theory yield to practice when theory jeoparded either one of these principles. He was a poet and a dreamer, as every man is who ever led a free people, and he never realized the practical difficulty of Democracy. The difficulty in believing in the people is that you know so many of them. It takes a man who can abstract the poetry from the most unpromising subject, namely, the person he knows, to construct a real, sound, water-tight theory of Democracy. I cannot make Democratic theory out of each of you, but I could make a Democratic theory out of all of you. And what Thomas Jefferson did was to learn the alchemy by which a great many imperfect persons are made to find impulse for the realization of visions and dreams. For, if you will compound with your neighbor the things which you and he believe, you will find that there is gathering in your head some little theory and vision of the destiny of the human race, if you will embark with him in a common enterprise and hope that common men, united, embody the progress of the race. It was thinking at once in visions and in concrete politics that made this man the great prototype of all true Democracy. Gentlemen, we do not return to Thomas Jefferson to borrow policies. We return to Thomas Jefferson to renew ideals.

It were impossible to apply the policies of the time of Thomas Jefferson to the time we live in. There are no common terms in which to describe his time and ours, and unless you are going to make light of the things which now exist you cannot return to the policies of Thomas Jefferson. But you can and must return to the ideals of Thomas Jefferson. If you do return to those ideals, what will you do? For we do not take counsel with each other as fellow citizens merely to ask each other what shall we think. There is something much more important than that in hand, and that is to determine what we shall *do*. For this country waits upon sound action for its salvation. We shall not be saved by good thinking, but we shall be saved by honest action. There are maladies in the body politic. They are not incurable, if the patient should obey the instructions of the physician, and we return to Thomas Jefferson to-night to hear the instructions of the physician. Many prescriptions of health, which are prescriptions of intellectual health as well as political wisdom, remain in the spirit of Thomas Jefferson.

For one thing, we shall reject, as we would reject poison itself, the prescriptions of Socialism. Thos. Jefferson's creed was a creed of individualism, not of Socialism. See what it is that you would do if you accepted the nostrums of the Socialists? You would enslave the individual by making him subject to the organization. You would make the biggest, most dangerous, corruptible organization that you could possibly conceive, combining the state along such lines that each one of us would constitute not an integer, but a fraction, not a whole man, but a fraction of a great body politic. The fundamental idea of Thos. Jefferson is individualism; is a vitalization of the parts, in order to a vitalization of the whole. You cannot vitalize a whole made up of individuals without first vitalizing the parts. Do you say that that is an abstract doctrine? Is it abstract doctrine? What are we struggling for now? To curb the power of corporations because we do not believe in corporations? No, I think not. I don't see how our modern civilization could dispense with corporations. I don't see anything but the utmost folly in entering upon a course of destruction in respect to the present organization of our economic life. We are not afraid of the corporations except in so far as we are afraid of the men who constitute them, and we are afraid of the men who constitute them because we have not picked them out for accountability by our laws, but have submerged them in the corporation to which they belong. We have organized corporations in such a way and administered law in such a way that men hide in the corporations; not only hide from the community, but hide from their own eyes, and are not themselves aware when they are dishonest. And courts tell you that you cannot pick out Mister A., the President of the corporation and Mr. B. the Secretary of the organization, can't put him in jail. And you know you can't put the organization into jail; you know that fines won't reach the disease. Somebody has got to go to jail. And the only way to get anybody into jail is to act upon Jeffersonian principles, and individualize men. Individualize men so that they will discover that if they are directors and don't direct they are going to be put in a place where they can't direct anything, not even their own selves; where men will find that the law don't deal with combinations, but with persons. It is persons who do wrong, not corporations, and when persons do wrong they should suffer the penalty of the law.

Do not answer to the Socialist, 'Yes, we will go further in the process yet, and so adjust our very politics that men will be dealt with still less as persons and become mere members of an organization.['] Will you carry this step of hiding the individual and sinking his individuality a step further so that we shall never discover the guilty person any more? The old, sane, tested processes of law are processes which have picked out the individual and said to him, 'There is nothing in which you take part for which you may not sooner or later be held responsible.' Why, gentlemen, what is it we have learned in recent investigations? That things were corrupt? No, we knew that already; but that men whom we trusted and still respect were dishonest and didn't know it. (Applause.) That men whom we still respect, I repeat, so merged their own individual sense of honor in the practices of the corporations they belonged to as not to be able to distinguish personal honor from corporate interest. This republic will not be recalled to the days of heroic achievement until every man knows that his honor cannot be compounded,—that he must stand by himself, singly, alone, ready to take any shocks of circumstances and any light of exposure. (Applause.) The men whom you really honor are not men who allow their consciences to be put in harness. This, it seems to me, is one of the best teachings of Thomas Jefferson,—the individualization of men and the basing of the law upon that individualization.

But what is going to govern our consciences? Merely a fear of being found out? Are we not going to be lifted to something better than that,—"something of a faith, some reverence for the laws ourselves have made?" Are we not to have a social sense of responsibility as well as an individual sense of responsibility? While we excercise our economic energy, through corporations, are we not to subordinate corporations to the public interest? Gentlemen, there is one thing that underlies a great deal of the corporation question, as you do not need to be told. I refer to the tariff. That has too much been made upon the principle of selecting particular interests for particular privileges. Certain interests which need not be named have been allowed to stand in the way of justice,—bare, naked justice— to the inhabitants of the Philippine Islands; and particular interests have been suffered both to check and to determine the economic growth of the United States. The Jeffersonian principle means this: all interests upon an equal footing and every man singled out for his personal responsibility. (Applause.)

Gentlemen, we do not, in my opinion, need more laws, but we do need laws which shall find the men. It seems to me to be of no little significance that we meet here to submit our selves to the spirit of a man who is dead and gone, for what we need in affairs is not so much a programme as a new spirit. We need a rejuvenation of the principles by which we have professed to live. We need to have the scales taken away from our eyes, to see the national life as it is, and to insist that the remedies, the old and tried remedies, be once more applied in public service.

We talk about the contest between capital and labor. I do not see anything essentially evil in that contest itself. Every good thing is worked out by contest. There is a pretty story of a gentleman who was watching a chrysalis—a little creature releasing itself from the chrysalis and becoming a butterfly. One wing had loosened itself and the creature, apparently with torture, was trying to loosen the other wing from the retaining chrysalis. The man in pity cut the chrysalis and the creature fell,—with but a single wing. It was maimed and imperfect because he had not permitted it to struggle to its perfect life.

There is nothing evil in struggle itself. The best service you can render me if I want something from you and you want something from me, is to lay your mind squarely alongside of mine and let each one of us determine his muscle and his virtue in the contest.

Capital will not discover its responsibilities if you aid it. Labor will not discover its limitations and ultimate conditions if you coddle it. You must see to it that your law does not take sides,—and that is Jeffersonian principle. Not that the law should intervene to ease the strain, but to prevent an unmanly advantage. Law is your umpire; it must not go into the ring until one or the other opponents hits below the belt. Law does not object to blows, but it objects to fraudulent or dirty blows. It insists that the contestants be manly, sportsmanlike, righteous, courteous. Its duty is fulfilled when it has enforced the rules of the game, not when it has entered and taken part in the game. Do not conceive for yourselves a commonwealth in which the law will assist its citizens class by class, but conceive to yourselves a commonwealth in which it will preside over the life of its citizens, condescending to assist nobody, but umpiring every move of the contest. We do not have to lay down policies; we have only to remind ourselves of principles that are as old as the world. And mark my word, insofar as modern states forget these old lessons, they will get deeper and deeper into the mire of hopeless struggle and men will see a time—God forbid that it should ever come—a time of despair, when we shall look in each other's faces and say, "Are we men no longer? Are we wards? Each of us wards of all of us? Can no man take care of himself? Must I always consult you and you always consult me? Must we seek to be children or seek to be men?' It was a principle of Thos. Jefferson's that there must be as little government as possible,— which did not mean that there must not be any government at all, but only that men must be taught to take care of themselves. I heartily subscribe—so heartily that if I could see the way to prevent litigation I would not take it, because moral muscle depends upon your showing men that there is nobody to take care of them except God and themselves.

The handsomest pictures in the history of individuals are the pictures of those who have stood out independent of Government,—individuals who made such replies as that historic reply of two recalcitrant subjects to whom the King said, "Do you know that I can hang you?" "Aye," they replied, "and we can die cursing you." We should crave the spirit that will not be subdued: only under the government of unsubdueable individual spirits shall we return to the great days of Jefferson.

Gentlemen, let us not forget the events of our youth, of the youth of our nation. Let not the complexity of modern circumstances obscure for us the memory of that heroic age—let us lift our eyes above the confusion of the signs that are about us and hark back to those simple and manly principles under which we were born and under which we shall prove worthy of our heritage.

"The Author and Signers of the Declaration of Independence"*

It is common to think of the Declaration of Independence as a highly speculative document; but no one can think it so who has read it. It is a strong, rhetorical statement of grievances against the English government. It does indeed open with the assertion that all men are equal and that they have certain inalienable rights, among them the right to life, liberty and the pursuit of happiness. It asserts that governments were instituted to secure these rights, and can derive their just powers only from the consent of the governed; and it solemnly declares that "whenever any government becomes destructive of these ends, it is the right of the people to alter or to abolish it, and to institute a new government, laying its foundations in such principles, and organizing its powers in such forms, as to them shall seem most likely to effect their safety and happiness." But this would not afford a general theory of government to formulate policies upon. No doubt we are meant to have liberty, but each generation must form its own conception of what liberty is. No doubt we shall always wish to be given leave to pursue happiness as we will, but we are not yet sure where or by what method we shall find it. That we are free to adjust government to these ends we know. But Mr. Jefferson and his colleagues in the Continental Congress prescribed the law of adjustment for no generation but their own. They left us to say whether we thought the government they had set up was founded on "such principles," its powers organized in "such forms" as seemed to us most likely to effect our safety and happiness. They did not attempt to dictate the aims and objects of any generation but their own.

* Published as "The Authors and Signers of the Declaration of Independence," *North American Review* CLXXXVI (September 1907): 22–33. The version presented here is reproduced from a typed manuscript in the Woodrow Wilson Collection of the Seeley G. Mudd Library at Princeton University. (Editor's note).

We are justified in looking back with a great satisfaction to the documents which spoke the purposes of the Revolution and formed the government which was to succeed to the authority of king and parliament. They speak the character of the men who drew them as clearly as they speak the circumstances of the times. The fifty-six men who put their names to the Declaration of Independence were not of the sort to meet an acute crisis in affairs with a treatise on government. They were accustomed to the practice of business, and as apt to go straight to their point as any minister over sea. They were of every calling;—men were apt in that day of beginnings to have been of several callings by the time they reached middle life. Lawyers predominated among them, men like James Wilson and John Adams and Edward Rutledge; but there were merchants too, like Robert Morris of Philadelphia and John Hancock of Boston; country gentlemen of large affairs like Benjamin Harrison and Charles Carroll; and physicians, like Benjamin Rush and Lyman Hall. Thomas Jefferson and Benjamin Franklin we cannot classify. Each stands unique and individual, a man supported by genius. And hard-headed Englishmen, like Button Gwinnet of Georgia; and men sure of their rights because they were Irishmen, born with an inclination to assert them, like James Smith and George Taylor, added to the handsome variety; and a man like John Witherspoon, the indomitable President of Princeton, turned statesman to authenticate the teaching he was giving lads like James Madison and Henry Lee, contributed his own flavour of unhesitating directness, both of thought and speech. Only Scotchmen seem able to be formidable at once in philosophy and in fact. The only professional politician among them was Samuel Adams, at home a master of agitation and political organization, but in the Congress quiet enough, a statesman of grievances, not of measures.

The genius of the new republic was expressed among these men as it was expressed eleven years later among the men who framed the Constitution of the United States, by practical capacity, thoughtful indeed and holding at its heart clear-cut, unmistakable conceptions of what government of free men ought to be, but not fanciful, a thing of action rather than of theory, suited to meet an exigency, not a mere turn in debate. We do not live in times as critical as theirs. We are not engaged in making a nation. But we are engaged in purging and preserving a nation, and an analysis of our duty in the situation in which we stand is in many ways more difficult than that which they attempted, the remedies to be applied left less obvious to our choice. They gave us the nation: we owe them, not empty eulogy, but the sincere flattery of imitation. If we are their descendants either in blood or in spirit, let us distinguish our ancestry from that of others by clear wisdom in counsel and fearless action taken upon plain principle.

No one now needs to be told what the principle of the American Revolution was: it was the principle of individual liberty. Though those men who signed the Declaration of Independence were no theorists but practical statesmen, a very definite conception of what the government of enlightened men ought to be lay back of everything they did, and that conception they held with a passionate conviction. They believed government to be a means by which the individual could realize at once his responsibility and his freedom from unnecessary restraint. Government should guard his rights, but it must not undertake to exercise them for him.

No doubt the most interesting spokesman of that conception was that eminent Virginian, that unique and singular author of the Declaration of Independence. No doubt Thomas Jefferson was an astute politician; no doubt he was a most interesting philosopher; certainly he was a most inscrutable man. It would be impossible to make a consistent picture of him that should include all sides of his varied genius and singular character. He took leave, like all great men of affairs, to be inconsistent and do what circumstances required, approaching the perfection of theory by the tedious indirections of imperfect practice, but the main base of his theories was the base upon which all thoughtful men in his day founded their thinking about politics and intended to found their measures also. He believed consistently and profoundly in the right of the individual to a free opportunity, and in the right of the nation to an unhampered development, and was ready to support every law or arrangement which promised to secure the people against any sort of monopoly in taking part in that development. Moreover, he knew that government was a thing conducted by individuals, men whose weaknesses and passions did not differ from the weaknesses and passions of the men whom they governed; and that government must operate upon individuals whose tangled rights and opportunities no government could look into too curiously or seek to control too intimately without intolerable consequences of paternalism and petty tyranny. Every man who signed the Declaration of Independence believed, as Mr. Jefferson did, that free men had a much more trustworthy capacity in taking care of themselves than any government had ever shown or was ever likely to show, in taking care of them; and upon that belief American government was built.

So far as the Declaration of Independence was a theoretical document, that is its theory. Do we still hold it? Does the doctrine of the Declaration of Independence still live in our principles of action, in the things we do, in the purposes we applaud, in the measures we approve? It is not a question of piety. We are not bound to adhere to the doctrines held by the signers of the Declaration of Independence: we are as free as they were to make and unmake governments. We are not here to worship men or a document. But neither are we here to indulge in a mere rhetorical and uncritical eulogy. Every Fourth of July should be a time for examining our standards, our purposes, for determining afresh what principles, what forms of power we think most likely to effect our safety and happiness. That and that alone is the obligation the Declaration lays upon us. It is no fetish; its words lay no compulsion upon the thought of any free man; but it was drawn by men who thought, and it obliges those who receive its benefits to think likewise.

What then do we think of our safety and of our happiness,— of the principles of action and the forms of power we are using to secure them? That we have come to a new age and a new attitude towards questions of government, no one can doubt,—to new definitions of constitutional power, new conceptions of legislative object, new schemes of individual and corporate regulation. Upon what principle of change do we act? Do we act upon definite calculations of purpose, or do we but stumble hesitatingly upon expedients? To what statements of principle would a declaration of our reasons and purposes commit us before the world: to those the signers of the Declaration of Independence would have avowed, or to others very different and not at all novel in the political history of the world? This is not a party question: there is apparently little difference between parties in regard to it. It is a national question,—a question touching the political principles of America. We ought not to hesitate to avow a change, if change there is to be; but we should be ashamed to act in radical fashion and not know that there was a change. Precedent is at least a guide by which to determine our direction.

There is much in our time that would cause men of the principles of Mr. Jefferson the bitterest disappointment. Individual opportunity is not unhampered. The nation has had in every respect an extraordinary material development, but the chief instrumentalities of that development have been at least virtually monopolized, and the people, though they created the opportunity and contributed the labor, have not shared the benefits of that development as they might have shared them. This has not been due to the operation of our institutions; it has been due to the operation of human nature, which is alike under all institutions and which has perhaps had freer play under our institutions than it would have had under any others, as Mr. Jefferson wished that it should have. Moreover, there is no doubt that we shall set all things right; but it is important we should inquire the way and not set them right by methods which may bring new trouble upon us, if the old methods will suffice for our safety and happiness. What were those methods? What was the spirit of the nation at its inception,—in 1776 when the great declaration of its intentions was framed, and in 1787 when it made deliberate choice of its form of government?

There is no difficulty in answering these questions; the answers to them have lain before us since we were children, in every book that spoke of our history or of our character as a nation. Let us use them as a mirror into which to look in order to make test whether we shall recognize our own features, disguised as they are by change of circumstance, in our present habit, as we live.

The most obvious characteristic of the men who gave the nation voice and power was their profound regard for law. That conviction is upon the surface and at the heart of everything they said or did in support of their purpose. They did not fling off from the mother country because they wanted new rights, but because the rights they had time out of mind enjoyed as free men under the laws and constitution of England, and the rights they had been promised as colonists in a new country with a life of its own, had been arbitrarily disregarded and withdrawn, and they knew not what ancient and undoubted liberties and privileges they could count upon. They wanted, not less law nor even better law, but law they could rely upon and live by. Their case was a case for legality, for the established understandings of law, upon which they knew that liberty had immemorially depended. There is no longer any need to debate what liberty really is; the question has been tried out again and again, both in theory and in practice,—in the council chamber and on the field of battle, where the air was calm and where it thrilled with passion,—and by no race more thoroughly than by that from which we derived our law; and we may say that we know. Affairs swing this way and that, sometimes with revolutionary force, as interests wage war for advantage, but we know where the midpoint of perfect poise lies and seek constantly to turn our lines of policy towards it. Liberty consists in the best possible adjustment between the power of the government and the privilege of the individual; and only law can effect that adjustment. Where liberty is, there must be a perfect understanding between the individual and those who would control him; and if either he or they can disregard the understanding, there is license or anarchy. It was in that knowledge that the founders of our government loved the law.

These same men, therefore, who revered law and depended upon its grants and definitions for their security and happiness, were deeply jealous of too much law. It is easy to talk of "society," of "communities," of "the people," but the fact is that these are but names we give to bodies made up of individuals. It is easy also to speak of "governments" as if they were forces set apart from us and above us; but governments also consist of individuals of like nature with ourselves. That is the reason, the very interesting and important reason, which the founders of our government needed not to have explained to [t]hem, why control of our affairs by the government and the regulation of our relations to each other by the law are two very different things and lead to sharply contrasted results. The history of liberty in the past, from which we may possibly gather some intimation of its history in the future, has been a history of resistance to too much governmental control and a careful discovery of the best forms and the most prudent degrees of legal regulations; and it is clear that the law which the signers of the Declaration of Independence loved was something which they regarded, not as a body of powers possessed by a government, but as a body of rules regulating the complex game of life, no more favorable to control than was necessary to make it a safeguard of individual privilege and a guarantee of equal rights. Too much law was too much government; and too much government was too little individual privilege,—as too much individual privilege in its turn was selfish license.

Now let us hold this mirror up to ourselves and see if we recognize in it the image of our own minds. In that mirror we see a conception of government which frankly puts the individual in the foreground, thinking of him as the person to be at once protected and heartened to make a free use of himself; the responsible administrator of his own liberties and his own responsibilities; and of government as the umpire; and which depends upon law for nothing else than a clear establishment of the rules of the game. That is hardly our notion. We are indeed in love with law,—more in love with it than were the makers of the government,—but hardly in love with it as a government of mere regulation. For us it is an instrument of reconstruction and control. The individual has eluded us, we seem to say, has merged and hidden himself in corporations and associations, through the intricacies of whose structure we have not time to thread our way in search of him; we will therefore meet the circumstances as we find them, treat him not as an integer but as a fraction, and deal with the association, not with the individual. We will prohibit corporations to do this or to do that, to be this or to be that, and punish them either with fine or with dissolution if they disobey. The morals of business and of law we will frankly accept as corporate morals, and we will not set these corporations, these new individuals of our modern law, to watch and sue one another for infractions of the law: they might combine, and there is no sufficient motive for them to check one another in illegal practices. Neither can we depend upon individuals: they are now too minute and weak. The moralizer and disciplinarian of corporations can in the nature of the case be none other than the government itself, and, because corporations spread from state to state, can be none other than the government of the United States.

It is amusing how we extend this new theory of law into some of the new details of our life,—extend it at any rate in our thinking, if not in our legislation. We hear it suggested on every side, for example, that the true and effective way to stop the driving of automobiles along our highways at excessive rates of speed is to lock up the automobiles themselves whenever the speed laws are violated, so that for a long time at least it may not be used again. I suppose we shall some day see officers of the law arresting electric cars and steam locomotives for the offences which their motormen and engineers have committed, and the faults of men everywhere corrected by locking up their tools. The trouble is that the tools are wanted, and the lives of all of us are inconvenienced if they are taken away. Even the automobile is useful, when used with sanity and caution. And there is exactly the same serious trouble about the way we now deal with our corporations, punishing inanimate things instead of persons. When we fine them, we merely take that much money out of their business,—that is, out of the business of the country,—and put it into the public treasury, where there is generally already a surplus and where it is likely to lie idle. When we dissolve them, we check and hamper legitimate undertakings and embarrass the business of the country much more than we should embarrass it were we to arrest locomotives and impound electric cars, the necessary vehicles of our intercourse. And all the while we know perfectly well that the iniquities we levy fines for were conceived and executed by particular individuals who go unpunished, unchecked even, in the enterprises which have led to the action of the courts. And so from one body of hidden individuals we turn to another, and say, "Go to, we will instruct the government to regulate this thing in place of boards of directors: if necessary, we will instruct the government to transact the business which these corporations have made the government interfere with on account of bad practices. We shall then have honesty: for are not the men who compose the government men of our own choice, our servants for our common business?"

It needs no prophet to predict that too much government lies that way, and nothing but too much government,—and no increased efficiency or improved business to be had in the bargain. And beyond too much government lies the old programme, repeated and repeated again and again every time the like thing has happened: a new struggle for liberty, a new eagerness for emancipation from the law that dictates, into the freedom of the law that umpires. No doubt the old cycle must some time be gone through again; but we ought not to be the people to go through it. We have had too much light: we have furnished the world with doctrines and example in this kind, and we cannot afford to illustrate our own principles by our mistakes after having illustrated them by our successes. Shall we return to our old standards, or shall we attempt arrangements which we know our children will be obliged to reject?

Can we return to our old standards in this strange and altered day, when all the face of circumstances seems changed and nothing remains as it was in the time when the government was hopefully set up? Undoubtedly we can. Not everything is changed: the biggest item of all remains unaltered,—human nature itself; and it is nothing to daunt a free people,—free to think and free to act, that the circumstances in which that old, unalterable nature now expresses itself are so complex and singular. The difficulty of the task is part of its desirability: it is a new enterprise upon which to stretch our powers and make proof of our sanity and strength. It is the task of making a new translation of our morals into the terms of our modern life, where individuality seems for the time being lost in complex organizations, and then making a new translation of our laws to match our new translation of morals. It is the task of finding the individual in the maize of modern social, commercial and industrial conditions; finding him with the probe of morals and with the probe of law. One really responsible man in jail, one real originator of the schemes and transactions which are contrary to public interest legally lodged in the penitentiary would be worth more than a thousand corporations mulcted in fines, if reform is to be genuine and permanent.

It is only in this way that we can escape socialism. If the individual is lost to our law, he is lost to our politics and to our social structure. If he is merged in the business group, he is merged in the state, the association that includes all others. Unless we can single him out again and make him once more the subject and object of law, we shall have to travel still further upon the road of government regulation which we have already traveled so far, and that road leads to state ownership. We have not even tried to extend the old roads into this vast new area of business and of corporate enterprise, which recent years have seen open up like a new continent of mind and achievement; and until we have tried, we cannot claim legitimate descent from the founders of the government. We have abandoned their principles without even making trial of their efficacy in a new situation.

The elaborate secret manipulations by means of which some of our so-called "financiers" get control of a voting majority of the stock of great railroad or manufacturing companies, in order to effect vast combinations of interest or properties, incidentally destroying the value of some stocks and fictitiously increasing the value of others, involve first or last acts which are in effect sheer thefts, making the property of thousands of stockholders so much waste paper, or arbitrarily decreasing the relative earning capacity of corporations for a share in whose earnings thousands of men and women had paid hard-earned cash; but we have never sought to bring the details of these transactions within the definition of the criminal law. Not to do so is like overlooking the highway robberies of the mediaeval barons. Moreover, it leaves an unjust stain of popular suspicion upon transactions similar to all outward appearance, but conceived in justice and fair-dealing. Every corporation is personally directed either by some one dominant person or by some group of persons, in respect of every essential step in its policy: somebody in particular is responsible for ordering or sanctioning every illegal act committed by its agents or officers; but neither our law of personal damages nor our criminal law has sought to seek the responsible persons out and hold them individually accountable for the acts complained of. It would require a careful hand and a minute knowledge of existing business conditions to draw the law, but statutes could oblige every corporation to make such public analysis of its organization as would enable both private individuals and officers of the law to fix legal responsibility upon the right person. We have never attempted such statutes. We indict corporations themselves, find them guilty of illegal practices, fine them, and leave the individuals who devise and execute the illegal acts free to discover new evasions and shape the policy of the corporations to practices not yet covered by the prohibitions of law. We complain that directors are too often mere names upon a list and that even when they attend the meetings of the boards to which they belong, they give no real heed to what is done and allow some committee to have its own way unquestioned; and yet the law could easily make them responsible, personally and individually responsible, to any extent it chose for acts which their votes authorized, and could thereby quickly change their nominal participation in the affairs of the corporations they pretend to govern, into real participation and watchful oversight. Let every corporation exactly define the obligations and powers of its directors, and then let the law fix responsibility upon them accordingly.

I need not multiply examples. We know that the vast majority of our business transactions are sound, the vast majority of our business men honest. In order to clear the way of unjust suspicion, give credit where credit is due, condemnation where condemnation; let us set ourselves to work to single out individuals and real personal responsibility, and we shall both lighten the difficulty of government and make a new platform of life. Governmental supervision there must be, but of the kind there has always been in District Attorneys' offices; not the kind that seeks to determine the processes of business, but the kind that brings home to individuals the obligations of the law.

It would be a happy emancipation. We should escape the burden of too much government, and we should regain our self-respect, our self-confidence, our sense of individual integrity; we should think straightway with regard to the moral aspect of conduct, and we should escape perplexities with regard to our political future; we should once more have the exhilarating freedom of governing our own lives, the law standing as umpire, not as master.

By such means we should prove ourselves indeed the spiritual descendants of the signers of the Declaration of Independence. It is fashionable, it is easy, to talk about Jeffersonian principles of government. Men of all kinds and of the most opposite doctrines call themselves by Mr. Jefferson's name; and it must be admitted that it is easy to turn many of Mr. Jefferson's opinions this way or that. But no man's name settles any principle, and Mr. Jefferson was originating no novel doctrine, announcing no discoveries in politics, when he wrote the Declaration of Independence. What it contains is in fact the common-place of political history. There can be no liberty if the individual is not free: there is no such thing as corporate liberty. There is no other possible formula for a free government than this: that the laws must deal with individuals, allowing them to choose their own lives under a definite personal responsibility to a common government set over them; and that government must regulate, not as a superintendent does, but as a judge does; it must safeguard, it must not direct. .

These thoughts ought still to linger in the very air of this place. The first English settlers came here while the breath of the "spacious times of great Elizabeth" was still in every man's lungs, and the quickening impulse of enterprise and adventure. The great Tudor queen had known how to deal with mettlesome men: she had given them leave to do what they pleased in the world, if only they would remember always her sovereignty and their allegiance, and deal always with each other's rights as the law commanded. The things which government fostered and sought to manage never throve in America, amongst the French colonists in Canada and the South, and amongst the Dutch and Danes on the North and South Rivers; but the free English energy throve like a thing bred for the wilderness. That breath of individual liberty has never gone out of our lungs. Too much government still suffocates us. We do not respect ourselves as much as fractions, as we do as integers. The future, like the past, is for individual energy and initiative; for men, not for corporations or for governments; and the law that has this ancient principle at its heart is the law that will endure.

The New Freedom*

Chapters 1 and 2

CHAPTER 1. THE OLD ORDER CHANGETH.

THERE is one great basic fact which underlies all the questions that are discussed on the political platform at the present moment. That singular fact is that nothing is done in this country as it was done twenty years ago.

We are in the presence of a new organization of society. Our life has broken away from the past. The life of America is not the life that it was twenty years ago; it is not the life that it was ten years ago. We have changed our economic conditions, absolutely, from top to bottom; and, with our economic society, the organization of our life. The old political formulas do not fit the present problems; they read now like documents taken out of a forgotten age. The older cries sound as if they belonged to a past age which men have almost forgotten. Things which used to be put into the party platforms of ten years ago would sound antiquated if put into a platform now. We are facing the necessity of fitting a new social organization, as we did once fit the old organization, to the happiness and prosperity of the great body of citizens; for we are conscious that the new order of society has not been made to fit and provide the convenience or prosperity of the average man. The life of the nation has grown infinitely varied. It does not centre now upon questions of governmental structure or of the distribution of governmental powers. It centres upon questions of the very structure and operation of society itself, of which government is only the instrument. Our development has run so fast and so far along the lines sketched in the earlier day of constitutional definition, has so crossed and interlaced those lines, has piled upon them such novel structures of trust and combination, has elaborated within them

---

* Chapters excerpted from *The New Freedom* (New York: Doubleday, Page and Company, 1913), 3–54. (Editor's note).

a life so manifold, so full of forces which transcend the boundaries of the country itself and fill the eyes of the world, that a new nation seems to have been created which the old formulas do not fit or afford a vital interpretation of.

We have come upon a very different age from any that preceded us. We have come upon an age when we do not do business in the way in which we used to do business,—when we do not carry on any of the operations of manufacture, sale, transportation, or communication as men used to carry them on. There is a sense in which in our day the individual has been submerged. In most parts of our country men work, not for themselves, not as partners in the old way in which they used to work, but generally as employees,—in a higher or lower grade,—of great corporations. There was a time when corporations played a very minor part in our business affairs, but now they play the chief part, and most men are the servants of corporations.

You know what happens when you are the servant of a corporation. You have in no instance access to the men who are really determining the policy of the corporation. If the corporation is doing the things that it ought not to do, you really have no voice in the matter and must obey the orders, and you have oftentimes with deep mortification to co-operate in the doing of things which you know are against the public interest. Your individuality is swallowed up in the individuality and purpose of a great organization.

It is true that, while most men are thus submerged in the corporation, a few, a very few, are exalted to a power which as individuals they could never have wielded. Through the great organizations of which they are the heads, a few are enabled to play a part unprecedented by anything in history in the control of the business operations of the country and in the determination of the happiness of great numbers of people.

Yesterday, and ever since history began, men were related to one another as individuals. To be sure there were the family, the Church, and the State, institutions which associated men in certain wide circles of relationship. But in the ordinary concerns of life, in the ordinary work, in the daily round, men dealt freely and directly with one another. To-day, the everyday relationships of men are largely with great impersonal concerns, with organizations, not with other individual men.

Now this is nothing short of a new social age, a new era of human relationships, a new stage-setting for the drama of life.

In this new age we find, for instance, that our laws with regard to the relations of employer and employee are in many respects wholly antiquated and impossible. They were framed for another age, which nobody now living remembers, which is, indeed, so remote from our life that it would be difficult for many of us to understand it if it were described to us. The employer is now generally a corporation or a huge company of some kind; the employee is one of hundreds or of thousands brought together, not by individual masters whom they know and with whom they have personal relations, but by agents of one sort or another. Workingmen are marshaled in great numbers for the performance of a multitude of particular tasks under a common discipline. They generally use dangerous and powerful machinery, over whose repair and renewal they have no control. New rules must be devised with regard to their obligations and their rights, their obligations to their employers and their responsibilities to one another. Rules must be devised for their protection, for their compensation when injured, for their support when disabled.

There is something very new and very big and very complex about these new relations of capital and labor. A new economic society has sprung up, and we must effect a new set of adjustments. We must not pit power against weakness. The employer is generally, in our day, as I have said, not an individual, but a powerful group; and yet the workingman when dealing with his employer is still, under our existing law, an individual.

Why is it that we have a labor question at all? It is for the simple and very sufficient reason that the laboring man and the employer are not intimate associates now as they used to be in time past. Most of our laws were formed in the age when employer and employees knew each other, knew each other's characters, were associates with each other, dealt with each other as man with man. That is no longer the case. You not only do not come into personal contact with the men who have the supreme command in those corporations, but it would be out of the question for you to do it. Our modern corporations employ thousands, and in some instances hundreds of thousands, of men. The only persons whom you see or deal with are local superintendents or local representatives of a vast organization, which is not like anything that the workingmen of the time in which our laws were framed knew anything about. A little group of workingmen, seeing their employer every day, dealing with him in a personal way, is one thing, and the modern body of labor engaged as employees of the huge enterprises that spread all over the country, dealing with men of whom they can form no personal conception, is another thing. A very different thing. You never saw a corporation, any more than you ever saw a government. Many a workingman to-day never saw the body of men who are conducting the industry in which he is employed. And they never saw him. What they know about him is written in ledgers and books and letters, in the correspondence of the office, in the reports of the superintendents. He is a long way off from them.

So what we have to discuss is, not wrongs which individuals intentionally do,—I do not believe there are a great many of those,—but the wrongs of a system. I want to record my protest against any discussion of this matter which would seem to indicate that there are bodies of our fellow-citizens who are trying to grind us down and do us injustice. There are some men of that sort. I don't know how they sleep o' nights, but there are men of that kind. Thank God, they are not numerous. The truth is, we are all caught in a great economic system which is heartless. The modern corporation is not engaged in business as an individual. When we deal with it, we deal with an impersonal element, an immaterial piece of society. A modern corporation is a means of co-operation in the conduct of an enterprise which is so big that no one man can conduct it, and which the resources of no one man are sufficient to finance. A company is formed; that company puts out a prospectus; the promoters expect to raise a certain fund as capital stock. Well, how are they going to raise it? They are going to raise it from the public in general, some of whom will buy their stock. The moment that begins, there is formed—what? A joint stock corporation. Men begin to pool their earnings, little piles, big piles. A certain number of men are elected by the stockholders to be directors, and these directors elect a president. This president is the head of the undertaking, and the directors are its managers.

Now, do the workingmen employed by that stock corporation deal with that president and those directors? Not at all. Does the public deal with that president and that board of directors? It does not. Can anybody bring them to account? It is next to impossible to do so. If you undertake it you will find it a game of hide and seek, with the objects of your search taking refuge now behind the tree of their individual personality, now behind that of their corporate irresponsibility.

And do our laws take note of this curious state of things? Do they even attempt to distinguish between a man's act as a corporation director and as an individual? They do not. Our laws still deal with us on the basis of the old system. The law is still living in the dead past which we have left behind. This is evident, for instance, with regard to the matter of employers' liability for workingmen's injuries. Suppose that a super[i]ntendent wants a workman to use a certain piece of machinery which it is not safe for him to use, and that the workman is injured by that piece of machinery. Some of our courts have held that the superintendent is a fellow-servant, or, as the law states it, a fellow-employee, and that, therefore, the man cannot recover damages for his injury. The superintendent who probably engaged the man is not his employer. Who is his employer? And whose negligence could conceivably come in there? The board of directors did not tell the employee to use that piece of machinery; and the president of the corporation did not tell him to use that piece of machinery. And so forth. Don't you see by that theory that a man never can get redress for negligence on the part of the employer? When I hear judges reason upon the analogy of the relationships that used to exist between workmen and their employers a generation ago, I wonder if they have not opened their eyes to the modern world. You know, we have a right to expect that judges will have their eyes open, even though the law which they administer hasn't awakened.

Yet that is but a single small detail illustrative of the difficulties we are in because we have not adjusted the law to the facts of the new order.

Since I entered politics, I have chiefly had men's views confided to me privately. Some of the biggest men in the United States, in the field of commerce and manufacture, are afraid of somebody, are afraid of something. They know that there is a power somewhere so organized, so subtle, so watchful, so interlocked, so complete, so pervasive, that they had better not speak above their breath when they speak in condemnation of it.

They know that America is not a place of which it can be said, as it used to be, that a man may choose his own calling and pursue it just as far as his abilities enable him to pursue it; because to-day, if he enters certain fields, there are organizations which will use means against him that will prevent his building up a business which they do not want to have built up; organizations that will see to it that the ground is cut from under him and the markets shut against him. For if he begins to sell to certain retail dealers, to any retail dealers, the monopoly will refuse to sell to those dealers, and those dealers, afraid, will not buy the new man's wares.

And this is the country which has lifted to the admiration of the world its ideals of absolutely free opportunity, where no man is supposed to be under any limitation except the limitations of his character and of his mind; where there is supposed to be no distinction of class, no distinction of blood, no distinction of social status, but where men win or lose on their merits.

I lay it very close to my own conscience as a public man whether we can any longer stand at our doors and welcome all newcomers upon those terms. American industry is not free, as once it was free; American enterprise is not free; the man with only a little capital is finding it harder to get into the field, more and more impossible to compete with the big fellow. Why? Because the laws of this country do not prevent the strong from crushing the weak. That is the reason, and because the strong have crushed the weak the strong dominate the industry and the economic life of this country. No man can deny that the lines of endeavor have more and more narrowed and stiffened; no man who knows anything about the development of industry in this country can have failed to observe that the larger kinds of credit are more and more difficult to obtain, unless you obtain them upon the terms of uniting your efforts with those who already control the industries of the country; and nobody can fail to observe that any man who tries to set himself up in competition with any process of manufacture which has been taken under the control of large combinations of capital will presently find himself either squeezed out or obliged to sell and allow himself to be absorbed.

There is a great deal that needs reconstruction in the United States. I should like to take a census of the business men,—I mean the rank and file of the business men,—as to whether they think that business conditions in this country, or rather whether the organization of business in this country, is satisfactory or not. I know what they would say if they dared. If they could vote secretly they would vote overwhelmingly that the present organization of business was meant for the big fellows and was not meant for the little fellows; that it was meant for those who are at the top and was meant to exclude those who are at the bottom; that it was meant to shut out beginners, to prevent new entries in the race, to prevent the building up of competitive enterprises that would interfere with the monopolies which the great trusts have built up.

What this country needs above everything else is a body of laws which will look after the men who are on the make rather than the men who are already made.

Because the men who are already made are not going to live indefinitely, and they are not always kind enough to leave sons as able and as honest as they are.

The originative part of America, the part of America that makes new enterprises, the part into which the ambitious and gifted workingman makes his way up, the class that saves, that plans, that organizes, that presently spreads its enterprises until they have a national scope and character,—that middle class is being more and more squeezed out by the processes which we have been taught to call processes of prosperity. Its members are sharing prosperity, no doubt; but what alarms me is that they are not *originating* prosperity. No country can afford to have its prosperity originated by a small controlling class. The treasury of America does not lie in the brains of the small body of men now in control of the great enterprises that have been concentrated under the direction of a very small number of persons. The treasury of America lies in those ambitions, those energies, that cannot be restricted to a special favored class. It depends upon the inventions of unknown men, upon the originations of unknown men, upon the ambitions of unknown men. Every country is renewed out of the ranks of the unknown, not out of the ranks of those already famous and powerful and in control.

There has come over the land that un-American set of conditions which enables a small number of men who control the government to get favors from the government; by those favors to exclude their fellows from equal business opportunity; by those favors to extend a network of control that will presently dominate every industry in the country, and so make men forget the ancient time when America lay in every hamlet, when America was to be seen in every fair valley, when America displayed her great forces on the broad prairies, ran her fine fires of enterprise up over the mountainsides and down into the bowels of the earth, and eager men were everywhere captains of industry, not employees; not looking to a distant city to find out what they might do, but looking about among their neighbors, finding credit according to their character, not according to their connections, finding credit in proportion to what was known to be in them and behind them, not in proportion to the securities they held that were approved where they were not known. In order to start an enterprise now, you have to be authenticated, in a perfectly impersonal way, not according to yourself, but according to what you own that somebody else approves of your owning. You cannot begin such an enterprise as those that have made America until you are so authenticated, until you have succeeded in obtaining the good-will of large allied capitalists. Is that freedom? That is dependence, not freedom.

We used to think in the old-fashioned days when life was very simple that all that government had to do was to put on a policeman's uniform, and say, "Now don't anybody hurt anybody else." We used to say that the ideal of government was for every man to be left alone and not interfered with, except when he interfered with somebody else; and that the best government was the government that did as little governing as possible. That was the idea that obtained in Jefferson's time. But we are coming now to realize that life is so complicated that we are not dealing with the old conditions, and that the law has to step in and create new conditions under which we may live, the conditions which will make it tolerable for us to live.

Let me illustrate what I mean: It used to be true in our cities that every family occupied a separate house of its own, that every family had its own little premises, that every family was separated in its life from every other family. That is no longer the case in our great cities. Families live in tenements, they live in flats, they live on floors; they are piled layer upon layer in the great tenement houses of our crowded districts, and not only are they piled layer upon layer, but they are associated room by room, so that there is in every room, sometimes, in our congested districts, a separate family. In some foreign countries they have made much more progress than we in handling these things. In the city of Glasgow, for example (Glasgow is one of the model cities of the world), they have made up their minds that the entries and the hallways of great tenements are public streets. Therefore, the policeman goes up the stairway, and patrols the corridors; the lighting department of the city sees to it that the halls are abundantly lighted. The city does not deceive itself into supposing that that great building is a unit from which the police are to keep out and the civic authority to be excluded, but it says: "These are public highways, and light is needed in them, and control by the authority of the city."

I liken that to our great modern industrial enterprises. A corporation is very like a large tenement house; it isn't the premises of a single commercial family; it is just as much a public affair as a tenement house is a network of public highways.

When you offer the securities of a great corporation to anybody who wishes to purchase them, you must open that corporation to the inspection of everybody who wants to purchase. There must, to follow out the figure of the tenement house, be lights along the corridors, there must be police patrolling the openings, there must be inspection wherever it is known that men may be deceived with regard to the contents of the premises. If we believe that fraud lies in wait for us, we must have the means of determining whether our suspicions are well founded or not. Similarly, the treatment of labor by the great corporations is not what it was in Jefferson's time. Whenever bodies of men employ bodies of men, it ceases to be a private relationship. So that when courts hold that workingmen cannot peaceably dissuade other workingmen from taking employment, as was held in a notable case in New Jersey, they simply show that their minds and understandings are lingering in an age which has passed away. This dealing of great bodies of men with other bodies of men is a matter of public scrutiny, and should be a matter of public regulation.

Similarly, it was no business of the law in the time of Jefferson to come into my house and see how I kept house. But when my house, when my so-called private property, became a great mine, and men went along dark corridors amidst every kind of danger in order to dig out of the bowels of the earth things necessary for the industries of a whole nation, and when it came about that no individual owned these mines, that they were owned by great stock companies, then all the old analogies absolutely collapsed and it became the right of the government to go down into these mines to see whether human beings were properly treated in them or not; to see whether accidents were properly safeguarded against; to see whether modern economical methods of using these inestimable riches of the earth were followed or were not followed. If somebody puts a derrick improperly secured on top of a building or overtopping the street, then the government of the city has the right to see that that derrick is so secured that you and I can walk under it and not be afraid that the heavens are going to fall on us. Likewise, in these great beehives where in every corridor swarm men of flesh and blood, it is the privilege of the government, whether of the State or of the United States, as the case may be, to see that human life is protected, that human lungs have something to breathe.

These, again, are merely illustrations of conditions. We are in a new world, struggling under old laws. As we go inspecting our lives to-day, surveying this new scene of centralized and complex society, we shall find many more things out of joint.

One of the most alarming phenomena of the time,—or rather it would be alarming if the nation had not awakened to it and shown its determination to control it,—one of the most significant signs of the new social era is the degree to which government has become associated with business. I speak, for the moment, of the control over the government exercised by Big Business. Behind the whole subject, of course, is the truth that, in the new order, government and business must be associated closely. But that association is at present of a nature absolutely intolerable; the precedence is wrong, the association is upside down. Our government has been for the past few years under the control of heads of great allied corporations with special interests. It has not controlled these interests and assigned them a proper place in the whole system of business; it has submitted itself to their control. As a result, there have g[r]own up vicious systems and schemes of governmental favoritism (the most obvious being the extravagant tariff), far-reaching in effect upon the whole fabric of life, touching to his injury every inhabitant of the land, laying unfair and impossible handicaps upon competitors, imposing taxes in every direction, stifling everywhere the free spirit of American enterprise.

Now this has come about naturally; as we go on we shall see how very naturally. It is no use denouncing anybody, or anything, except human nature. Nevertheless, it is an intolerable thing that the government of the republic should have got so far out of the hands of the people; should have been captured by interests which are special and not general. In the train of this capture follow the troops of scandals, wrongs, indecencies, with which our politics swarm.

There are cities in America of whose government we are ashamed. There are cities everywhere, in every part of the land, in which we feel that, not the interests of the public, but the interests of special privileges, of selfish men, are served; where contracts take precedence over public interest. Not only in big cities is this the case. Have you not noticed the growth of socialistic sentiment in the smaller towns? Not many months ago I stopped at a little town in Nebraska, and while my train lingered I met on the platform a very engaging young fellow dressed in overalls who introduced himself to me as the mayor of the town, and added that he was a Socialist. I said, "What does that mean? Does that mean that this town is socialistic?" "No, sir," he said; "I have not deceived myself; the vote by which I was elected was about 20 per cent. socialistic and 80 per cent. protest." It was protest against the treachery to the people of those who led both the other parties of that town.

All over the Union people are coming to feel that they have no control over the course of affairs. I live in one of the greatest States in the union, which was at one time in slavery. Until two years ago we had witnessed with increasing concern the growth in New Jersey of a spirit of almost cynical despair. Men said: "We vote; we are offered the platform we want; we elect the men who stand on that platform, and we get absolutely nothing." So they began to ask: "What is the use of voting? We know that the machines of both parties are subsidized by the same persons, and therefore it is useless to turn in either direction."

This is not confined to some of the state governments and those of some of the towns and cities. We know that something intervenes between the people of the United States and the control of their own affairs at Washington. It is not the people who have been ruling there of late.

Why are we in the presence, why are we at the threshold, of a revolution? Because we are profoundly disturbed by the influences which we see reigning in the determination of our public life and our public policy. There was a time when America was blithe with self-confidence. She boasted that she, and she alone, knew the processes of popular government; but now she sees her sky overcast; she sees that there are at work forces which she did not dream of in her hopeful youth.

Don't you know that some man with eloquent tongue, without conscience, who did not care for the nation, could put this whole country into a flame? Don't you know that this country from one end to the other believes that something is wrong? What an opportunity it would be for some man without conscience to spring up and say: "This is the way. Follow me!"—and lead in paths of destruction!

The old order changeth—changeth under our very eyes, not quietly and equably, but swiftly and with the noise and heat and tumult of reconstruction.

I suppose that all struggle for law has been conscious, that very little of it has been blind or merely instinctive. It is the fashion to say, as if with superior knowledge of affairs and of human weakness, that every age has been an age of transition, and that no age is more full of change than another; yet in very few ages of the world can the struggle for change have been so widespread, so deliberate, or upon so great a scale as in this in which we are taking part.

The transition we are witnessing is no equable transition of growth and normal alteration; no silent, unconscious unfolding of one age into another, its natural heir and successor. Society is looking itself over, in our day, from top to bottom; is making fresh and critical analysis of its very elements; is questioning its oldest practices as freely as its newest, scrutinizing every arrangement and motive of its life; and it stands ready to attempt nothing less than a radical reconstruction, which only frank and honest counsels and the forces of generous co-operation can hold back from becoming a revolution. We are in a temper to reconstruct economic society, as we were once in a temper to reconstruct political society, and political society may itself undergo a radical modification in the process. I doubt if any age was ever more conscious of its task or more unanimously desirous of radical and extended changes in its economic and political practice.

We stand in the presence of a revolution,—not a bloody revolution; America is not given to the spilling of blood,—but a silent revolution, whereby America will insist upon recovering in practice those ideals which she has always professed, upon securing a government devoted to the general interest and not to special interests.

We are upon the eve of a great reconstruction. It calls for creative statesmanship as no age has done since that great age in which we set up the government under which we live, that government which was the admiration of the world until it suffered wrongs to grow up under it which have made many of our own compatriots question the freedom of our institutions and preach revolution against them. I do not fear revolution. I have unshaken faith in the power of America to keep its self-possession. Revolution will come in peaceful guise, as it came when we put aside the crude government of the Confederation and created the great Federal Union which governs individuals, not States, and which has been these hundred and thirty years our vehicle of progress. Some radical changes we must make in our law and practice. Some reconstructions we must push forward, which a new age and new circumstances impose upon us. But we can do it all in calm and sober fashion, like statesmen and patriots.

I do not speak of these things in apprehension, because all is open and aboveboard. This is not a day in which great forces rally in secret. The whole stupendous program must be publicly planned and canvassed. Good temper, the wisdom that comes of sober counsel, the energy of thoughtful and unselfish men, the habit of co-operation and of compromise which has been bred in us by long years of free government, in which reason rather than passion has been made to prevail by the sheer virtue of candid and universal debate, will enable us to win through to still another great age without violence.

CHAPTER 2. WHAT IS PROGRESS?

In that sage and veracious chronicle, "Alice Through the Looking-Glass," it is recounted how, on a noteworthy occasion, the little heroine is seized by the Red

Chess Queen, who races her off at a terrific pace. They run until both of them are out of breath; then they stop, and Alice looks around her and says, "Why, we are just where we were when we started!" "Oh, yes," says the Red Queen; "you have to run twice as fast as that to get anywhere else."

That is a parable of progress. The laws of this country have not kept up with the change of economic circumstances in this country; they have not kept up with the change of political circumstances; and therefore we are not even where we were when we started. We shall have to run, not until we are out of breath, but until we have caught up with our own conditions, before we shall be where we were when we started; when we started this great experiment which has been the hope and the beacon of the world. And we should have to run twice as fast as any rational program I have seen in order to get anywhere else.

I am, therefore, forced to be a progressive, if for no other reason, because we have not kept up with our changes of conditions, either in the economic field or in the political field. We have not kept up as well as other nations have. We have not kept our practices adjusted to the facts of the case, and until we do, and unless we do, the facts of the case will always have the better of the argument; because if you do not adjust your laws to the facts, so much the worse for the laws, not for the facts, because law trails along after the facts. Only that law is unsafe which runs ahead of the facts and beckons to it and makes it follow the will-o'-the-wisps of imaginative projects.

Business is in a situation in America which it was never in before; it is in a situation to which we have not adjusted our laws. Our laws are still meant for business done by individuals; they have not been satisfactorily adjusted to business done by great combinations, and we have got to adjust them. I do not say we may or may not; I say we must; there is no choice. If your laws do not fit your facts, the facts are not injured, the law is damaged; because the law, unless I have studied it amiss, is the expression of the facts in legal relationships. Laws have never altered the facts; laws have always necessarily expressed the facts; adjusted interests as they have arisen and have changed toward one another.

Politics in America is in a case which sadly requires attention. The system set up by our law and our usage doesn't work,—or at least it can't be depended on; it is made to work only by a most unreasonable expenditure of labor and pains. The government, which was designed for the people, has got into the hands of bosses and their employers, the special interests. An invisible empire has been set up above the forms of democracy.

There are serious things to do. Does any man doubt the great discontent in this country? Does any man doubt that there are grounds and justifications for discontent? Do we dare stand still? Within the past few months we have witnessed (along with other strange political phenomena, eloquently significant of popular uneasiness) on one side a doubling of the Socialist vote and on the other the posting on dead walls and hoardings all over the country of certain very attractive and diverting bills warning citizens that it was "better to be safe than sorry" and advising them to "let well enough alone." Apparently a good many citizens doubted whether the situation they were advised to let alone was really well enough, and concluded that they would take a chance of being sorry. To me, these counsels of do-nothingism, these counsels of sitting still for fear something would happen, these counsels addressed to the hopeful, energetic people of the United States, telling them that they are not wise enough to touch their own affairs without marring them, constitute the most extraordinary argument of fatuous ignorance I ever heard. Americans are not yet cowards. True, their self-reliance has been sapped by years of submission to the doctrine that prosperity is something that benevolent magnates provide for them with the aid of the government; their self-reliance has been weakened, but not so utterly destroyed that you can twit them about it. The American people are not naturally stand-patters. Progress is the word that charms their ears and stirs their hearts.

There are, of course, Americans who have not yet heard that anything is going on. The circus might come to town, have the big parade and go, without their catching a sight of the camels or a note of the calliope. There are people, even Americans, who never move themselves or know that anything else is moving.

A friend of mine who had heard of the Florida "cracker," as they call a certain ne'er-do-weel portion of the population down there, when passing through the State in a train, asked some one to point out a "cracker" to him. The man asked replied, "Well, if you see something off in the woods that looks brown, like a stump, you will know it is either a stump or a cracker; if it moves, it is a stump."

Now, movement has no virtue in itself. Change is not worth while for its own sake. I am not one of those who love variety for its own sake. If a thing is good to-day, I should like to have it stay that way to-morrow. Most of our calculations in life are dependent upon things staying the way they are. For example, if, when you got up this morning, you had forgotten how to dress, if you had forgotten all about those ordinary things which you do almost automatically, which you can almost do half awake, you would have to find out what you did yesterday. I am told by the psychologists that if I did not remember who I was yesterday, I should not know who I am to-day, and that, therefore, my very identity depends upon my being able to tally to-day with yesterday. If they do not tally, then I am confused; I do not know who I am, and I have to go around and ask somebody to tell me my name and where I came from.

I am not one of those who wish to break connection with the past; I am not one of those who wish to change for the mere sake of variety. The only men who do that are the men who want to forget something, the men who filled yesterday with something they would rather not recollect to-day, and so go about seeking diversion, seeking abstraction in something that will blot out recollection, or seeking to put something into them which will blot out all recollection. Change is not worth while unless it is improvement. If I move out of my present house because I do not like it, then I have got to choose a better house, or build a better house, to justify the change.

It would seem a waste of time to point out that ancient distinction,—between mere change and improvement. Yet there is a class of mind that is prone to confuse them. We have had political leaders whose conception of greatness was to be forever frantically doing something,—it mattered little what; restless, vociferous men, without sense of the energy of concentration, knowing only the energy of succession. Now, life does not consist of eternally running to a fire. There is no virtue in going anywhere unless you will gain something by being there. The direction is just as important as the impetus of motion.

All progress depends on how fast you are going, and where you are going, and I fear there has been too much of this thing of knowing neither how fast we were going or where we were going. I have my private belief that we have been doing most of our progressiveness after the fashion of those things that in my boyhood days we called "treadmills," a treadmill being a moving platform, with cleats on it, on which some poor devil of a mule was forced to walk forever without getting anywhere. Elephants and even other animals have been known to turn treadmills, making a good deal of noise, and causing certain wheels to go round, and I daresay grinding out some sort of product for somebody, but without achieving much progress. Lately, in an effort to persuade the elephant to move, really, his friends tried dynamite. It moved,—in separate and scattered parts, but it moved.

A cynical but witty Englishman said, in a book, not long ago, that it was a mistake to say of a conspicuously successful man, eminent in his line of business, that you could not bribe a man like that, because, he said, the point about such men is that they have been bribed—not in the ordinary meaning of that word, not in any gross, corrupt sense, but they have achieved their great success by means of the existing order of things and therefore they have been put under bonds to see that that existing order of things is not changed; they are bribed to maintain the *status quo*.

It was for that reason that I used to say, when I had to do with the administration of an educational institution, that I should like to make the young gentlemen of the rising generation as unlike their fathers as possible. Not because their fathers lacked character or intelligence or knowledge or patriotism, but because their fathers, by reason of their advancing years and their established position in society, had lost touch with the processes of life; they had forgotten what it was to begin; they had forgotten what it was to rise; they had forgotten what it was to be dominated by the circumstances of their life on their way up from the bottom to the top, and, therefore, they were out of sympathy with the creative, formative and progressive forces of society.

Progress! Did you ever reflect that that word is almost a new one? No word comes more often or more naturally to the lips of modern man, as if the thing it stands for were almost synonymous with life itself, and yet men through many thousand years never talked or thought of progress. They thought in the other direction. Their stories of heroisms and glory were tales of the past. The ancestor wore the heavier armor and carried the larger spear. "There were giants in those days." Now all that has altered. We think of the future, not the past, as the more glorious time in comparison with which the present is nothing. Progress, development,—those are modern words. The modern idea is to leave the past and press onward to something new.

But what is progress going to do with the past, and with the present? How is it going to treat them? With ignominy, or respect? Should it break with them altogether, or rise out of them, with its roots still deep in the older time? What attitude shall progressives take toward the existing order, toward those institutions of conservatism, the Constitution, the laws, and the courts?

Are those thoughtful men who fear that we are now about to disturb the ancient foundations of our institutions justified in their fear? If they are, we ought to go very slowly about the processes of change. If it is indeed true that we have grown tired of the institutions which we have so carefully and sedulously built up, then we ought to go very slowly and very carefully about the very dangerous task of altering them. We ought, therefore, to ask ourselves, first of all, whether thought in this country is tending to do anything by which we shall retrace our steps, or by which we shall change the whole direction of our development?

I believe, for one, that you cannot tear up ancient rootages and safely plant the tree of liberty in soil which is not native to it. I believe that the ancient traditions of a people are its ballast; you cannot make a *tabula rasa* upon which to write a political program. You cannot take a new sheet of paper and determine what your life shall be to-morrow. You must knit the new into the old. You cannot put a new patch on an old garment without ruining it; it must be not a patch, but something woven into the old fabric, of practically the same pattern, of the same texture and intention. If I did not believe that to be progressive was to preserve the essentials of our institutions, I for one could not be a progressive.

One of the chief benefits I used to derive from being president of a university was that I had the pleasure of entertaining thoughtful men from all over the world. I cannot tell you how much has dropped into my granary by their presence. I had been casting around in my mind for something by which to draw several parts of my political thought together when it was my good fortune to entertain a very interesting Scotsman who had been devoting himself to the philosophical thought of the seventeenth century. His talk was so engaging that it was delightful to hear him speak of anything, and presently there came out of the unexpected region of his thought the thing I had been waiting for. He called my attention to the fact that in every generation all sorts of speculation and thinking tend to fall under the formula of the dominant thought of the age. For example, after the Newtonian Theory of the universe had been developed, almost all thinking tended to express itself in the analogies of the Newtonian Theory, and since the Darwinian Theory has reigned amongst us, everybody is likely to express whatever he wishes to expound in terms of development and accommodation to environment.

Now, it came to me, as this interesting man talked, that the Constitution of the United States had been made under the dominion of the Newtonian Theory. You have only to read the papers of *The Federalist* to see that fact written on every page. They speak of the "checks and balances" of the Constitution, and use to express their idea the simile of the organization of the universe, and particularly of the solar system,—how by the attraction of gravitation the various parts are held in their orbits; and then they proceed to represent Congress, the Judiciary, and the President as a sort of imitation of the solar system.

They were only following the English Whigs, who gave Great Britain its modern constitution. Not that those Englishmen analyzed the matter, or had any theory about it; Englishmen care little for theories. It was a Frenchman, Montesquieu, who pointed out to them how faithfully they had copied Newton's description of the mechanism of the heavens.

The makers of our Federal Constitution read Montesquieu with true scientific enthusiasm. They were scientists in their way,—the best way of their age,—those fathers of the nation. Jefferson wrote of "the laws of Nature,"—and then by way of afterthought,—"and of Nature's God." And they constructed a government as they would have constructed an orrery,—to display the laws of nature. Politics in their thought was a variety of mechanics. The Constitution was founded on the law of gravitation. The government was to exist and move by virtue of the efficacy of "checks and balances."

The trouble with the theory is that government is not a machine, but a living thing. It falls, not under the theory of the universe, but under the theory of organic life. It is accountable to Darwin, not to Newton. It is modified by its environment, necessitated by its tasks, shaped to its functions by the sheer pressure of life. No living thing can have its organs offset against each other, as checks, and live. On the contrary, its life is dependent upon their quick co-operation, their ready response to the commands of instinct or intelligence, their amicable community of purpose. Government is not a body of blind forces; it is a body of men, with highly differentiated functions, no doubt, in our modern day, of specialization, with a common task and purpose. Their co-operation is indispensable, their warfare fatal. There can be no successful government without the intimate, instinctive co-ordination of the organs of life and action. This is not theory, but fact, and displays its force as fact, whatever theories may be thrown across its track. Living political constitutions must be Darwinian in structure and in practice. Society is a living organism and must obey the laws of life, not of mechanics; it must develop.

All that progressives ask or desire is permission—in an era when "development," "evolution," is the scientific word—to interpret the Constitution according to the Darwinian principle; all they ask is recognition of the fact that a nation is a living thing and not a machine.

Some citizens of this country have never got beyond the Declaration of Independence, signed in Philadelphia, July 4th, 1776. Their bosoms swell against George III, but they have no consciousness of the war for freedom that is going on to-day.

The Declaration of Independence did not mention the questions of our day. It is of no consequence to us unless we can translate its general terms into examples of the present day and substitute them in some vital way for the examples it itself gives, so concrete, so intimately involved in the circumstanc[e]s of the day in which it was conceived and written. It is an eminently practical document, meant for the use of practical men; not a thesis for philosophers, but a whip for tyrants; not a theory of government, but a program of action. Unless we can translate it into the questions of our own day, we are not worthy of it, we are not the sons of the sires who acted in response to its challenge.

What form does the contest between tyranny and freedom take to-day? What is the special form of tyranny we now fight? How does it endanger the rights of the people, and what do we mean to do in order to make our contest against it effectual? What are to be the items of our new declaration of independence?

By tyranny, as we now fight it, we mean control of the law, of legislation and adjudication, by organizations which do not represent the people, by means which are private and selfish. We mean, specifically, the conduct of our affairs and the shaping of our legislation in the interest of special bodies of capital and those who organize their use. We mean the alliance, for this purpose, of political machines with selfish business. We mean the exploitation of the people by legal and political means. We have seen many of our governments under these influences cease to be representative governments, cease to be governments representative of the people, and become governments representative of special interests, controlled by machines, which in their turn are not controlled by the people.

Sometimes, when I think of the growth of our economic system, it seems to me as if, leaving our law just about where it was before any of the modern inventions or developments took place, we had simply at haphazard extended the family residence, added an office here and a workroom there, and a new set of sleeping rooms there, built up higher on our foundations, and put out little lean-tos on the side, until we have a structure that has no character whatever. Now, the problem is to continue to live in the house and yet change it.

Well, we are architects in our time, and our architects are also engineers. We don't have to stop using a railroad terminal because a new station is being built. We don't have to stop any of the processes of our lives because we are rearranging the structures in which we conduct those processes. What we have to undertake is to systematize the foundations of the house, then to thread all the old parts of the structure with the steel which will be laced together in modern fashion, accommodated to all the modern knowledge of structural strength and elasticity, and then slowly change the partitions, relay the walls, let in the light through new apertures, improve the ventilation; until finally, a generation or two from now, the scaffolding will be taken away, and there will be the family in a great building whose noble architecture will at last be disclosed, where men can live as a single community, co-operative as in a perfected, co-ordinated beehive, not afraid of any storm of nature, not afraid of any artificial storm, any imitation of thunder and lightning, knowing that the foundations go down to the bedrock of principle, and knowing that whenever they please they can change that plan again and accommodate it as they please to the altering necessities of their lives.

But there are a great many men who don't like the idea. Some wit recently said, in view of the fact that most of our American architects are trained in a certain *École* in Paris, that all American architecture in recent years was either bizarre or "Beaux Arts." I think that our economic architecture is decidedly bizarre; and I am afraid that there is a good deal to learn about matters other than architecture from the same source from which our architects have learned a great many things. I don't mean the School of Fine Arts at Paris, but the experience of France; for from the other side of the water men can now hold up against us the reproach that we have not adjusted our lives to modern conditions to the same extent that they have adjusted theirs. I was very much interested in some of the reasons given by our friends across the Canadian border for being very shy about the reciprocity arrangements. They said: "We are not sure whither these arrangements will lead, and we don't care to associate too closely with the economic conditions of the United States until those conditions are as modern as ours." And when I resented it, and asked for particulars, I had, in regard to many matters, to retire from the debate. Because I found that they had adjusted their regulations of economic development to conditions we had not yet found a way to meet in the United States.

Well, we have started now at all events. The procession is under way. The stand-patter doesn't know there is a procession. He is asleep in the back part of his house. He doesn't know that the road is resounding with the tramp of men going to the front. And when he wakes up, the country will be empty. He will be deserted, and he will wonder what has happened. Nothing has happened. The world has been going on. The world has a habit of going on. The world has a habit of leaving those behind who won't go with it. The world has always neglected stand-patters. And, therefore, the stand-patter does not excite my indignation; he excites my sympathy. He is going to be so lonely before it is all over. And we are good fellows, we are good company; why doesn't he come along? We are not going to do him any harm. We are going to show him a good time. We are going to climb the slow road until it reaches some upland where the air is fresher, where the whole talk of mere politicians is stilled, where men can look in each other's faces and see that there is nothing to conceal, that all they have to talk about they are willing to talk about in the open and talk about with each other; and whence, looking back over the road, we shall see at last that we have fulfilled our promise to mankind. We had said to all the world, "America was created to break every kind of monopoly, and to set men free, upon a footing of equality, upon a footing of opportunity, to match their brains and their energies." and now we have proved that we meant it.

Part III
Institutional Reform

"Cabinet Government in the United States"*

Our patriotism seems of late to have been exchanging its wonted tone of confident hope for one of desponding solicitude. Anxiety about the future of our institutions seems to be daily becoming stronger in the minds of thoughtful Americans. A feeling of uneasiness is undoubtedly prevalent, sometimes taking the shape of a fear that grave, perhaps radical, defects in our mode of government are militating against our liberty and prosperity. A marked and alarming decline in statesmanship, a rule of levity and folly instead of wisdom and sober forethought in legislation, threaten to shake our trust not only in the men by whom our national policy is controlled, but also in the very principles upon which our Government rests. Both State and National legislatures are looked upon with nervous suspicion, and we hail an adjournment of Congress as a temporary immunity from danger. In casting about for the chief cause of the admitted evil, many persons have convinced themselves that it is to be found in the principle of universal suffrage. When Dr. Woolsey, in his admirable work on Political Science, speaks with despondency of the influence of this principle upon our political life, he simply gives clear expression to misgivings which he shares with a growing minority of his countrymen. We must, it is said, purge the constituencies of their ignorant elements, if we would have high-minded, able, worthy representatives. We see adventurers, who in times of revolution and confusion were suffered to climb to high and responsible places, still holding positions of trust; we perceive that our institutions, when once thrown out of gear, seem to possess no power of self-readjustment,—and we hasten to cast discredit upon that principle the establishment of which has been regarded as America's greatest claim to political honor,—the right of every man to a voice in the Government under which he

* "Cabinet Government in the United States," *International Review* VI (August 1879): 146–63. (Editor's note).

lives. The existence of such sentiments is in itself an instructive fact. But while it is indisputably true that universal suffrage is a constant element of weakness, and exposes us to many dangers which we might otherwise escape, its operation does not suffice alone to explain existing evils. Those who make this the scapegoat of all our national grievances have made too superficial an analysis of the abuses about which they so loudly complain.

What is the real cause of this solicitude and doubt? It is, in our opinion, to be found in the absorption of all power by a legislature which is practically irresponsible for its acts. But even this would not necessarily be harmful, were it not for the addition of a despotic principle which it is my present purpose to consider.

At its highest development, *representative* government is that form which best enables a free people to govern themselves. The main object of a representative assembly, therefore, should be the discussion of public business. They should legislate as if in the presence of the whole country, because they come under the closest scrutiny and fullest criticism of all the representatives of the country speaking in open and free debate. Only in such an assembly, only in such an atmosphere of publicity, only by means of such a vast investigating machine, can the different sections of a great country learn each other's feelings and interests. It is not enough that the general course of legislation is known to all. Unless during its progress it is subjected to a thorough, even a tediously prolonged, process of public sifting, to the free comment of friend and foe alike, to the ordeal of battle among those upon whose vote its fate depends, an act of open legislation may have its real intent and scope completely concealed by its friends and undiscovered by its enemies, and it may be as fatally mischievous as the darkest measures of an oligarchy or a despot. Nothing can be more obvious than the fact that the very life of free, popular institutions is dependent upon their breathing the bracing air of thorough, exhaustive, and open discussions, or that select Congressional committees, whose proceedings must from their very nature be secret, are, as means of legislation, dangerous and unwholesome. Parliaments are forces for freedom; for "talk is persuasion, persuasion is force, the one force which can sway freemen to deeds such as those which have made England what she is," or our English stock what it is.

Congress is a deliberative body in which there is little real deliberation; a legislature which legislates with no real discussion of its business. Our Government is practically carried on by irresponsible committees. Too few Americans take the trouble to inform themselves as to the methods of Congressional management; and, as a consequence, not many have perceived that almost *absolute* power has fallen into the hands of men whose irresponsibility prevents the regulation of their conduct by the people from whom they derive their authority. The most important, most powerful man in the government of the United States in time of peace is the Speaker of the House of Representatives. Instead of being merely an executive officer, whose principal duties are those immediately connected with the administration of the rules of order, he is a potent party chief, the only chief of any real potency,—and must of necessity be so. He must be the strongest and shrewdest member of his party in the lower House; for almost all the real business of that House is transacted by committees whose members are his nominees. Unless the rules of the House be suspended by a special two-thirds vote, every bill introduced must be referred, without debate, to the proper Standing Committee, with whom rests the privilege of embodying it, or any part of it, in their reports, or of rejecting it altogether. The House very seldom takes any direct action upon any measures introduced by individual members; its votes and discussions are almost entirely confined to committee reports and committee dictation. The whole attitude of business depends upon forty-seven Standing Committees. Even the discussions upon their directive reports are merely nominal,—liberal forms, at most. Take, as an example of the workings of the system, the functions and privileges of the Committee of Ways and Means. To it is intrusted the financial policy of the country; its chairman is, in reality, our Chancellor of the Exchequer. With the aid of his colleagues he determines the course of legislation upon finance; in English political phrase, he draws up the *budget*. All the momentous questions connected with our finance are debated in the private sessions of this committee, and there only. For, when the budget is submitted to the House for its consideration, only a very limited time is allowed for its discussion; and, besides the member of the committee to whom its introduction is intrusted, no one is permitted to speak save those to whom he through courtesy yields the floor, and who must have made arrangements beforehand with the Speaker to be recognized. Where, then, is there room for thorough discussion,—for discussion of any kind? If carried, the provisions of the budget must be put into operation by the Secretary of the Treasury, who may be directly opposed to the principles which it embodies. If lost, no one save Congress itself is responsible for the consequent embarrassment into which the nation is brought,—and Congress as a body is not readily punishable.

It must at once be evident to every thinking man that a policy thus regulated cannot be other than vacillating, uncertain, devoid of plan or consistency. This is certainly a phase of representative government peculiar to ourselves. And yet its development was most natural and apparently necessary. It is hardly possible for a body of several hundred men, without official or authoritative leaders, to determine upon any line of action without interminable wrangling and delays injurious to the interests under their care. Left to their own resources, they would be as helpless as any other mass meeting. Without leaders having authority to guide their deliberations and give a definite direction to the movement of legislation; and, moreover, with none of that sense of responsibility which constantly rests upon those whose duty it is to work out to a successful issue the policies which they themselves originate, yet with full power to dictate policies which others must carry into execution,—a recognition of the need of some sort of leadership, and of a division of labor, led to the formation of these Standing Committees, to which are intrusted the shaping of the national policy in the several departments of administration, as well as the prerogatives of the initiative in legislation and leadership in debate. When theoretically viewed, this is an ingenious and apparently harmless device, but one which, in practice, subverts that most fundamental of all the principles of a free State,—the right of the people to a potential voice in their own government. Great measures of legislation are discussed and determined, not conspicuously in public session of the people's representatives, but in the unapproachable privacy of committee rooms.

But what less imperfect means of representative government can we find without stepping beyond the bounds of a true republicanism? Certainly none other than those which were rejected by the Constitutional Convention. When the Convention of 1787, upon the submission of the report of the Committee of Detail, came to consider the respective duties and privileges of the legislative and executive departments, and the relations which these two branches of the Government should sustain towards each other, many serious questions presented themselves for solution. One of the gravest of these was, whether or not the interests of the public service would be furthered by *allowing some of the higher officers of State to occupy seats in the legislature*. The propriety and practical advantage of such a course were obviously suggested by a similar arrangement under the British Constitution, to which our political fathers often and wisely looked for useful hints. But since the spheres of the several departments were in the end defined with all the clearness, strictness, and care possible to a written instrument, the opinion prevailed among the members of the Convention that it would be unadvisable to establish any such connection between the Executive and Congress. They thought, in their own fervor of patriotism and intensity of respect for written law, that paper barriers would prove sufficient to prevent the encroachments of any one department upon the prerogatives of any other; that these vaguely broad laws—or principles of law—would be capable of securing and maintaining the harmonious and mutually helpful co-operation of the several branches; that the exhibition of these general views of government would be adequate to the stupendous task of preventing the legislature from rising to the predominance of influence, which, nevertheless, constantly lay within its reach. But, in spite of constitutional barriers, the legislature has become the imperial power of the State, as it must of necessity become under every representative system; and experience of the consequences of a complete separation of the legislative and executive branches long since led that able and sagacious commentator upon the Constitution, Chief-Justice Story, to remark that, "if it would not have been safe to trust the heads of departments, as representatives, to the choice of the people, as their constituents, it would have been at least some gain to have allowed them seats, like territorial delegates, in the House of Representatives, where they might freely debate without a title to vote." In short, the framers of the Constitution, in endeavoring to act in accordance with the principle of Montesquieu's celebrated and unquestionably just political maxim,—that the legislative, executive, and judicial departments of a free State should be *separate*,—made their separation so complete as to amount to *isolation*. To the methods of representative government which have sprung from these provisions of the Constitution, by which the Convention thought so carefully to guard and limit the powers of the legislature, we must look for an explanation, in a large measure, of the evils over which we now find ourselves lamenting.

What, then, is Cabinet government? What is the change proposed? Simply to give to the heads of the Executive departments—the members of the Cabinet— seats in Congress, with the privilege of the initiative in legislation and some part of the unbounded privileges now commanded by the Standing Committees. But the advocates of such a change—and they are now not a few—deceive themselves when they maintain that it would not necessarily involve the principle of ministerial responsibility,—that is, the resignation of the Cabinet upon the defeat of any important part of their plans. For, if Cabinet officers sit in Congress as official representatives of the Executive, this principle of responsibility must of necessity come sooner or later to be recognized. Experience would soon demonstrate the practical impossibility of their holding their seats, and continuing to represent the Administration, after they had found themselves unable to gain the consent of a majority to their policy. Their functions would be peculiar. They would constitute a link between the legislative and executive branches of the general Government, and, as representatives of the Executive, must hold the right of the initiative in legislation. Otherwise their position would be an anomalous one, indeed. There would be little danger and evident propriety in extending to them the first right of introducing measures relative to the administration of the several departments; and they could possess such a right without denying the fullest privileges to other members. But, whether granted this initiative or not, the head of each department would undoubtedly find it necessary to take a decided and open stand for or against every measure bearing upon the affairs of his department, by whomsoever introduced. No high-spirited man would long remain in an office in the business of which he was not permitted to pursue a policy which tallied with his own principles and convictions. If defeated by both Houses, he would naturally resign; and not many years would pass before resignation upon defeat would have become an established precedent,—and resignation upon defeat is the essence of responsible government. In arguing, therefore, for the admission of Cabinet officers into the legislature, we are logically brought to favor *responsible Cabinet government* in the United States.

But, to give to the President the right to choose whomsoever he pleases as his constitutional advisers, after having constituted Cabinet officers *ex officio* members of Congress, would be to empower him to appoint a limited number of representatives, and would thus be plainly at variance with republican principles. The highest order of responsible government could, then, be established in the United States only by laying upon the President the necessity of selecting his Cabinet from among the number of representatives already chosen by the people, or by the legislatures of the States.

Such a change in our legislative system would not be so radical as it might at first appear: it would certainly be very far from revolutionary. Under our present system we suffer all the inconveniences, are hampered by all that is defective in the machinery, of responsible government, without securing any of the many benefits which would follow upon its complete establishment. Cabinet officers are now appointed only with the consent of the Senate. Such powers as a Cabinet with responsible leadership must possess are now divided among the forty-seven Standing Committees, whose prerogatives of irresponsible leadership savor of despotism, because exercised for the most part within the secret precincts of a committee room, and not under the eyes of the whole House, and thus of the whole country. These committees, too, as has been said, rule without any of that freedom of public debate which is essential to the liberties of the people. Their measures are too often mere partisan measures, and are hurried through the forms of voting by a party majority whose interest it is that all serious opposition, all debate that might develop obstructive antagonism, should be suppressed. Under the conditions of Cabinet government, however, full and free debates are sure to take place. For what are these conditions? According as their policy stands or falls, the ministers themselves stand or fall; to the party which supports them each discussion involves a trial of strength with their opponents; upon it depends the amount of their success as a party: while to the opposition the triumph of ministerial plans means still further exclusion from office; their overthrow, accession to power. To each member of the assembly every debate offers an opportunity for placing himself, by able argument, in a position to command a place in any future Cabinet that may be formed from the ranks of his own party; each speech goes to the building up (or the tearing down) of his political fortunes. There is, therefore, an absolute certainty that every phase of every subject will be drawn carefully and vigorously, will be dwelt upon with minuteness, will be viewed from every possible standpoint. The legislative, holding full power of final decision, would find itself in immediate contact with the executive and its policy. Nor would there be room for factious government or factious opposition. Plainly, ministers must found their policies, an opposition must found its attacks, upon well-considered principles; for in this open sifting of debate, when every feature of every measure, even to the motives which prompted it, is the subject of outspoken discussion and keen scrutiny, no chicanery, no party craft, no questionable principles can long hide themselves. Party trickery, legislative jobbery, are deprived of the very air they breathe, the air of secrecy, of concealment. The public is still surprised whenever they find that dishonest legislation has been allowed to pass unchallenged. Why surprised? As things are, measures are determined in the interests of corporations, and the suffering people know almost nothing of them until their evil tendencies crop out in actual execution. Under lobby pressure from interested parties, they have been cunningly concocted in the closet sessions of partisan committees, and, by the all-powerful aid of party machinery, have been hurried through the stages of legislation without debate; so that even

Press correspondents are often as ignorant of the real nature of such special measures as the outside public. Any searching debate of such questions would at once have brought the public eye upon them, and how could they then have stood? Lifting the lid of concealment must have been the discovery to all concerned of their unsavory character. Light would have killed them.

We are thus again brought into the presence of the cardinal fact of this discussion,—that *debate* is the essential function of a popular representative body. In the severe, distinct, and sharp enunciation of underlying principles, the unsparing examination and telling criticism of opposite positions, the careful, painstaking unravelling of all the issues involved, which are incident to the free discussion of questions of public policy, we see the best, the only effective, means of educating public opinion. Can any one suppose for one moment that, in the late heated and confused discussions of the Bland silver bill, the Western papers would have had any color of justification in claiming that the Resumption Act of 1875 was passed secretly and without the knowledge of the people, if we had then had responsible government? Although this all-important matter was before the country for more than a year; was considered by two Congresses, recommended by more than one Congressional committee; was printed and circulated for the perusal of the people; was much spoken of, though little understood by the Press at the time,—the general mass of our population knew little or nothing about it, for it elicited almost no statesmanlike comment upon the floor of Congress, was exposed to none of the analysis of earnest debate. What, however, would have been its history under a well-ordered Cabinet government? It would have been introduced—if introduced at House by the Secretary of the Treasury as a part of the financial policy of the Administration, supported by the authority and sanction of the entire Cabinet. At once it would have been critically scanned by the leaders of the opposition; at each reading of the bill, and especially in Committee of the Whole, its weak points would have been mercilessly assailed, and its strong features urged in defence; attacks upon its principle by the opposition would have been met by an unequivocal avowal of "soft money" principles from the majority; and, defended by men anxious to win honors in support of the ministry, it would have been dissected by all those who were at issue with the financial doctrines of the majority, discussed and re-discussed until all its essential, all its accidental features, and all its remotest tendencies, had been dinned into the public ear, so that no man in the nation could have pretended ignorance of its meaning and object. The educational influence of such discussions is two-fold, and operates in two directions,—upon the members of the legislature themselves, and upon the people whom they represent. Thus do the merits of the two systems— Committee government and government by a responsible Cabinet—hinge upon this matter of a full and free discussion of all subjects of legislation; upon the principle stated by Mr. Bagehot, that "free government is self-government,—a government of the people by the people." It is perhaps safe to say, that the Government which secures the most thorough discussions of public interests,—whose administration most nearly conforms to the opinions of the governed,—is the freest and the best. And certainly, when judged by this principle, government by irresponsible Standing Committees can bear no comparison with government by means of a responsible ministry; for, as we have seen,—and as others besides Senator Hoar have shown,—its essential feature is a vicious suppression of debate.

Only a single glance is necessary to discover how utterly Committee government must fail to give effect to public opinion. In the first place, the exclusion of debate prevents the intelligent formation of opinion on the part of the nation at large; in the second place, public opinion, when once formed, finds it impossible to exercise any immediate control over the action of its representatives. There is no one in Congress to speak for the nation. Congress is a conglomeration of inharmonious elements; a collection of men representing each his neighborhood, each his local interest; an alarmingly large proportion of its legislation is "special"; all of it is at best only a limping compromise between the conflicting interests of the innumerable localities represented. There is no guiding or harmonizing power. Are the people in favor of a particular policy,—what means have they of forcing it upon the sovereign legislature at Washington? None but the most imperfect. If they return representatives who favor it (and this is the most they can do), these representatives being under no directing power will find a mutual agreement impracticable among so many, and will finally settle upon some policy which satisfies nobody, removes no difficulty, and makes little definite or valuable provision for the future. They must, indeed, be content with whatever measure the appropriate committee chances to introduce. Responsible ministries, on the other hand, form the policy of their parties; the strength of their party is at their command; the course of legislation turns upon the acceptance or rejection by the Houses of definite and consistent plans upon which they determine. In forming its judgment of their policy, the nation knows whereof it is judging; and, with biennial Congresses, it may soon decide whether any given policy shall stand or fall. The question would then no longer be, What representatives shall we choose to represent our chances in this haphazard game of legislation? but, What plans of national administration shall we sanction? Would not party programmes mean something then? Could they be constructed only to deceive and bewilder?

But, above and beyond all this, a responsible Cabinet constitutes a link between the executive and legislative departments of the Government which experience declares in the clearest tones to be absolutely necessary in a well-regulated, well-proportioned body politic. None can so well judge of the perfections or imperfections of a law as those who have to administer it. Look, for example, at the important matter of taxation. The only legitimate object of taxation is the support of Government; and who can so well determine the requisite revenue as those who conduct the Government? Who can so well choose feasible means of taxation, available sources of revenue, as those who have to meet the practical difficulties of tax-collection? And what surer guarantee against exorbitant estimates and unwise taxation, than the necessity of full explanation and defence before the whole House? The same principles, of course, apply to all legislation upon matters connected with any of the Executive departments.

Thus, then, not only can Cabinet ministers meet the needs of their departments more adequately and understandingly, and conduct their administration better than can irresponsible committees, but they are also less liable to misuse their powers. Responsible ministers must secure from the House and Senate an intelligent, thorough, and practical treatment of their affairs; must vindicate their principles in open battle on the floor of Congress. The public is thus enabled to exercise a direct scrutiny over the workings of the Executive departments, to keep all their operations under a constant stream of daylight. Ministers could do nothing under the shadow of darkness; committees do all in the dark. It can easily be seen how constantly ministers would be plied with questions about the conduct of public affairs, and how necessary it would be for them to satisfy their questioners if they did not wish to fall under suspicion, distrust, and obloquy.

But, while the people would thus be able to defend themselves through their representatives against malfeasance or inefficiency in the management of their business, the heads of the departments would also have every opportunity to defend their administration of the people's affairs against unjust censure or crippling legislation. Corruption in office would court concealment in vain; vicious trifling with the administration of public business by irresponsible persons would meet with a steady and effective check. The ground would be clear for a manly and candid defence of ministerial methods; wild schemes of legislation would meet with a cold repulse from ministerial authority. The salutary effect of such a change would most conspicuously appear in the increased effectiveness of our now crumbling civil, military, and naval services; for we should no longer be cursed with tardy, insufficient, and misapplied appropriations. The ministers of War, of the Navy, of the Interior, would be able to submit their estimates in person, and to procure speedy and regular appropriations; and half the abuses at present connected with appropriative legislation would necessarily disappear with the present committee system. Appropriations now, though often inadequate, are much oftener wasteful and fraudulent. Under responsible government, every appropriation asked by an Executive chief, as well as the reasons by which he backed his request, would be subjected to the same merciless sifting processes of debate as would characterize the consideration of other questions. Always having their responsible agents thus before them, the people would at once know how much they were spending, and for what it was spent.

When we come to speak of the probable influence of responsible Cabinet government upon the development of statesmanship and the renewal of the now perishing growth of statesmanlike qualities, we come upon a vital interest of the whole question. Will it bring with it worthy successors of Hamilton and Webster? Will it replace a leadership of trickery and cunning device by one of ability and moral strength? If it will not, why advocate it? If it will, how gladly and eagerly and imperatively ought we to demand it! The most despotic of Governments under the control of wise statesmen is preferable to the freest ruled by demagogues. Now, there are few more common, and perhaps few more reasonable, beliefs than that at all times, among the millions of population who constitute the body of this great nation, there is here and there to be found a man with all the genius, all the deep and strong patriotism, all the moral vigor, and all the ripeness of knowledge and variety of acquisition which gave power and lasting fame to the greater statesmen of our past history. We bewail and even wonder at the fact that these men do not find their way into public life, to claim power and leadership in the service of their country. We naturally ascribe their absence to the repugnance which superior minds must feel for the intrigues, the glaring publicity, and the air of unscrupulousness and even dishonesty which are the characteristics, or at least the environments, of political life. In our disappointment and vexation that they do not, even at the most distressing sacrifice of their personal convenience and peace, devote themselves to the study and practice of state-craft, we turn for comfort to re-read history's lesson,—that many countries find their greatest statesmen in times of extraordinary crisis or rapid transition and progress; the intervals of slow growth and uninteresting everyday administration of the government being noted only for the elevation of mediocrity, or at most of shrewd cunning, to high administrative places. We take cold consolation from the hope that times of peril—which sometimes seem close enough at hand—will not find us without strong leaders worthy of the most implicit confidence. Thus we are enabled to arrive at the comfortable and fear-quieting conclusion that it is from no fault of ours, certainly from no defects in our forms of government, that we are ruled by scheming, incompetent, political tradesmen, whose aims and ambitions are merely personal, instead of by broad-minded, masterful statesmen, whose sympathies and purposes are patriotic and national.

To supply the conditions of statesmanship is, we conclude, beyond our power; for the causes of its decline and the means necessary to its development are beyond our ken. Let us take a new departure. Let us, drawing light from every source within the range of our knowledge, make a little independent analysis of the conditions of statesmanship, with a view to ascertaining whether or not it is in reality true that we cannot contribute to its development, or even perchance give it a perennial growth among us. We learn from a critical survey of the past, that, so far as political affairs are concerned, great critical epochs are the man-making epochs of history, that revolutionary influences are man-making influences. And why? If this be the law, it must have some adequate reason underlying it; and we seem to find the reason a very plain and conspicuous one. Crises give birth and a new growth to statesmanship because they are peculiarly periods of action, in which talents find the widest and the freest scope. They are periods not only of action, but also of unusual opportunity for gaining leadership and a controlling and guiding influence. It is opportunity for transcendent influence, therefore, which calls into active public life a nation's greater minds,—minds which might otherwise remain absorbed in the smaller affairs of private life. And we thus come upon the principle,—a principle which will appear the more incontrovertible the more it is looked into and tested,—that governmental forms will call to the work of administration able minds and strong hearts constantly or infrequently, according as they do or do not afford them at all times an opportunity of gaining and retaining a commanding authority and an undisputed leadership in the nation's councils. Now it certainly needs no argument to prove that government by supreme committees, whose members are appointed at the caprice of an irresponsible party chief, by seniority, because of reputation gained in entirely different fields, or because of partisan shrewdness, is not favorable to a full and strong development of statesmanship. Certain it is that statesmanship has been steadily dying out in the United States since that stupendous crisis during which its government felt the first throbs of life. In the government of the United States there is no place found for the leadership of men of real ability. Why, then, complain that we have no leaders? The President can seldom make himself recognized as a leader; he is merely the executor of the sovereign legislative will; his Cabinet officers are little more than chief clerks, or superintendents, in the Executive departments, who advise the President as to matters in most of which he has no power of action independently of the concurrence of the Senate. The most ambitious representative can rise no higher than the chairmanship of the Committee of Ways and Means, or the Speakership of the House. The cardinal feature of Cabinet government, on the other hand, is responsible leadership,—the leadership and authority of a small body of men who have won the foremost places in their party by a display of administrative talents, by evidence of high ability upon the floor of Congress in the stormy play of debate. None but the ablest can become leaders and masters in this keen tournament in which arguments are the weapons, and the people the judges. Clearly defined, definitely directed policies arouse bold and concerted opposition; and leaders of oppositions become in time leaders of Cabinets. Such a recognized leadership it is that is necessary to the development of statesmanship under popular, republican institutions; for only such leadership can make politics seem worthy of cultivation to men of high mind and aim.

And if party success in Congress—the ruling body of the nation—depends upon power in debate, skill and prescience in policy, successful defence of or attacks upon ruling ministries, how ill can contending parties spare their men of ability from Congress! To keep men of the strongest mental and moral fibre in Congress would become a party necessity. Party triumph would then be a matter of might in debate, not of supremacy in subterfuge. The two great national parties—and upon the existence of two great parties, with clashings and mutual jealousies and watchings, depends the health of free political institutions—are dying for want of unifying and vitalizing principles. Without leaders, they are also without policies, without aims. With leaders there must be followers, there must be parties. And with leaders whose leadership was earned in an open war of principle against principle, by the triumph of one opinion over all opposing opinions, parties must from the necessities of the case have definite policies. Platforms, then, must mean something. Broken promises will then end in broken power. A

Cabinet without a policy that is finding effect in progressive legislation is, in a country of frequent elections, inviting its own defeat. Or is there, on the other hand, a determined, aggressive opposition? Then the ministry have a right to ask them what they would do under similar circumstances, were the reins of government to fall to them. And if the opposition are then silent, they cannot reasonably expect the country to intrust the government to them. Witness the situation of the Liberal party in England during the late serious crisis in Eastern affairs. Not daring to propose any policy,—having indeed, because of the disintegration of the party, no policy to propose,—their numerical weakness became a moral weakness, and the nation's ear was turned away from them. Eight words contain the sum of the present degradation of our political parties: *No leaders, no principles; no principles, no parties.* Congressional leadership is divided infinitesimally; and with divided leadership there can be no great party units. Drill in debate, by giving scope to talents, invites talents; raises up a race of men habituated to the methods of public business, skilled parliamentary chiefs. And, more than this, it creates a much-to-be-desired class who early make attendance upon public affairs the business of their lives, devoting to the service of their country all their better years. Surely the management of a nation's business will, in a well-ordered society, be as properly a matter of life-long training as the conduct of private affairs.

These are but meagre and insufficient outlines of some of the results which would follow upon the establishment of responsible Cabinet government in the United States. Its establishment has not wanted more or less outspoken advocacy from others; nor, of course, have there been lacking those who are ready to urge real or imaginary objections against it, and proclaim it an exotic unfit to thrive in American soil. It has certainly, in common with all other political systems, grave difficulties and real evils connected with it. Difficulties and evils are inseparable from every human scheme of government; and, in making their choice, a people can do no more than adopt that form which affords the largest measure of real liberty, whose machinery is least imperfect, and which is most susceptible to the control of their sovereign will.

Few, however, have discovered the real defects of such a responsible government as that which I now advocate. It is said, for instance, that it would render the President a mere figure-head, with none of that stability of official tenure, or that traditional dignity, which are necessary to such figure-heads. Would the President's power be curtailed, then, if his Cabinet ministers simply took the place of the Standing Committees? Would it not rather be enlarged? He would then be in fact, and not merely in name, the head of the Government. Without the consent of the Senate, he now exercises no sovereign functions that would be taken from him by a responsible Cabinet.

The apparently necessary existence of a partisan Executive presents itself to many as a fatal objection to the establishment of the forms of responsible Cabinet government in this country. The President must continue to represent a political party, and must continue to be anxious to surround himself with Cabinet officers who shall always substantially agree with him on all political questions. It must be admitted that the introduction of the principle of ministerial responsibility might, on this account, become at times productive of mischief, unless the tenure of the presidential office were made more permanent than it now is. Whether or not the presidential term should, under such a change of conditions, be lengthened would be one of several practical questions which would attend the adoption of a system of this sort. But it must be remembered that such a state of things as now exists, when we find the Executive to be of one party and the majority in Congress to be of the opposite party, is the exception, by no means the rule. Moreover we must constantly keep before our minds the fact that the choice now lies between this responsible Cabinet government and the rule of irresponsible committees which actually exists. It is not hard to believe that most presidents would find no greater inconvenience, experience no greater unpleasantness, in being at the head of a Cabinet composed of political opponents than in presiding, as they must now occasionally do, over a Cabinet of political friends who are compelled to act in all matters of importance according to the dictation of Standing Committees which are ruled by the opposite party. In the former case, the President may, by the exercise of whatever personal influence he possesses, affect the action of the Cabinet, and, through them, the action of the Houses; in the latter he is absolutely helpless. Even now it might prove practically impossible for a President to gain from a hostile majority in the Senate a confirmation of his appointment of a strongly partisan Cabinet drawn from his own party. The President must now, moreover, acting through his Cabinet, simply do the bidding of the committees in directing the business of the departments. With a responsible Cabinet—even though that Cabinet were of the opposite party—he might, if a man of ability, exercise great power over the conduct of public affairs; if not a man of ability, but a *mere* partisan, he would in any case be impotent. From these considerations it would appear that government by Cabinet ministers who represent the majority in Congress is no more incompatible with a partisan Executive than is government by committees representing such a majority. Indeed, a partisan President might well prefer legislation through a hostile body at whose deliberations he might himself be present, and whose course he might influence, to legislation through hostile committees over whom he could have no manner of control, direct or indirect. And such conditions would be exceptional.

But the encroachment of the legislative upon the executive is deemed the capital evil of our Government in its later phases; and it is asked, Would not the power of Congress be still more dangerously enlarged, and these encroachments made easier and surer, by thus making its relations with the Executive closer? By no means. The several parts of a perfect mechanism must actually interlace and be in strong union in order mutually to support and check each other. Here again permanent, dictating committees are the only alternative. On the one hand, we have committees directing policies for whose miscarriage they are not responsible; on the other, we have a ministry asking for legislation for whose results they are responsible. In both cases there is full power and authority on the part of the legislature to determine all the main lines of administration: there is no more real control of Executive acts in the one case than in the other; but there is an all-important difference in the character of the agents employed. When carrying out measures thrust upon them by committees, administrative officers can throw off all sense of responsibility; and the committees are safe from punishment, safe even from censure, whatever the issue. But in administering laws which have passed under the influence of their own open advocacy, ministers must shoulder the responsibilities and face the consequences. We should not, then, be giving Congress powers or opportunities of encroachment which it does not now possess, but should, on the contrary, be holding its powers in constant and effective check by putting over it responsible leaders. A complete separation of the executive and legislative is not in accord with the true spirit of those essentially English institutions of which our Government is a characteristic offshoot. The Executive is in constant need of legislative co-operation; the legislative must be aided by an Executive who is in a position intelligently and vigorously to execute its acts. There must needs be, therefore, as a binding link between them, some body which has no power to coerce the one and is interested in maintaining the independent effectiveness of the other. Such a link is the responsible Cabinet.

Again, it is objected that we should be cursed with that instability of government which results from a rapid succession of ministries, a frequent shifting of power from the hands of one party to the hands of another. This is not necessarily more likely to occur under the system of responsibility than now. We should be less exposed to such fluctuations of power than is the English government. The elective system which regulates the choice of United States Senators prevents more than one third of the seats becoming vacant at once, and this third only once every two years. The political complexion of the Senate can be changed only by a succession of elections.

But against such a responsible system the alarm-bell of *centralization* is again sounded, and all those who dread seeing too much authority, too complete control, placed within the reach of the central Government sternly set their faces against any such change. They deceive themselves. There could be no more despotic authority wielded under the forms of free government than our national Congress now exercises. It is a despotism which uses its power with all the caprice, all the scorn for settled policy, all the wild unrestraint which mark the methods of other tyrants as hateful to freedom.

Few of us are ready to suggest a remedy for the evils all deplore. We hope that our system is self-adjusting, and will not need our corrective interference. This is a vain hope! It is no small part of wisdom to know how long an evil ought to be tolerated, to see when the time has come for the people, from whom springs all authority, to speak its doom or prescribe its remedy. If that time be allowed to slip unrecognized, our dangers may overwhelm us, our political maladies may prove incurable.

Thomas W. Wilson.

Congressional Government*
Chapter 2 and Conclusion

CHAPTER 2. THE HOUSE OF REPRESENTATIVES.

No more vital truth was ever uttered than that freedom and free institutions cannot long be maintained by any people who do not understand the nature of their own government.

Like a vast picture thronged with figures of equal prominence and crowded with elaborate and obtrusive details, Congress is hard to see satisfactorily and appreciatively at a single view and from a single stand-point. Its complicated forms and diversified structure confuse the vision, and conceal the system which underlies its composition. It is too complex to be understood without an effort, without a careful and systematic process of analysis. Consequently, very few people do understand it, and its doors are practically shut against the comprehension of the public at large. If Congress had a few authoritative leaders whose figures were very distinct and very conspicuous to the eye of the world, and who could represent and stand for the national legislature in the thoughts of that very numerous, and withal very respectable, class of persons who must think specifically and in concrete forms when they think at all, those persons who can make something out of men but very little out of intangible generalizations, it would be quite within the region of possibilities for the majority of the nation to follow the course of legislation without any very serious confusion of thought. I suppose that almost everybody who just now gives any heed to the policy of Great Britain, with regard even to the reform of the franchise and other like strictly legislative questions, thinks of Mr. Gladstone and his colleagues rather than of the House of Commons, whose servants they are. The question is not, What will Parliament

* Chapters excerpted from *Congressional Government*, 15th edition (Boston: Houghton Mifflin, 1900 [orig. pub. 1885]), 58–129, 294–333. (Editor's note).

do? but, What will Mr. Gladstone do? And there is even less doubt that it is easier and more natural to look upon the legislative designs of Germany as locked up behind Bismarck's heavy brows than to think of them as dependent upon the determinations of the Reichstag, although as a matter of fact its consent is indispensable even to the plans of the imperious and domineering Chancellor.

But there is no great minister or ministry to represent the will and being of Congress in the common thought. The Speaker of the House of Representatives stands as near to leadership as any one; but his will does not run as a formative and imperative power in legislation much beyond the appointment of the committees who are to lead the House and do its work for it, and it is, therefore, not entirely satisfactory to the public mind to trace all legislation to him. He may have a controlling hand in starting it; but he sits too still in his chair, and is too evidently not on the floor of the body over which he presides, to make it seem probable to the ordinary judgment that he has much immediate concern in legislation after it is once set afoot. Everybody knows that he is a staunch and avowed partisan, and that he likes to make smooth, whenever he can, the legislative paths of his party; but it does not seem likely that all important measures originate with him, or that he is the author of every distinct policy. And in fact he is not. He is a great party chief, but the hedging circumstances of his official position as presiding officer prevent his performing the part of active leadership. He appoints the leaders of the House, but he is not himself its leader.

The leaders of the House are the chairmen of the principal Standing Committees. Indeed, to be exactly accurate, the House has as many leaders as there are subjects of legislation; for there are as many Standing Committees as there are leading classes of legislation, and in the consideration of every topic of business the House is guided by a special leader in the person of the chairman of the Standing Committee, charged with the superintendence of measures of the particular class to which that topic belongs. It is this multiplicity of leaders, this many-headed leadership, which makes the organization of the House too complex to afford uninformed people and unskilled observers any easy clue to its methods of rule. For the chairmen of the Standing Committees do not constitute a cooperative body like a ministry. They do not consult and concur in the adoption of homogeneous and mutually helpful measures; there is no thought of acting in concert. Each Committee goes its own way at its own pace. It is impossible to discover any unity or method in the disconnected and therefore unsystematic, confused, and desultory action of the House, or any common purpose in the measures which its Committees from time to time recommend.

And it is not only to the unanalytic thought of the common observer who looks at the House from the outside that its doings seem helter-skelter, and without comprehensible rule; it is not at once easy to understand them when they are scrutinized in their daily headway through open session by one who is inside the House. The newly-elected member, entering its doors for the first time, and with no more knowledge of its rules and customs than the more intelligent of his con-

stituents possess, always experiences great difficulty in adjusting his preconceived ideas of congressional life to the strange and unlooked-for conditions by
which he finds himself surrounded after he has been sworn in and has become a
part of the great legislative machine. Indeed there are generally many things connected with his career in Washington to disgust and dispirit, if not to aggrieve, the
new member. In the first place, his local reputation does not follow him to the federal capital. Possibly the members from his own State know him, and receive him
into full fellowship; but no one else knows him, except as an adherent of this or
that party, or as a new-comer from this or that State. He finds his station in-
significant, and his identity indistinct. But this social humiliation which he experiences in circles in which to be a congressman does not of itself confer distinction, because it is only to be one among many, is probably not to be compared
with the chagrin and disappointment which come in company with the inevitable
discovery that he is equally without weight or title to consideration in the House
itself. No man, when chosen to the membership of a body possessing great powers and exalted prerogatives, likes to find his activity repressed, and himself suppressed, by imperative rules and precedents which seem to have been framed for
the deliberate purpose of making usefulness unattainable by individual members.
Yet such the new member finds the rules and precedents of the House to be. It
matters not to him, because it is not apparent on the face of things, that those rules
and precedents have grown, not out of set purpose to curtail the privileges of new
members as such, but out of the plain necessities of business; it remains the fact
that he suffers under their curb, and it is not until "custom hath made it in him a
property of easiness" that he submits to them with anything like good grace.

Not all new members suffer alike, of course, under this trying discipline; because it is not every new member that comes to his seat with serious purposes of
honest, earnest, and duteous work. There are numerous tricks and subterfuges,
soon learned and easily used, by means of which the most idle and self-indulgent
members may readily make such show of exemplary diligence as will quite satisfy, if it does not positively delight, constituents in Buncombe. But the number
of congressmen who deliberately court uselessness and counterfeit well-doing is
probably small. The great majority doubtless have a keen enough sense of their
duty, and a sufficiently unhesitating desire to do it; and it may safely be taken for
granted that the zeal of new members is generally hot and insistent. If it be not
hot to begin with, it is like to become so by reason of friction with the rules, because such men must inevitably be chafed by the bonds of restraint drawn about
them by the inexorable observances of the House.

Often the new member goes to Washington as the representative of a particular line of policy, having been elected, it may be, as an advocate of free trade, or
as a champion of protection; and it is naturally his first care upon entering on his
duties to seek immediate opportunity for the expression of his views and immediate means of giving them definite shape and thrusting them upon the attention
of Congress. His disappointment is, therefore, very keen when he finds both

opportunity and means denied him. He can introduce his bill; but that is all he can do, and he must do that at a particular time and in a particular manner. This he is likely to learn through rude experience, if he be not cautious to inquire before-hand the details of practice. He is likely to make a rash start, upon the supposi-tion that Congress observes the ordinary rules of parliamentary practice to which he has become accustomed in the debating clubs familiar to his youth, and in the mass-meetings known to his later experience. His bill is doubtless ready for pre-sentation early in the session, and some day, taking advantage of a pause in the proceedings, when there seems to be no business before the House, he rises to read it and move its adoption. But he finds getting the floor an arduous and pre-carious undertaking. There are certain to be others who want it as well as he; and his indignation is stirred by the fact that the Speaker does not so much as turn to-wards him, though he must have heard his call, but recognizes some one else readily and as a matter of course. If he be obstreperous and persistent in his cries of "Mr. Speaker," he may get that great functionary's attention for a moment,—only to be told, however, that he is out of order, and that his bill can be introduced at that stage only by unanimous consent: immediately there are mechanically-uttered but emphatic exclamations of objection, and he is forced to sit down con-fused and disgusted. He has, without knowing it, obtruded himself in the way of the "regular order of business," and been run over in consequence, without being quite clear as to how the accident occurred.

Moved by the pain and discomfiture of this first experience to respect, if not to fear, the rules, the new member casts about, by study or inquiry, to find out, if possible, the nature and occasion of his privileges. He learns that his only safe day is Monday. On that day the roll of the States is called, and members may in-troduce bills as their States are reached in the call. So on Monday he essays an-other bout with the rules, confident this time of being on their safe side, mayhap indiscreetly and unluckily over-confident. For if he supposes, as he naturally will, that after his bill has been sent up to be read by the clerk he may say a few words in its behalf, and in that belief sets out upon his long-considered remarks, he will be knocked down by the rules as surely as he was on the first occasion when he gained the floor for a brief moment. The rap of Mr. Speaker's gavel is sharp, im-mediate, and peremptory. He is curtly informed that no debate is in order; the bill can only be referred to the appropriate Committee.

This is, indeed, disheartening; it is his first lesson in committee government, and the master's rod smarts; but the sooner he learns the prerogatives and pow-ers of the Standing Committees the sooner will he penetrate the mysteries of the rules and avoid the pain of further contact with their thorny side. The privileges of the Standing Committees are the beginning and the end of the rules. Both the House of Representatives and the Senate conduct their business by what may fig-uratively, but not inaccurately, be called an odd device of *disintegration*. The House virtually both deliberates and legislates in small sections. Time would fail it to discuss all the bills brought in, for they every session number thousands; and it is to be doubted whether, even if time allowed, the ordinary processes of debate and amendment would suffice to sift the chaff from the wheat in the bushels of bills every week piled upon the clerk's desk. Accordingly, no futile attempt is made to do anything of the kind. The work is parceled out, most of it to the forty-seven Standing Committees which constitute the regular organization of the House, some of it to select committees appointed for special and temporary purposes. Each of the almost numberless bills that come pouring in on Mondays is "read a first and second time,"—simply perfunctorily read, that is, by its title, by the clerk, and passed by silent assent through its first formal courses, for the purpose of bringing it to the proper stage for commitment,—and referred without debate to the appropriate Standing Committee. Practically, no bill escapes commitment—save, of course, bills introduced by committees, and a few which may now and then be crowded through under a suspension of the rules, granted by a two-thirds vote—though the exact disposition to be made of a bill is not always determined easily and as a matter of course. Besides the great Committee of Ways and Means and the equally great Committee on Appropriations, there are Standing Committees on Banking and Currency, on Claims, on Commerce, on the Public Lands, on Post-Offices and Post-Roads, on the Judiciary, on Public Expenditures, on Manufactures, on Agriculture, on Military Affairs, on Naval Affairs, on Mines and Mining, on Education and Labor, on Patents, and on a score of other branches of legislative concern; but careful and differential as is the topical division of the subjects of legislation which is represented in the titles of these Committees, it is not always evident to which Committee each particular bill should go. Many bills affect subjects which may be regarded as lying as properly within the jurisdiction of one as of another of the Committees; for no hard and fast lines separate the various classes of business which the Committees are commissioned to take in charge. Their jurisdictions overlap at many points, and it must frequently happen that bills are read which cover just this common ground. Over the commitment of such bills sharp and interesting skirmishes often take place. There is active competition for them, the ordinary, quiet routine of matter-of-course reference being interrupted by rival motions seeking to give very different directions to the disposition to be made of them. To which Committee should a bill "to fix and establish the maximum rates of fares of the Union Pacific and Central Pacific Railroads" be sent,—to the Committee on Commerce or to the Committee on the Pacific Railroads? Should a bill which prohibits the mailing of certain classes of letters and circulars go to the Committee on Post-Offices and Post-Roads, because it relates to the mails, or to the Committee on the Judiciary, because it proposes to make any transgression of its prohibition a crime? What is the proper disposition of any bill which thus seems to lie within two distinct committee jurisdictions?

The fate of bills committed is generally not uncertain. As a rule, a bill committed is a bill doomed. When it goes from the clerk's desk to a committee-room it crosses a parliamentary bridge of sighs to dim dungeons of silence whence it will never return. The means and time of its death are unknown, but its friends never see it again. Of course no Standing Committee is privileged to take upon itself the full powers of the House it represents, and formally and decisively reject a bill referred to it; its disapproval, if it disapproves, must be reported to the House in the form of a recommendation that the bill "do not pass." But it is easy, and therefore common, to let the session pass without making any report at all upon bills deemed objectionable or unimportant, and to substitute for reports upon them a few bills of the Committee's own drafting; so that thousands of bills expire with the expiration of each Congress, not having been rejected, but having been simply neglected. There was not time to report upon them.

Of course it goes without saying that the practical effect of this Committee organization of the House is to consign to each of the Standing Committees the entire direction of legislation upon those subjects which properly come to its consideration. As to those subjects it is entitled to the intitiative, and all legislative action with regard to them is under its overruling guidance. It gives shape and course to the determinations of the House. In one respect, however, its initiative is limited. Even a Standing Committee cannot report a bill whose subject-matter has not been referred to it by the House, "by the rules or otherwise"; it cannot volunteer advice on questions upon which its advice has not been asked. But this is not a serious, not even an operative, limitation upon its functions of suggestion and leadership; for it is a very simple matter to get referred to it any subject it wishes to introduce to the attention of the House. Its chairman, or one of its leading members, frames a bill covering the point upon which the Committee wishes to suggest legislation; brings it in, in his capacity as a private member, on Monday, when the call of States is made; has it referred to his Committee; and thus secures an opportunity for the making of the desired report.

It is by this imperious authority of the Standing Committees that the new member is stayed and thwarted whenever he seeks to take an active part in the business of the House. Turn which way he may, some privilege of the Committees stands in his path. The rules are so framed as to put all business under their management; and one of the discoveries which the new member is sure to make, albeit after many trying experiences and sobering adventures and as his first session draws towards its close, is, that under their sway freedom of debate finds no place of allowance, and that his long-delayed speech must remain unspoken. For even a long congressional session is too short to afford time for a full consideration of all the reports of the forty-seven Committees, and debate upon them must be rigidly cut short, if not altogether excluded, if any considerable part of the necessary business is to be gotten through with before adjournment. There are some subjects to which the House must always give prompt attention; therefore reports from the Committees on Printing and on Elections are always in order; and there are some subjects to which careful consideration must always be accorded; therefore the Committee of Ways and Means and the Committee on Appropriations are clothed with extraordinary privileges; and revenue and supply bills may be reported, and will ordinarily be considered, at any time. But these four are the only specially licensed Committees. The rest must take their turns in fixed order as they are called on by the Speaker, contenting themselves with such crumbs of time as fall from the tables of the four Committees of highest prerogative.

Senator Hoar, of Massachusetts, whose long congressional experience entitles him to speak with authority, calculates[1] that, "supposing the two sessions which make up the life of the House to last ten months," most of the Committees have at their disposal during each Congress but two hours apiece in which "to report upon, debate, and dispose of all the subjects of general legislation committed to their charge." For of course much time is wasted. No Congress gets immediately to work upon its first assembling. It has its officers to elect, and after their election some time must elapse before its organization is finally completed by the appointment of the Committees. It adjourns for holidays, too, and generally spares itself long sittings. Besides, there are many things to interrupt the call of the Committees upon which most of the business waits. That call can proceed only during the morning hours,—the hours just after the reading of the "Journal,"—on Tuesdays, Wednesdays, and Thursdays; and even then it may suffer postponement because of the unfinished business of the previous day which is entitled to first consideration. The call cannot proceed on Mondays because the morning hour of Mondays is devoted invariably to the call of the States for the introduction of bills and resolutions; nor on Fridays, for Friday is "private bill day," and is always engrossed by the Committee on Claims, or by other fathers of bills which have gone upon the "private calendar." On Saturdays the House seldom sits.

The reports made during these scant morning hours are ordered to be printed, for future consideration in their turn, and the bills introduced by the Committees are assigned to the proper calendars, to be taken up in order at the proper time. When a morning hour has run out, the House hastens to proceed with the business on the Speaker's table.

These are some of the plainer points of the rules. They are full of complexity, and of confusion to the uninitiated, and the confusions of practice are greater than the confusions of the rules. For the regular order of business is constantly being interrupted by the introduction of resolutions offered "by unanimous consent," and of bills let in under a "suspension of the rules." Still, it is evident that there is one principle which runs through every stage of procedure, and which is never disallowed or abrogated,—the principle that the Committees shall rule without let or hindrance. And this is a principle of extraordinary formative power. It is the mould of all legislation. In the first place, the speeding of business under the direction of the Committees determines the character and the amount of the discussion to which legislation shall be subjected. The House is conscious that time presses. It knows that, hurry as it may, it will hardly get through with one eighth

---

[1] In an article entitled "The Conduct of Business in Congress" (*North American Review*, vol. cxxviii, p. 113), to which I am indebted for many details of the sketch in the text.

of the business laid out for the session, and that to pause for lengthy debate is to allow the arrears to accumulate. Besides, most of the members are individually anxious to expedite action on every pending measure, because each member of the House is a member of one or more of the Standing Committees, and is quite naturally desirous that the bills prepared by his Committees, and in which he is, of course, specially interested by reason of the particular attention which he has been compelled to give them, should reach a hearing and a vote as soon as possible. It must, therefore, invariably happen that the Committee holding the floor at any particular time is the Committee whose proposals the majority wish to dispose of as summarily as circumstances will allow, in order that the rest of the forty-two unprivileged Committees to which the majority belong may gain the earlier and the fairer chance of a hearing. A reporting Committee, besides, is generally as glad to be pushed as the majority are to push it. It probably has several bills matured, and wishes to see them disposed of before its brief hours of opportunity[2] are passed and gone.

Consequently, it is the established custom of the House to accord the floor for one hour to the member of the reporting Committee who has charge of the business under consideration; and that hour is made the chief hour of debate. The reporting committee-man seldom, if ever, uses the whole of the hour himself for his opening remarks; he uses part of it, and retains control of the rest of it; for by undisputed privilege it is his to dispose of, whether he himself be upon the floor or not. No amendment is in order during that hour, unless he consent to its presentation; and he does not, of course, yield his time indiscriminately to any one who wishes to speak. He gives way, indeed, as in fairness he should, to opponents as well as to friends of the measure under his charge; but generally no one is accorded a share of his time who has not obtained his previous promise of the floor; and those who do speak must not run beyond the number of minutes he has agreed to allow them. He keeps the course both of debate and of amendment thus carefully under his own supervision, as a good tactician, and before he finally yields the floor, at the expiration of his hour, he is sure to move the previous question. To neglect to do so would be to lose all control of the business in hand; for unless the previous question is ordered the debate may run on at will, and his Committee's chance for getting its measures through slip quite away; and that would be nothing less than his disgrace. He would be all the more blameworthy because he had but to ask for the previous question to get it. As I have said, the House is as eager to hurry business as he can be, and will consent to almost any limitation of discussion that he may demand; though, probably, if he were to throw the reins upon its neck, it would run at large from very wantonness, in scorn of such a driver. The previous question once ordered, all amendments are

---

[2] No Committee is entitled, when called, to occupy more than the morning hours of two successive days with the measures which it has prepared; though if its second morning hour expire while the House is actually considering one of its bills, that single measure may hold over from morning hour to morning hour until it is disposed of.

precluded, and one hour remains for the summing-up of this same privileged committee-man before the final vote is taken and the bill disposed of.

These are the customs which baffle and perplex and astound the new member. In these precedents and usages, when at length he comes to understand them, the novice spies out the explanation of the fact, once so confounding and seemingly inexplicable, that when he leaped to his feet to claim the floor other members who rose after him were coolly and unfeelingly preferred before him by the Speaker. Of course it is plain enough now that Mr. Speaker knew beforehand to whom the representative of the reporting Committee had agreed to yield the floor; and it was no use for any one else to cry out for recognition. Whoever wished to speak should, if possible, have made some arrangement with the Committee before the business came to a hearing, and should have taken care to notify Mr. Speaker that he was to be granted the floor for a few moments.

Unquestionably this, besides being a very interesting, is a very novel and significant method of restricting debate and expediting legislative action,— a method of very serious import, and obviously fraught with far-reaching constitutional effects. The practices of debate which prevail in its legislative assembly are manifestly of the utmost importance to a self-governing people; for that legislation which is not thoroughly discussed by the legislating body is practically done in a corner. It is impossible for Congress itself to do wisely what it does so hurriedly; and the constituencies cannot understand what Congress does not itself stop to consider. The prerogatives of the Committees represent something more than a mere convenient division of labor. There is only one part of its business to which Congress, as a whole, attends,— that part, namely, which is embraced under the privileged subjects of revenue and supply. The House never accepts the proposals of the Committee of Ways and Means, or of the Committee on Appropriations, without due deliberation; but it allows almost all of its other Standing Committees virtually to legislate for it. In form, the Committees only digest the various matter introduced by individual members, and prepare it, with care, and after thorough investigation, for the final consideration and action of the House; but, in reality, they dictate the course to be taken, prescribing the decisions of the House not only, but measuring out, according to their own wills, its opportunities for debate and deliberation as well. The House sits, not for serious discussion, but to sanction the conclusions of its Committees as rapidly as possible. It legislates in its committee-rooms; not by the determinations of majorities, but by the resolutions of specially-commissioned minorities; so that it is not far from the truth to say that Congress in session is Congress on public exhibition, whilst Congress in its committee-rooms is Congress at work.

Habit grows fast, even upon the unconventional American, and the nature of the House of Representatives has, by long custom, been shaped to the spirit of its rules. Representatives have attained, by rigorous self-discipline, to the perfect stature of the law under which they live, having purged their hearts as completely as may be of all desire to do that which it is the chief object of that law to forbid by giving over a vain lust after public discussion. The entire absence of the instinct of debate amongst them, and their apparent unfamiliarity with the idea of combating a proposition by argument, was recently illustrated by an incident which was quite painfully amusing. The democratic majority of the House of the Forty-eighth Congress desired the immediate passage of a pension bill of rather portentous proportions; but the republican minority disapproved of the bill with great fervor, and, when it was moved by the Pension Committee, late one afternoon, in a thin House, that the rules be suspended, and an early day set for a consideration of the bill, the Republicans addressed themselves to determined and persistent "filibustering" to prevent action. First they refused to vote, leaving the Democrats without an acting quorum; then, all night long, they kept the House at roll-calling on dilatory and obstructive motions, the dreary dragging of the time being relieved occasionally by the amusement of hearing the excuses of members who had tried to slip off to bed, or by the excitement of an angry dispute between the leaders of the two parties as to the responsibility for the dead-lock. Not till the return of morning brought in the delinquents to recruit the democratic ranks did business advance a single step. Now, the noteworthy fact about this remarkable scene is, that the minority were not manœuvring to gain opportunity or time for debate, in order that the country might be informed of the true nature of the obnoxious bill, but were simply fighting a preliminary motion with silent, dogged obstruction. After the whole night had been spent in standing out against action, the House is said to have been "in no mood for the thirty-minutes' debate allowed by the rules," and a final vote was taken, with only a word or two said. It was easier and more natural, as everybody saw, to direct attention to the questionable character of what was being attempted by the majority by creating a somewhat scandalous "scene," of which every one would talk, than by making speeches which nobody would read. It was a notable commentary on the characteristic methods of our system of congressional government.

One very noteworthy result of this system is to shift the theatre of debate upon legislation from the floor of Congress to the privacy of the committee-rooms. Provincial gentlemen who read the Associated Press dispatches in their morning papers as they sit over their coffee at breakfast are doubtless often very sorely puzzled by certain of the items which sometimes appear in the brief telegraphic notes from Washington. What can they make of this for instance: "The House Committee on Commerce to-day heard arguments from the congressional delegation from" such and such States "in advocacy of appropriations for river and harbor improvements which the members desire incorporated in the River and Harbor Appropriations Bill"? They probably do not understand that it would have been useless for members not of the Committee on Commerce to wait for any opportunity to make their suggestions on the floor of Congress, where the measure to which they wish to make additions would be under the authoritative control of the Committee, and where, consequently, they could gain a hearing only by the courteous sufferance of the committee-man in charge of the report. Whatever is to be done must be done by or through the Committee.

It would seem, therefore, that practically Congress, or at any rate the House of Representatives, delegates not only its legislative but also its deliberative functions to its Standing Committees. The little public debate that arises under the stringent and urgent rules of the House is formal rather than effective, and it is the discussions which take place in the Committees that give form to legislation. Undoubtedly these siftings of legislative questions by the Committees are of great value in enabling the House to obtain "undarkened counsel" and intelligent suggestions from authoritative sources. All sober, purposeful, business-like talk upon questions of public policy, whether it take place in Congress or only before the Committees of Congress, is of great value; and the controversies which spring up in the committee-rooms, both amongst the committee-men themselves and between those who appear before the Committees as advocates of special measures, cannot but contribute to add clearness and definite consistency to the reports submitted to the House.

There are, however, several very obvious reasons why the most thorough canvass of business by the Committees, and the most exhaustive and discriminating discussion of all its details in their rooms, cannot take the place or fulfill the uses of amendment and debate by Congress in open session. In the first place, the proceedings of the Committees are private and their discussions unpublished. The chief, and unquestionably the most essential, object of all discussion of public business is the enlightenment of public opinion; and of course, since it cannot hear the debates of the Committees, the nation is not apt to be much instructed by them. Only the Committees are enlightened. There is a conclusive objection to the publication of the proceedings of the Committees, which is recognized as of course by all parliamentary lawyers, namely, that those proceedings are of no force till confirmed by the House. A Committee is commissioned, not to instruct the public, but to instruct and guide the House.

Indeed it is not usual for the Committees to open their sittings often to those who desire to be heard with regard to pending questions; and no one can demand a hearing as of right. On the contrary, they are privileged and accustomed to hold their sessions in absolute secrecy. It is made a breach of order for any member to allude on the floor of the House to anything that has taken place in committee, "unless by a written report sanctioned by a majority of the Committee"; and there is no place in the regular order of business for a motion instructing a Committee to conduct its investigations with open doors. Accordingly, it is only by the concession of the Committees that arguments are made before them.

When they do suffer themselves to be approached, moreover, they generally extend the leave to others besides their fellow-congressmen. The Committee on Commerce consents to listen to prominent railroad officials upon the subject of the regulation of freight charges and fares; and scores of interested persons telegraph inquiries to the chairman of the Committee of Ways and Means as to the time at which they are to be permitted to present to the Committee their views upon the revision of the tariff. The speeches made before the Committees at their open sessions are, therefore, scarcely of such a kind as would be instructive to the public, and on that account worth publishing. They are as a rule the pleas of special pleaders, the arguments of advocates. They have about them none of the searching, critical, illuminating character of the higher order of parliamentary debate, in which men are pitted against each other as equals, and urged to sharp contest and masterful strife by the inspiration of political principle and personal ambition, through the rivalry of parties and the competition of policies. They represent a joust between antagonistic interests, not a contest of principles. They could scarcely either inform or elevate public opinion, ever if they were to obtain its heed.

For the instruction and elevation of public opinion, in regard to national affairs, there is needed something more than special pleas for special privileges. There is needed public discussion of a peculiar sort: a discussion by the sovereign legislative body itself, a discussion in which every feature of each mooted point of policy shall be distinctly brought out, and every argument of significance pushed to the farthest point of insistence, by recognized leaders in that body; and, above all, a discussion upon which something—something of interest or importance, some pressing question of administration or of law, the fate of a party or the success of a conspicuous Politician—evidently depends. It is only a discussion of this sort that the public will heed; no other sort will impress it.

There could, therefore, be no more unwelcome revelation to one who has anything approaching a statesman-like appreciation of the essential conditions of intelligent self-government than just that which must inevitably be made to every one who candidly examines our congressional system; namely, that, under that system, such discussion is impossible. There are, to begin with, physical and *architectural* reasons why business-like debate of public affairs by the House of Representatives is out of the question. To those who visit the galleries of the representative chamber during a session of the House these reasons are as obvious as they are astonishing. It would be natural to expect that a body which meets ostensibly for consultation and deliberation should hold its sittings in a room small enough to admit of an easy interchange of views and a ready concert of action, where its members would be brought into close, sympathetic contact; and it is nothing less than astonishing to find it spread at large through the vast spaces of such a chamber as the hall of the House of Representatives, where there are no close ranks of coöperating parties, but each member has a roomy desk and an easy revolving chair; where broad aisles spread and stretch themselves; where ample, soft-carpeted areas lie about the spacious desks of the Speaker and clerks; where deep galleries reach back from the outer limits of the wide passages which lie beyond "the bar": an immense, capacious chamber, disposing its giant dimensions freely beneath the great level lacunar ceiling through whose glass panels the full light of day pours in. The most vivid impression the visitor gets in looking over that vast hall is the impression of space. A speaker must needs have a voice like O'Connell's, the practical visitor is apt to think, as he sits in the gallery, to fill even the silent spaces of that room; how much more to overcome the disorderly noises that buzz and rattle through it when the representatives are assembled,—a voice clear, sonorous, dominant, like the voice of a clarion. One who speaks there with the voice and lungs of the ordinary mortal must content himself with the audience of those members in his own immediate neighborhood, whose ears he rudely assails in vehement efforts to command the attention of those beyond them, and who, therefore, cannot choose but hear him.

It is of this magnitude of the hall of the representatives that those news telegrams are significant which speak of an interesting or witty speech in Congress as having drawn about the speaker listeners from all parts of the House. As one of our most noted wits would say, a member must needs take a Sabbath day's journey to get within easy hearing distance of a speaker who is addressing the House from the opposite side of the hall; for besides the space there are the noises intervening, the noises of loud talking and of the clapping of hands for the pages, making the task of the member who is speaking "very like trying to address the people in the omnibuses from the curbstone in front of the Astor House."[3]

But these physical limitations to debate, though serious and real, are amongst the least important, because they are amongst the least insuperable. If effective and business-like public discussions were considered indispensable by Congress, or even desirable, the present chamber could readily be divided into two halls: the one a commodious reading-room where the members might chat and write at ease as they now do in the House itself; and the other a smaller room suitable for debate and earnest business. This, in fact, has been several times proposed, but the House does not feel that there is any urgency about providing facilities for debate, because it sees no reason to desire an increase of speech-making, in view of the fact that, notwithstanding all the limitations now put upon discussion, its business moves much too slowly. The early Congresses had time to talk; Congresses of to-day have not. Before that wing of the Capitol was built in which the representative chamber now is, the House used to sit in the much smaller room, now empty save for the statuary to whose exhibition it is devoted; and there much speech-making went on from day to day; there Calhoun and Randolph and Webster and Clay won their reputations as statesmen and orators. So earnest and interesting were the debates of those days, indeed, that the principal speeches delivered in Congress seem to have been usually printed at length in the metropolitan journals.[4] But the number and length of the speeches was even then very much deplored; and so early as 1828 a writer in the "North American Review" condemns what he calls "the habit of congressional debating," with the air of one who speaks against some abuse which every one acknowledges to be a nuisance.[5] Eleven years later a contributor to the "Democratic Review"[6] declared that it had

---

[3] Quoted from an exceedingly life-like and picturesque description of the House which appeared in the New York *Nation* for April 4, 1878.

[4] *North American Review*, vol. xxvi, p. 162.

[5] Id., the same article.

[6] "Glances at Congress," *Democratic Review*, March, 1839.

"been gravely charged upon" Mr. Samuel Cushman, then a member of the Twenty-fifth Congress from New Hampshire, "that he moves the previous question. Truly," continues the essayist, "he does, and for that very service, if he had never done anything else, he deserves a monument as a public benefactor. One man who can arrest a tedious, long-winded, factious, time-killing debate, is worth forty who can provoke or keep one up. It requires some moral courage, some spirit, and some tact also, to move the previous questions, and to move it, too, at precisely the right point of time."

This ardent and generous defense of Mr. Cushman against the odious accusation of moving the previous question would doubtless be exquisitely amusing to the chairman of one of the Standing Committees of the Forty-eighth Congress, to whom the previous question seems one of the commonest necessities of life. But, after all, he ought not to laugh at the ingenuous essayist, for that was not the heydey of the rules; they then simply served and did not tyrannize over the House. They did not then have the opportunity of empire afforded them by the scantiness of time which hurries the House, and the weight of business which oppresses it; and they were at a greater disadvantage in a room where oratory was possible than they are in a vast chamber where the orator's voice is drowned amidst the noises of disorderly inattention. Nowadays would-be debaters are easily thrust out of Congress and forced to resort to the printing-office; are compelled to content themselves with speaking from the pages of the "Record" instead of from their places in the House. Some people who live very far from Washington may imagine that the speeches which are spread at large in the columns of the "Congressional Record," or which their representative sends them in pamphlet form, were actually delivered in Congress; but every one else knows that they were not; that Congress is constantly granting leave to its members to insert in the official reports of the proceedings speeches which it never heard and does not care to hear, but which it is not averse from printing at the public expense, if it is desirable that constituents and the country at large should read them. It will not stand between a member and his constituents so long as it can indulge the one and satisfy the others without any inconvenience to itself or any serious drain upon the resources of the Treasury. The public printer does not object.

But there are other reasons still more organic than these why the debates of Congress cannot, under our present system, have that serious purpose of search into the merits of policies and that definite and determinate party—or, if you will, partisan—aim without which they can never be effective for the instruction of public opinion, or the cleansing of political action. The chief of these reasons, because the parent of all the rest, is that there are in Congress no authoritative leaders who are the recognized spokesmen of their parties. Power is nowhere concentrated; it is rather deliberately and of set policy scattered amongst many small chiefs. It is divided up, as it were, into forty-seven seigniories, in each of which a Standing Committee is the court-baron and its chairman lord-proprietor. These petty barons, some of them not a little powerful, but none of them within reach of the full powers of rule, may at will exercise an almost despotic sway within their own shires, and may sometimes threaten to convulse even the realm itself; but both their mutual jealousies and their brief and restricted opportunities forbid their combining, and each is very far from the office of common leader.

I know that to some this scheme of distributed power and disintegrated rule seems a very excellent device whereby we are enabled to escape a dangerous "one-man power" and an untoward concentration of functions; and it is very easy to see and appreciate the considerations which make this view of committee government so popular. It is based upon a very proper and salutary fear of *irresponsible* power; and those who most resolutely maintain it always fight from the position that all leadership in legislation is hard to restrain in proportion to its size and to the strength of its prerogatives, and that to divide it is to make it manageable. They aver, besides, that the less a man has to do—that is to say, the more he is confined to single departments and to definite details—the more intelligent and thorough will his work be. They like the Committees, therefore, just because they are many and weak, being quite willing to abide their being despotic within their narrow spheres.

It seems evident, however, when the question is looked at from another standpoint, that, as a matter of fact and experience, the more power is divided the more irresponsible it becomes. A mighty baron who can call half the country to arms is watched with greater jealousy, and, therefore, restrained with more vigilant care than is ever vouchsafed the feeble master of a single and solitary castle. The one cannot stir abroad upon an innocent pleasure jaunt without attracting the suspicious attention of the whole country-side; the other may vex and harry his entire neighborhood without fear of let or hindrance. It is ever the little foxes that spoil the grapes. At any rate, to turn back from illustration to the facts of the argument, it is plain enough that the petty character of the leadership of each Committee contributes towards making its despotism sure by making its duties uninteresting. The Senate almost always discusses its business with considerable thoroughness; and even the House, whether by common consent or by reason of such persistent "filibustering" on the part of the minority as compels the reporting Committee and the majority to grant time for talk, sometimes stops to debate committee reports at length; but nobody, except, perhaps, newspaper editors, finds these debates interesting reading.

Why is it that many intelligent and patriotic people throughout this country, from Virginia to California,—people who, beyond all question, love their State and the Union more than they love our cousin state over sea,—subscribe for the London papers in order to devour the parliamentary debates, and yet would never think of troubling themselves to make tedious progress through a single copy of the "Congressional Record"? Is it because they are captivated by the old-world dignity of royal England with its nobility and its court pageantry, or because of a vulgar desire to appear better versed than their neighbors in foreign affairs, and to affect familiarity with British statesmen? No; of course not. It is because the parliamentary debates are interesting and ours are not. In the British House of Commons the functions and privileges of our Standing Committees are all concentrated in the hands of the Ministry, who have, besides, some prerogatives of leadership which even our Committees do not possess, so that they carry all responsibility as well as great power, and all debate wears an intense personal and party interest. Every important discussion is an arraignment of the Ministry by the Opposition,—an arraignment of the majority by the minority; and every important vote is a party defeat and a party triumph. The whole conduct of the government turns upon what is said in the Commons, because the revelations of debate often change votes, and a Ministry loses hold upon power as it loses hold upon the confidence of the Commons. This great Standing Committee goes out whenever it crosses the will of the majority. It is, therefore, for these very simple and obvious reasons that the parliamentary debates are read on this side of the water in preference to the congressional debates. They affect the ministers, who are very conspicuous persons, and in whom, therefore, all the intelligent world is interested; and they determine the course of politics in a great empire. The season of a parliamentary debate is a great field day on which Liberals and Conservatives pit their full forces against each other, and people like to watch the issues of the contest.

Our congressional debates, on the contrary, have no tithe of this interest, because they have no tithe of such significance and importance. The committee reports, upon which the debates take place, are backed by neither party; they represent merely the recommendations of a small body of members belonging to both parties, and are quite as likely to divide the vote of the party to which the majority of the Committee belong as they are to meet with opposition from the other side of the chamber. If they are carried, it is no party triumph; if they are lost, it is no party discomfiture. They are no more than the proposals of a mixed Committee, and may be rejected without political inconvenience to either party or reproof to the Committee; just as they may be passed without compliment to the Committee or political advantage to either side of the House. Neither party has any great stake in the controversy. The only importance that can attach to the vote must hang upon its relation to the next general election. If the report concern a question which is at the time so much in the public eye that all action upon it is likely to be marked and remembered against the day of popular action, parties are careful to vote as solidly as possible on what they conceive to be the safe side; but all other reports are disposed of without much thought of their influence upon the fortunes of distant elections, because that influence is remote and problematical.

In a word, the national parties do not act in Congress under the restraint of a sense of immediate responsibility. Responsibility is spread thin; and no vote or debate can gather it. It rests not so much upon parties as upon individuals; and it rests upon individuals in no such way as would make it either just or efficacious to visit upon them the iniquity of any legislative act. Looking at government from a practical and business-like, rather than from a theoretical and abstractly-ethical point of view,—treating the business of government as a business,—it seems to be unquestionably and in a high degree desirable that all legislation should distinctly represent the action of parties as parties. I know that it has been proposed by enthusiastic, but not too practical, reformers to do away with parties by some legerdemain of governmental reconstruction, accompanied and supplemented by some rehabilitation, devoutly to be wished, of the virtues least commonly controlling in fallen human nature; but it seems to me that it would be more difficult and less desirable than these amiable persons suppose to conduct a government of the many by means of any other device than party organization, and that the great need is, not to get rid of parties, but to find and use some expedient by which they can be managed and made amenable from day to day to public opinion. Plainly this cannot be effected by punishing here and there a member of Congress who has voted for a flagrantly dishonest appropriation bill, or an obnoxious measure relating to the tariff. Unless the punishment can be extended to the party—if any such be recognizable—with which these members have voted, no advantage has been won for self-government, and no triumph has been gained by public opinion. It should be desired that parties should act in distinct organizations, in accordance with avowed principles, under easily recognized leaders, in order that the voters might be able to declare by their ballots, not only their condemnation of any past policy, by withdrawing all support from the party responsible for it; but also and particularly their will as to the future administration of the government, by bringing into power a party pledged to the adoption of an acceptable policy.

It is, therefore, a fact of the most serious consequence that by our system of congressional rule no such means of controlling legislation is afforded. Outside of Congress the organization of the national parties is exceedingly well-defined and tangible; no one could wish it, and few could imagine it, more so; but within Congress it is obscure and intangible. Our parties marshal their adherents with the strictest possible discipline for the purpose of carrying elections, but their discipline is very slack and indefinite in dealing with legislation. At least there is within Congress no *visible*, and therefore no *controllable* party organization. The only bond of cohesion is the caucus, which occasionally whips a party together for coöperative action against the time for casting its vote upon some critical question. There is always a majority and a minority, indeed, but the legislation of a session does not represent the policy of either; it is simply an aggregate of the bills recommended by Committees composed of members from both sides of the House, and it is known to be usually, not the work of the majority men upon the Committees, but compromise conclusions bearing some shade or tinge of each of the variously-colored opinions and wishes of the committee-men of both parties. . . .

CHAPTER 6. CONCLUSION.

Political philosophy must analyze political history; it must distinguish what is due to the excellence of the people, and what to the excellence of the laws; it must carefully calculate the exact effect of each part of the constitution, though thus it may destroy many an idol of the multitude, and detect the secret of utility where but few imagined it to lie.—BAGEHOT.

Congress always makes what haste it can to legislate. It is the prime object of its rules to expedite law-making. Its customs are fruits of its characteristic diligence in enactment. Be the matters small or great, frivolous or grave, which busy it, its aim is to have laws always a-making. Its temper is strenuously legislative. That it cannot regulate all the questions to which its attention is weekly invited is its misfortune, not its fault; is due to the human limitation of its faculties, not to any narrow circumscription of its desires. If its committee machinery is inadequate to the task of bringing to action more than one out of every hundred of the bills introduced, it is not because the quick clearance of the docket is not the motive of its organic life. If legislation, therefore, were the only or the chief object for which it should live, it would not be possible to withhold admiration from those clever hurrying rules and those inexorable customs which seek to facilitate it. Nothing but a doubt as to whether or not Congress should confine itself to lawmaking can challenge with a question the utility of its organization as a facile statute-devising machine.

The political philosopher of these days of self-government has, however, something more than a doubt with which to gainsay the usefulness of a sovereign representative body which confines itself to legislation to the exclusion of all other functions. Buckle declared, indeed, that the chief use and value of legislation nowadays lay in its opportunity and power to remedy the mistakes of the legislation of the past; that it was beneficent only when it carried healing in its wings; that repeal was more blessed than enactment. And it is certainly true that the greater part of the labor of legislation consists in carrying the loads recklessly or bravely shouldered in times gone by, when the animal which is now a bull was only a calf, and in completing, if they may be completed, the tasks once undertaken in the shape of unambitious schemes which at the outset looked innocent enough. Having got his foot into it, the legislator finds it difficult, if not impossible, to get it out again. "The modern industrial organization, including banks, corporations, joint-stock companies, financial devices, national debts, paper currency, national systems of taxation, is largely the creation of legislation (not in its historical origin, but in the mode of its existence and in its authority), and is largely regulated by legislation. Capital is the breath of life to this organization, and every day, as the organization becomes more complex and delicate, the folly of assailing capital or credit becomes greater. At the same time it is evident that the task of the legislator to embrace in his view the whole system, to adjust his rules so that the play of the civil institutions shall not alter the play of the economic forces, requires more training and more acumen. Furthermore, the greater the complication and delicacy of the industrial system, the greater the chances for cupidity when backed by craft, and the task of the legislator to meet and defeat the attempts of this cupidity is one of constantly increasing difficulty."[7]

Legislation unquestionably generates legislation. Every statute may be said to have a long lineage of statutes behind it; and whether that lineage be honorable or of ill repute is as much a question as to each individual statute as it can be with regard to the ancestry of each individual legislator. Every statute in its turn has a numerous progeny, and only time and opportunity can decide whether its offspring will bring it honor or shame. Once begin the dance of legislation, and you must struggle through its mazes as best you can to its breathless end,—if any end there be.

It is not surprising, therefore, that the enacting, revising, tinkering, repealing of laws should engross the attention and engage the entire energy of such a body as Congress. It is, however, easy to see how it might be better employed; or, at least, how it might add others to this overshadowing function, to the infinite advantage of the government. Quite as important as legislation is vigilant oversight of administration; and even more important than legislation is the instruction and guidance in political affairs which the people might receive from a body which kept all national concerns suffused in a broad daylight of discussion. There is no similar legislature in existence which is so shut up to the one business of lawmaking as is our Congress. As I have said, it in a way superintends administration by the exercise of semi-judicial powers of investigation, whose limitations and insufficiency are manifest. But other national legislatures command administration and verify their name of "parliaments" by talking official acts into notoriety. Our extra-constitutional party conventions, short-lived and poor in power as they are, constitute our only machinery for that sort of control of the executive which consists in the award of personal rewards and punishments. This is the cardinal fact which differentiates Congress from the Chamber of Deputies and from Parliament, and which puts it beyond the reach of those eminently useful functions whose exercise would so raise it in usefulness and in dignity.

An effective representative body, gifted with the power to rule, ought, it would seem, not only to speak the will of the nation, which Congress does, but also to lead it to its conclusions, to utter the voice of its opinions, and to serve as its eyes in superintending all matters of government,—which Congress does not do. The discussions which take place in Congress are aimed at random. They now and again strike rather sharply the tender spots in this, that, or the other measure; but, as I have said, no two measures consciously join in purpose or agree in character, and so debate must wander as widely as the subjects of debate. Since there is little

---

[7] Professor [William Graham] Sumner's [*Life of*] *Andrew Jackson*, (American Statesmen Series), [(Boston, 1882),] p. 226. "Finally," adds Prof. S., "the methods and machinery of democratic republican self-government—caucuses, primaries, committees, and conventions—lend themselves perhaps more easily than any other methods and machinery to the uses of selfish cliques which seek political influence for interested purposes."

coherency about the legislation agreed upon, there can be little coherency about the debates. There is no one policy to be attacked or defended, but only a score or two of separate bills. To attend to such discussions is uninteresting; to be instructed by them is impossible. There is some scandal and discomfort, but infinite advantage, in having every affair of administration subjected to the test of constant examination on the part of the assembly which represents the nation. The chief use of such inquisition is, not the direction of those affairs in a way with which the country will be satisfied (though that itself is of course all-important), but the enlightenment of the people, which is always its sure consequence. Very few men are unequal to a danger which they see and understand; all men quail before a threatening which is dark and unintelligible, and suspect what is done behind a screen. If the people could have, through Congress, daily knowledge of all the more important transactions of the governmental offices, an insight into all that now seems withheld and private, their confidence in the executive, now so often shaken, would, I think, be very soon established. Because dishonesty *can* lurk under the privacies now vouchsafed our administrative agents, much that is upright and pure suffers unjust suspicion. Discoveries of guilt in a bureau cloud with doubts the trustworthiness of a department. As nothing is open enough for the quick and easy detection of peculation or fraud, so nothing is open enough for the due vindication and acknowledgment of honesty. The isolation and privacy which shield the one from discovery cheat the other of reward.

Inquisitiveness is never so forward, enterprising, and irrepressible as in a popular assembly which is given leave to ask questions and is afforded ready and abundant means of getting its questions answered. No cross-examination is more searching than that to which a minister of the Crown is subjected by the all-curious Commons. "Sir Robert Peel once asked to have a number of questions carefully written down which they asked him one day in succession in the House of Commons. They seemed a list of everything that could occur in the British empire or to the brain of a member of parliament."[8] If one considered only the wear and tear upon ministers of state, which the plague of constant interrogation must inflict, he could wish that their lives, if useful, might be spared this blight of unending explanation; but no one can overestimate the immense advantage of a facility so unlimited for knowing all that is going on in the places where authority lives. The conscience of every member of the representative body is at the service of the nation. All that he feels bound to know he can find out; and what he finds out goes to the ears of the country. The question is his, the answer the nation's. And the inquisitiveness of such bodies as Congress is the best conceivable source of information. Congress is the only body which has the proper motive for inquiry, and it is the only body which has the power to act effectively upon the knowledge which its inquiries secure. The Press is merely curious or merely par-

---

[8] [Walter] Bagehot: *Essay on Sir Robert Peel*, [in Bagehot, *Biographical Studies*, ed. Richard Holt Hutton (London: Longmans, Green & Co., 1881),] p. 24.

tisan. The people are scattered and unorganized. But Congress is, as it were, the corporate people, the mouthpiece of its will. It is a sovereign delegation which could ask questions with dignity, because with authority and with power to act.

Congress is fast becoming the governing body of the nation, and yet the only power which it possesses in perfection is the power which is but a part of government, the power of legislation. Legislation is but the oil of government. It is that which lubricates its channels and speeds its wheels; that which lessens the friction and so eases the movement. Or perhaps I shall be admitted to have hit upon a closer and apter analogy if I say that legislation is like a foreman set over the forces of government. It issues the orders which others obey. It directs, it admonishes, but it does not do the actual heavy work of governing. A good foreman does, it is true, himself take a hand in the work which he guides; and so I suppose our legislation must be likened to a poor foreman, because it stands altogether apart from that work which it is set to see well done. Members of Congress ought not to be censured too severely, however, when they fail to check evil courses on the part of the executive. They have been denied the means of doing so promptly and with effect. Whatever intention may have controlled the compromises of constitution-making in 1787, their result was to give us, not government by discussion, which is the only tolerable sort of government for a people which tries to do its own governing, but only *legislation* by discussion, which is no more than a small part of government by discussion. What is quite as indispensable as the debate of problems of legislation is the debate of all matters of administration. It is even more important to know how the house is being built than to know how the plans of the architect were conceived and how his specifications were calculated. It is better to have skillful work—stout walls, reliable arches, unbending rafters, and windows sure to "expel the winter's flaw"—than a drawing on paper which is the admiration of all the practical artists in the country. The discipline of an army depends quite as much upon the temper of the troops as upon the orders of the day.

It is the proper duty of a representative body to look diligently into every affair of government and to talk much about what it sees. It is meant to be the eyes and the voice, and to embody the wisdom and will of its constituents. Unless Congress have and use every means of acquainting itself with the acts and the disposition of the administrative agents of the government, the country must be helpless to learn how it is being served; and unless Congress both scrutinize these things and sift them by every form of discussion, the country must remain in embarrassing, crippling ignorance of the very affairs which it is most important that it should understand and direct. The informing function of Congress should be preferred even to its legislative function. The argument is not only that discussed and interrogated administration is the only pure and efficient administration, but, more than that, that the only really self-governing people is that people which discusses and interrogates its administration. The talk on the part of Congress which we sometimes justly condemn is the profitless squabble of words over frivolous bills or selfish party issues. It would be hard to conceive of there being too much talk about the practical concerns and processes of government. Such talk it is which, when earnestly and purposefully conducted, clears the public mind and shapes the demands of public opinion.

Congress could not be too diligent about such talking; whereas it may easily be too diligent in legislation. It often overdoes that business. It already sends to its Committees bills too many by the thousand to be given even a hasty thought; but its immense committee facilities and the absence of all other duties but that of legislation make it omnivorous in its appetite for new subjects for consideration. It is greedy to have a taste of every possible dish that may be put upon its table, as an "extra" to the constitutional bill of fare. This disposition on its part is the more notable because there is certainly less need for it to hurry and overwork itself at lawmaking than exists in the case of most other great national legislatures. It is not state and national legislature combined, as are the Commons of England and the Chambers of France. Like the Reichstag of our cousin Germans, it is restricted to subjects of imperial scope. Its thoughts are meant to be kept for national interests. Its time is spared the waste of attention to local affairs. It is even forbidden the vast domain of the laws of property, of commercial dealing, and of ordinary crime. And even in the matter of caring for national interests the way has from the first been made plain and easy for it. There are no clogging feudal institutions to embarrass it. There is no long-continued practice of legal or of royal tyranny for it to cure,—no clearing away of old debris of any sort to delay it in its exercise of a common-sense dominion over a thoroughly modern and progressive nation. It is easy to believe that its legislative purposes might be most fortunately clarified and simplified, were it to square them by a conscientious attention to the paramount and controlling duty of understanding, discussing, and directing administration.

If the people's authorized representatives do not take upon themselves this duty, and by identifying themselves with the actual work of government stand between it and irresponsible, half-informed criticism, to what harassments is the executive not exposed? Led and checked by Congress, the prurient and fearless, because anonymous, animadversions of the Press, now so often premature and inconsiderate, might be disciplined into serviceable capacity to interpret and judge. Its energy and sagacity might be tempered by discretion, and strengthened by knowledge. One of our chief constitutional difficulties is that, in opportunities for informing and guiding public opinion, the freedom of the Press is greater than the freedom of Congress. It is as if newspapers, instead of the board of directors, were the sources of information for the stockholders of a corporation. We look into correspondents' letters instead of into the Congressional Record to find out what is a-doing and a-planning in the departments. Congress is altogether excluded from the arrangement by which the Press declares what the executive is, and conventions of the national parties decide what the executive shall be. Editors are self-constituted our guides, and caucus delegates our government directors.

Since all this curious scattering of functions and contrivance of frail, extra-constitutional machinery of government is the result of that entire separation of the legislative and executive branches of the system which is with us so characteristically and essentially constitutional, it is exceedingly interesting to inquire and important to understand how that separation came to be insisted upon in the making of the Constitution. Alexander Hamilton has in our own times, as well as before, been "severely reproached with having said that the British government was the 'best model in existence.' In 1787 this was a mere truism. However much the men of that day differed they were all agreed in despising and distrusting *a priori* constitutions and ideally perfect governments, fresh from the brains of visionary enthusiasts, such as sprang up rankly in the soil of the French revolution. The Convention of 1787 was composed of very able men of the English-speaking race. They took the system of government with which they had been familiar, improved it, adapted it to the circumstances with which they had to deal, and put it into successful operation. Hamilton's plan, then, like the others, was on the British model, and it did not differ essentially in details from that finally adopted."[9] It is needful, however, to remember in this connection what has already been alluded to, that when that convention was copying the English Constitution, that Constitution was in a stage of transition, and had by no means fully developed the features which are now recognized as most characteristic of it. Mr. Lodge is quite right in saying that the Convention, in adapting, improved upon the English Constitution with which its members were familiar,—the Constitution of George III. and Lord North, the Constitution which had failed to crush Bute. It could hardly be said with equal confidence, however, that our system as then made was an improvement upon that scheme of responsible cabinet government which challenges the admiration of the world to-day, though it was quite plainly a marked advance upon a parliament of royal nominees and pensionaries and a secret cabinet of "king's friends." The English Constitution of that day had a great many features which did not invite republican imitation. It was suspected, if not known, that the ministers who sat in parliament were little more than the tools of a ministry of royal favorites who were kept out of sight behind the strictest confidences of the court. It was notorious that the subservient parliaments of the day represented the estates and the money of the peers and the influence of the King rather than the intelligence and purpose of the nation. The whole "form and pressure" of the time illustrated only too forcibly Lord Bute's sinister suggestion, that "the forms of a free and the ends of an arbitrary government are things not altogether incompatible." It was, therefore, perfectly natural that the warnings to be so easily drawn from the sight of a despotic monarch binding the usages and privileges of self-government to the service of his own intemperate purposes should be given grave heed by Americans, who were the very

---

[9] H[enry] C[abot] Lodge's [*Life of*] *Alexander Hamilton* (Am. Statesmen Series), [(Boston, 1882)], pp. 60, 61.

persons who had suffered most from the existing abuses. It was something more than natural that the Convention of 1787 should desire to erect a Congress which would not be subservient and an executive which could not be despotic. And it was equally to have been expected that they should regard an absolute separation of these two great branches of the system as the only effectual means for the accomplishment of that much desired end. It was impossible that they could believe that executive and legislature could be brought into close relations of coöperation and mutual confidence without being tempted, nay, even bidden, to collude. How could either maintain its independence of action unless each were to have the guaranty of the Constitution that its own domain should be absolutely safe from invasion, its own prerogatives absolutely free from challenge? "They shrank from placing sovereign power anywhere. They feared that it would generate tyranny; George III. had been a tyrant to them, and come what might they would not make a George III."[10] They would conquer, by dividing, the power they so much feared to see in any single hand.

"The English Constitution, in a word," says our most astute English critic, "is framed on the principle of choosing a single sovereign authority, and making it good; the American, upon the principle of having many sovereign authorities, and hoping that their multitude may atone for their inferiority. The Americans now extol their institutions, and so defraud themselves of their due praise. But if they had not a genius for politics, if they had not a moderation in action singularly curious where superficial speech is so violent, if they had not a regard for law, such as no great people have ever evinced, and infinitely surpassing ours, the multiplicity of authorities in the American Constitution would long ago have brought it to a bad end. Sensible shareholders, I have heard a shrewd attorney say, can work any deed of settlement; and so the men of Massachusetts could, I believe, work *any* constitution."[11] It is not necessary to assent to Mr. Bagehot's strictures; but it is not possible to deny the clear-sighted justice of this criticism. In order to be fair to the memory of our great constitution-makers, however, it is necessary to remember that when they sat in convention in Philadelphia the English Constitution, which they copied, was not the simple system which was before Mr. Bagehot's eyes when he wrote. Its single sovereign authority was not then a twice-reformed House of Commons truly representative of the nation and readily obeyed by a responsible Ministry. The sovereignty was at see-saw between the throne and the parliament,—and the throne-end of the beam was generally uppermost. Our device of separated, individualized powers was very much better than a nominal sovereignty of the Commons which was suffered to be overridden by force, fraud, or craft, by the real sovereignty of the King. The English Constitution was at that time in reality much worse than our own; and, if it is now superior, it is so because its growth has not been hindered or destroyed by the too tight ligaments of a written fundamental law.

[10] Bagehot, *Eng[lish] Const[itution]*, p. 293.
[11] Bagehot, *Eng[lish] Const[itution]*, p. 296.

The natural, the inevitable tendency of every system of self-government like our own and the British is to exalt the representative body, the people's parliament, to a position of absolute supremacy. That tendency has, I think, been quite as marked in our own constitutional history as in that of any other country, though its power has been to some extent neutralized, and its progress in great part stayed, by those denials of that supremacy which we respect because they are written in our law. The political law written in our hearts is here at variance with that which the Constitution sought to establish. A written constitution may and often will be violated in both letter and spirit by a people of energetic political talents and a keen instinct for progressive practical development; but so long as they adhere to the forms of such a constitution, so long as the machinery of government supplied by it is the only machinery which the legal and moral sense of such a people permits it to use, its political development must be in many directions narrowly restricted because of an insuperable lack of open or adequate channels. Our Constitution, like every other constitution which puts the authority to make laws and the duty of controlling the public expenditure into the hands of a popular assembly, practically sets that assembly to rule the affairs of the nation as supreme overlord. But, by separating it entirely from its executive agencies, it deprives it of the opportunity and means for making its authority complete and convenient. The constitutional machinery is left of such a pattern that other forces less than that of Congress may cross and compete with Congress, though they are too small to overcome or long offset it; and the result is simply an unpleasant, wearing friction which, with other adjustments, more felicitous and equally safe, might readily be avoided.

Congress, consequently, is still lingering and chafing under just such embarrassments as made the English Commons a nuisance both to themselves and to everybody else immediately after the Revolution Settlement had given them their first sure promise of supremacy. The parallel is startlingly exact. "In outer seeming the Revolution of 1688 had only transferred the sovereignty over England from James to William and Mary. In actual fact it had given a powerful and decisive impulse to the great constitutional progress which was transferring the sovereignty from the King to the House of Commons. From the moment when its sole right to tax the nation was established by the Bill of Rights, and when its own resolve settled the practice of granting none but annual supplies to the Crown, the House of Commons became the supreme power in the State. . . . But though the constitutional change was complete, the machinery of government was far from having adapted itself to the new conditions of political life which such a change brought about. However powerful the will of the Commons might be, it had no means of bringing its will directly to bear on the control of public affairs. The ministers who had charge of them were not its servants but the servants of the Crown; it was from the King that they looked for direction, and to the King that they held themselves responsible. By impeachment or more indirect means the Commons could force a king to remove a minister who contradicted their will;

but they had no constitutional power to replace the fallen statesman by a minister who would carry out their will.

"The result was the growth of a temper in the Lower House which drove William and his ministers to despair. It became as corrupt, as jealous of power, as fickle in its resolves and factious in its spirit as bodies always become whose consciousness of the possession of power is untempered by a corresponding consciousness of the practical difficulties or the moral responsibilities of the power which they possess. It grumbled . . . and it blamed the Crown and its ministers for all at which it grumbled. But it was hard to find out what policy or measures it would have preferred. Its mood changed, as William bitterly complained, with every hour. . . . The Houses were in fact without the guidance of recognized leaders, without adequate information, and destitute of that organization out of which alone a definite policy can come."[12]

The cure for this state of things which Sunderland had the sagacity to suggest, and William the wisdom to apply, was the mediation between King and Commons of a cabinet representative of the majority of the popular chamber,—a first but long and decisive step towards responsible cabinet government. Whether a similar remedy would be possible or desirable in our own case it is altogether aside from my present purpose to inquire. I am pointing out facts,—diagnosing, not prescribing remedies. My only point just now is, that no one can help being struck by the closeness of the likeness between the incipient distempers of the first parliaments of William and Mary and the developed disorders now so plainly discernible in the constitution of Congress. Though honest and diligent, it is meddlesome and inefficient; and it is meddlesome and inefficient for exactly the same reasons that made it natural that the post-Revolutionary parliaments should exhibit like clumsiness and like temper: namely, because it is "without the guidance of recognized leaders, without adequate information, and destitute of that organization out of which alone a definite policy can come."

The dangers of this serious imperfection in our governmental machinery have not been clearly demonstrated in our experience hitherto; but now their delayed fulfillment seems to be close at hand. The plain tendency is towards a centralization of all the greater powers of government in the hands of the federal authorities, and towards the practical confirmation of those prerogatives of supreme overlordship which Congress has been gradually arrogating to itself. The central government is constantly becoming stronger and more active, and Congress is establishing itself as the one sovereign authority in that government. In constitutional theory and in the broader features of past practice, ours has been what Mr. Bagehot has called a "composite" government. Besides state and federal authorities to dispute as to sovereignty, there have been within the federal system itself rival and irreconcilable powers. But gradually the strong are overcoming the

---

[12] [John R.] Green: [*A Short*] *Hist[ory]* *of the English People* (Harper's ed.), [(London, 1875),] iv, pp. 58, 59.

weak. If the signs of the times are to be credited, we are fast approaching an adjustment of sovereignty quite as "simple" as need be. Congress is not only to retain the authority it already possesses, but is to be brought again and again face to face with still greater demands upon its energy, its wisdom, and its conscience, is to have ever-widening duties and responsibilities thrust upon it, without being granted a moment's opportunity to look back from the plough to which it has set its hands.

The sphere and influence of national administration and national legislation are widening rapidly. Our populations are growing at such a rate that one's reckoning staggers at counting the possible millions that may have a home and a work on this continent ere fifty more years shall have filled their short span. The East will not always be the centre of national life. The South is fast accumulating wealth, and will faster recover influence. The West has already achieved a greatness which no man can gainsay, and has in store a power of future growth which no man can estimate. Whether these sections are to be harmonious or dissentient depends almost entirely upon the methods and policy of the federal government. If that government be not careful to keep within its own proper sphere and prudent to square its policy by rules of national welfare, sectional lines must and will be known; citizens of one part of the country may look with jealousy and even with hatred upon their fellow-citizens of another part; and faction must tear and dissension distract a country which Providence would bless, but which man may curse. The government of a country so vast and various must be strong, prompt, wieldy, and efficient. Its strength must consist in the certainty and uniformity of its purposes, in its accord with national sentiment, in its unhesitating action, and in its honest aims. It must be steadied and approved by open administration diligently obedient to the more permanent judgments of public opinion; and its only active agency, its representative chambers, must be equipped with something besides abundant powers of legislation.

As at present constituted, the federal government lacks strength because its powers are divided, lacks promptness because its authorities are multiplied, lacks wieldiness because its processes are roundabout, lacks efficiency because its responsibility is indistinct and its action without competent direction. It is a government in which every officer may talk about every other officer's duty without having to render strict account for not doing his own, and in which the masters are held in check and offered contradiction by the servants. Mr. Lowell has called it "government by declamation." Talk is not sobered by any necessity imposed upon those who utter it to suit their actions to their words. There is no day of reckoning for words spoken. The speakers of a congressional majority may, without risk of incurring ridicule or discredit, condemn what their own Committees are doing; and the spokesmen of a minority may urge what contrary courses they please with a well-grounded assurance that what they say will be forgotten before they can be called upon to put it into practice. Nobody stands sponsor for the policy of the government. A dozen men originate it; a dozen compromises twist and alter it; a dozen offices whose names are scarcely known outside of Washington put it into execution.

This is the defect to which, it will be observed, I am constantly recurring; to which I recur again and again because every examination of the system, at whatsoever point begun, leads inevitably to it as to a central secret. It is the defect which interprets all the rest, because it is their common product. It is exemplified in the extraordinary fact that the utterances of the Press have greater weight and are accorded greater credit, though the Press speaks entirely without authority, than the utterances of Congress, though Congress possesses all authority. The gossip of the street is listened to rather than the words of the law-makers. The editor directs public opinion, the congressman obeys it. When a presidential election is at hand, indeed, the words of the political orator gain temporary heed. He is recognized as an authority in the arena, as a professional critic competent to discuss the good and bad points, and to forecast the fortunes of the contestants. There is something definite in hand, and he is known to have studied all its bearings. He is one of the managers, or is thought to be well acquainted with the management. He speaks "from the card." But let him talk, not about candidates, but about measures or about the policy of the government, and his observations sink at once to the level of a mere individual expression of opinion, to which his political occupations seem to add very little weight. It is universally recognized that he speaks without authority, about things which his vote may help to settle, but about which several hundred other men have votes quite as influential as his own. Legislation is not a thing to be known beforehand. It depends upon the conclusions of sundry Standing Committees. It is an aggregate, not a simple, production. It is impossible to tell how many persons' opinions and influences have entered into its composition. It is even impracticable to determine from this year's law-making what next year's will be like.

Speaking, therefore, without authority, the political orator speaks to little purpose when he speaks about legislation. The papers do not report him carefully; and their editorials seldom take any color from his arguments. The Press, being anonymous and representing a large force of inquisitive news-hunters, is much more powerful than he chiefly because it *is* impersonal and seems to represent a wider and more thorough range of information. At the worst, it can easily compete with any ordinary individual. Its individual opinion is quite sure to be esteemed as worthy of attention as any other individual opinion. And, besides, it is almost everywhere strong enough to deny currency to the speeches of individuals whom it does not care to report. It goes to its audience; the orator must depend upon his audience coming to him. It can be heard at every fireside; the orator can be heard only on the platform or the hustings. There is no imperative demand on the part of the reading public in this country that the newspapers should report political speeches in full. On the contrary, most readers would be disgusted at finding their favorite columns so filled up. By giving even a notice of more than an item's length to such a speech, an editor runs the risk of being denounced as dull.

And I believe that the position of the American Press is in this regard quite singular. The English newspapers are so far from being thus independent and self-sufficient powers,—a law unto themselves,—in the politics of the empire that they are constrained to do homage to the political orator whether they will or no. Conservative editors must spread before their readers *verbatim* reports not only of the speeches of the leaders of their own party, but also of the principal speeches of the leading Liberal orators; and Liberal journals have no choice but to print every syllable of the more important public utterances of the Conservative leaders. The nation insists upon knowing what its public men have to say, even when it is not so well said as the newspapers which report them could have said it. There are only two things which can give any man a right to expect that when he speaks the whole country will listen: namely, genius and authority. Probably no one will ever contend that Sir Stafford Northcote was an orator, or even a good speaker. But by proof of unblemished character, and by assiduous, conscientious, and able public service he rose to be the recognized leader of his party in the House of Commons; and it is simply because he speaks as one having authority,— and not as the scribes of the Press,—that he is as sure of a heedful hearing as is Mr. Gladstone, who adds genius and noble oratory to the authority of established leadership. The leaders of English public life have something besides weight of character, prestige of personal service and experience, and authority of individual opinion to exalt them above the anonymous Press. They have definite authority and power in the actual control of government. They are directly commissioned to control the policy of the administration. They stand before the country, in parliament and out of it, as the responsible chiefs of their parties. It is their business to lead those parties, and it is the matter-of-course custom of the constituencies to visit upon the parties the punishment due for the mistakes made by these chiefs. They are at once the servants and scapegoats of their parties.

It is these well-established privileges and responsibilities of theirs which make their utterances considered worth hearing,—nay, necessary to be heard and pondered. Their public speeches are their parties' platforms. What the leader promises his party stands ready to do, should it be intrusted with office. This certainty of audience and of credit gives spice to what such leaders have to say, and lends elevation to the tone of all their public utterances. They for the most part avoid buncombe, which would be difficult to translate into Acts of Parliament. It is easy to see how great an advantage their station and influence give them over our own public men. We have no such responsible party leadership on this side the sea; we are very shy about conferring much authority on anybody, and the consequence is that it requires something very like genius to secure for any one of our statesmen a universally recognized right to be heard and to create an ever-active desire to hear him whenever he talks, not about candidates, but about measures. An extraordinary gift of eloquence, such as not every generation may hope to see, will always hold, because it will always captivate, the attention of the people. But genius and eloquence are too rare to be depended upon for the instruction and guidance of the masses; and since our politicians lack the credit of authority and responsibility, they must give place, except at election-time, to the Press, which is everywhere, generally well-informed, and always talking. It is necessarily "government by declamation" and editorial-writing.

It is probably also this lack of leadership which gives to our national parties their curious, conglomerate character. It would seem to be scarcely an exaggeration to say that they are homogeneous only in name. Neither of the two principal parties is of one mind with itself. Each tolerates all sorts of difference of creed and variety of aim within its own ranks. Each pretends to the same purposes and permits among its partisans the same contradictions to those purposes. They are grouped around no legislative leaders whose capacity has been tested and to whose opinions they loyally adhere. They are like armies without officers, engaged upon a campaign which has no great cause at its back. Their names and traditions, not their hopes and policy, keep them together.

It is to this fact, as well as to short terms which allow little time for differences to come to a head, that the easy agreement of congressional majorities should be attributed. In other like assemblies the harmony of majorities is constantly liable to disturbance. Ministers lose their following and find their friends falling away in the midst of a session. But not so in Congress. There, although the majority is frequently simply conglomerate, made up of factions not a few, and bearing in its elements every seed of discord, the harmony of party voting seldom, if ever, suffers an interruption. So far as outsiders can see, legislation generally flows placidly on, and the majority easily has its own way, acting with a sort of matter-of-course unanimity, with no suspicion of individual freedom of action. Whatever revolts may be threatened or accomplished in the ranks of the party outside the House at the polls, its power is never broken inside the House. This is doubtless due in part to the fact that there is no freedom of debate in the House; but there can be no question that it is principally due to the fact that debate is without aim, just because legislation is without consistency. Legislation is conglomerate. The absence of any concert of action amongst the Committees leaves legislation with scarcely any trace of determinate party courses. No two schemes pull together. If there is a coincidence of principle between several bills of the same session, it is generally accidental; and the confusion of policy which prevents intelligent coöperation also, of course, prevents intelligent differences and divisions. There is never a transfer of power from one party to the other during a session, because such a transfer would mean almost nothing. The majority remains of one mind so long as a Congress lives, because its mind is very vaguely ascertained, and its power of planning a split consequently very limited. It has no common mind, and if it had, has not the machinery for changing it. It is led by a score or two of Committees whose composition must remain the same to the end; and who are too numerous, as well as to[o] disconnected, to fight against. It stays on one side because it hardly knows where the boundaries of that side are or how to cross them.

Moreover, there is a certain well-known piece of congressional machinery long ago invented and applied for the special purpose of keeping both majority and minority compact. The legislative caucus has almost as important a part in our system as have the Standing Committees, and deserves as close study as they. Its functions are much more easily understood in all their bearings than those of the Committees, however, because they are much simpler. The caucus is meant as an antidote to the Committees. It is designed to supply the cohesive principle which the multiplicity and mutual independence of the Committees so powerfully tend to destroy. Having no Prime Minister to confer with about the policy of the government, as they see members of parliament doing, our congressmen confer with each other in caucus. Rather than imprudently expose to the world the differences of opinion threatened or developed among its members, each party hastens to remove disrupting debate from the floor of Congress, where the speakers might too hastily commit themselves to insubordination, to quiet conferences behind closed doors, where frightened scruples may be reassured and every disagreement healed with a salve of compromise or subdued with the whip of political expediency. The caucus is the drilling-ground of the party. There its discipline is renewed and strengthened, its uniformity of step and gesture regained. The voting and speaking in the House are generally merely the movements of a sort of dress parade, for which the exercises of the caucus are designed to prepare. It is easy to see how difficult it would be for the party to keep its head amidst the confused cross-movements of the Committees without thus now and again pulling itself together in caucus, where it can ask itself its own mind and pledge itself anew to eternal agreement.

The credit of inventing this device is probably due to the Democrats. They appear to have used it so early as the second session of the eighth Congress. Speaking of that session, a reliable authority says: "During this session of Congress there was far less of free and independent discussion on the measures proposed by the friends of the administration than had been previously practiced in both branches of the national legislature. It appeared that on the most important subjects, the course adopted by the majority was the effect of caucus arrangement, or, in other words, had been previously agreed upon at meetings of the Democratic members held in private. Thus the legislation of Congress was constantly swayed by a party following feelings and pledges rather than according to sound reason or personal conviction."[13] The censure implied in this last sentence may have seemed righteous at the time when such caucus pledges were in disfavor as new-fangled shackles, but it would hardly be accepted as just by the intensely practical politicians of to-day. They would probably prefer to put it thus: That the silvern speech spent in caucus secures the golden silence maintained on the floor of Congress, making each party rich in concord and happy in coöperation.

The fact that makes this defense of the caucus not altogether conclusive is that it is shielded from all responsibility by its sneaking privacy. It has great power

---

[13] *Statesman's Manual*, i, p. 244.

without any balancing weight of accountability. Probably its debates would constitute interesting and instructive reading for the public, were they published; but they never get out except in rumors often rehearsed and as often amended. They are, one may take it for granted, much more candid and go much nearer the political heart of the questions discussed than anything that is ever said openly in Congress to the reporters' gallery. They approach matters without masks and handle them without gloves. It might hurt, but it would enlighten us to hear them. As it is, however, there is unhappily no ground for denying their power to override sound reason and personal conviction. The caucus cannot always silence or subdue a large and influential minority of dissentients, but its whip seldom fails to reduce individual malcontents and mutineers into submission. There is no place in congressional jousts for the free lance. The man who disobeys his party caucus is understood to disavow his party allegiance altogether, and to assume that dangerous neutrality which is so apt to degenerate into mere caprice, and which is almost sure to destroy his influence by bringing him under the suspicion of being unreliable,—a suspicion always conclusively damning in practical life. Any individual, or any minority of weak numbers or small influence, who has the temerity to neglect the decisions of the caucus is sure, if the offense be often repeated, or even once committed upon an important issue, to be read out of the party, almost without chance of reinstatement. And every one knows that nothing can be accomplished in politics by mere disagreement. The only privilege such recalcitrants gain is the privilege of disagreement; they are forever shut out from the privilege of confidential cooperation. They have chosen the helplessness of a faction.

It must be admitted, however, that, unfortunate as the necessity is for the existence of such powers as those of the caucus, that necessity actually exists and cannot be neglected. Against the fatal action of so many elements of disintegration it would seem to be imperatively needful that some energetic element of cohesion should be provided. It is doubtful whether in any other nation, with a shorter inheritance of political instinct, parties could long successfully resist the centrifugal forces of the committee system with only the varying attraction of the caucus to detain them. The wonder is that, despite the forcible and unnatural divorcement of legislation and administration and the consequent distraction of legislation from all attention to anything like an intelligent planning and superintendence of policy, we are not cursed with as many factions as now almost hopelessly confuse French politics. That we have had, and continue to have, only two national parties of national importance or real power is fortunate rather than natural. Their names stand for a fact, but scarcely for a reason.

An intelligent observer of our politics[14] has declared that there is in the United States "a class, including thousands and tens of thousands of the best men in the country, who think it possible to enjoy the fruits of good government without

---

[14] Mr. Dale, of Birmingham.

working for them." Every one who has seen beyond the outside of our American life must recognize the truth of this; to explain it is to state the sum of all the most valid criticisms of congressional government. Public opinion has no easy vehicle for its judgments, no quick channels for its action. Nothing about the system is direct and simple. Authority is perplexingly subdivided and distributed, and responsibility has to be hunted down in out-of-the-way corners. So that the sum of the whole matter is that the means of working for the fruits of good government are not readily to be found. The average citizen may be excused for esteeming government at best but a haphazard affair, upon which his vote and all of his influence can have but little effect. How is his choice of a representative in Congress to affect the policy of the country as regards the questions in which he is most interested, if the man for whom he votes has no chance of getting on the Standing Committee which has virtual charge of those questions? How is it to make any difference who is chosen President? Has the President any very great authority in matters of vital policy? It seems almost a thing of despair to get any assurance that any vote he may cast will even in an infinitesimal degree affect the essential courses of administration. There are so many cooks mixing their ingredients in the national broth that it seems hopeless, this thing of changing one cook at a time.

The charm of our constitutional ideal has now been long enough wound up to enable sober men who do not believe in political witchcraft to judge what it has accomplished, and is likely still to accomplish, without further winding. The Constitution is not honored by blind worship. The more open-eyed we become, as a nation, to its defects, and the prompter we grow in applying with the unhesitating courage of conviction all thoroughly-tested or well-considered expedients necessary to make self-government among us a straightforward thing of simple method, single, unstinted power, and clear responsibility, the nearer will we approach to the sound sense and practical genius of the great and honorable statesmen of 1787. And the first step towards emancipation from the timidity and false pride which have led us to seek to thrive despite the defects of our national system rather than seem to deny its perfection is a fearless criticism of that system. When we shall have examined all its parts without sentiment, and gauged all its functions by the standards of practical common sense, we shall have established anew our right to the claim of political sagacity; and it will remain only to act intelligently upon what our opened eyes have seen in order to prove again the justice of our claim to political genius.

Constitutional Government
in the United States*
Chapters 3 and 8

CHAPTER 3. THE PRESIDENT OF THE UNITED STATES.

It is difficult to describe any single part of a great governmental system without describing the whole of it. Governments are living things and operate as organic wholes. Moreover, governments have their natural evolution and are one thing in one age, another in another. The makers of the Constitution constructed the federal government upon a theory of checks and balances which was meant to limit the operation of each part and allow to no single part or organ of it a dominating force; but no government can be successfully conducted upon so mechanical a theory. Leadership and control must be lodged somewhere; the whole art of statesmanship is the art of bringing the several parts of government into effective cooperation for the accomplishment of particular common objects,—and party objects at that. Our study of each part of our federal system, if we are to discover our real government as it lives, must be made to disclose to us its operative coördination as a whole: its places of leadership, its method of action, how it operates, what checks it, what gives it energy and effect. Governments are what politicians make them, and it is easier to write of the President than of the presidency.

The government of the United States was constructed upon the Whig theory of political dynamics, which was a sort of unconscious copy of the Newtonian theory of the universe. In our own day, whenever we discuss the structure or development of anything, whether in nature or in society, we consciously or unconsciously follow Mr. Darwin; but before Mr. Darwin, they followed Newton. Some single law, like the law of gravitation, swung each system of thought and gave it its principle of unity. Every sun, every planet, every free body in the spaces of the

* Chapters excerpted from *Constitutional Government in the United States* (New York: Columbia University Press, 1908), 54–81, 198–222. (Editor's note).

heavens, the world itself, is kept in its place and reined to its course by the attraction of bodies that swing with equal order and precision about it, themselves governed by the nice poise and balance of forces which give the whole system of the universe its symmetry and perfect adjustment. The Whigs had tried to give England a similar constitution. They had had no wish to destroy the throne, no conscious desire to reduce the king to a mere figurehead, but had intended only to surround and offset him with a system of constitutional checks and balances which should regulate his otherwise arbitrary course and make it at least always calculable.

They had made no clear analysis of the matter in their own thoughts; it has not been the habit of English politicians, or indeed of English-speaking politicians on either side of the water, to be clear theorists. It was left to a Frenchman to point out to the Whigs what they had done. They had striven to make Parliament so influential in the making of laws and so authoritative in the criticism of the king's policy that the king could in no matter have his own way without their coöperation and assent, though they left him free, the while, if he chose, to interpose an absolute veto upon the acts of Parliament. They had striven to secure for the courts of law as great an independence as possible, so that they might be neither over-awed by parliament nor coerced by the king. In brief, as Montesquieu pointed out to them in his lucid way, they had sought to balance executive, legislature, and judiciary off against one another by a series of checks and counterpoises, which Newton might readily have recognized as suggestive of the mechanism of the heavens.

The makers of our federal Constitution followed the scheme as they found it expounded in Montesquieu, followed it with genuine scientific enthusiasm. The admirable expositions of the *Federalist* read like thoughtful applications of Montesquieu to the political needs and circumstances of America. They are full of the theory of checks and balances. The President is balanced off against Congress, Congress against the President, and each against the courts. Our statesmen of the earlier generations quoted no one so often as Montesquieu, and they quoted him always as a scientific standard in the field of politics. Politics is turned into mechanics under his touch. The theory of gravitation is supreme.

The trouble with the theory is that government is not a machine, but a living thing. It falls, not under the theory of the universe, but under the theory of organic life. It is accountable to Darwin, not to Newton. It is modified by its environment, necessitated by its tasks, shaped to its functions by the sheer pressure of life. No living thing can have its organs offset against each other as checks, and live. On the contrary, its life is dependent upon their quick coöperation, their ready response to the commands of instinct or intelligence, their amicable community of purpose. Government is not a body of blind forces; it is a body of men, with highly differentiated functions, no doubt, in our modern day of specialization, but with a common task and purpose. Their coöperation is indispensable, their warfare fatal. There can be no successful government without leadership or without the intimate, almost instinctive, coördination of the organs of life and action. This is not theory, but fact, and displays its force as fact, whatever theories may be thrown across its track. Living political constitutions must be Darwinian in structure and in practice.

Fortunately, the definitions and prescriptions of our constitutional law, though conceived in the Newtonian spirit and upon the Newtonian principle, are sufficiently broad and elastic to allow for the play of life and circumstance. Though they were Whig theorists, the men who framed the federal Constitution were also practical statesmen with an experienced eye for affairs and a quick practical sagacity in respect of the actual structure of government, and they have given us a thoroughly workable model. If it had in fact been a machine governed by mechanically automatic balances, it would have had no history; but it was not, and its history has been rich with the influences and personalities of the men who have conducted it and made it a living reality. The government of the United States has had a vital, and normal organic growth and has proved itself eminently adapted to express the changing temper and purposes of the American people from age to age.

That is the reason why it is easier to write of the President than of the presidency. The presidency has been one thing at one time, another at another, varying with the man who occupied the office and with the circumstances that surrounded him. One account must be given of the office during the period 1789 to 1825, when the government was getting its footing both at home and abroad, struggling for its place among the nations and its full credit among its own people; when English precedents and traditions were strongest; and when the men chosen for the office were men bred to leadership in a way that attracted to them the attention and confidence of the whole country. Another account must be given of it during Jackson's time, when an imperious man, bred not in deliberative assemblies or quiet councils, but in the field and upon a rough frontier, worked his own will upon affairs, with or without formal sanction of law, sustained by a clear undoubting conscience and the love of a people who had grown deeply impatient of the régime he had supplanted. Still another account must be given of it during the years 1836 to 1861, when domestic affairs of many debatable kinds absorbed the country, when Congress necessarily exercised the chief choices of policy, and when the Presidents who followed one another in office lacked the personal force and initiative to make for themselves a leading place in counsel. After that came the Civil War and Mr. Lincoln's unique task and achievement, when the executive seemed for a little while to become by sheer stress of circumstances the whole government, Congress merely voting supplies and assenting to necessary laws, as Parliament did in the time of the Tudors. From 1865 to 1898 domestic questions, legislative matters in respect of which Congress had naturally to make the initial choice, legislative leaders the chief decisions of policy, came once more to the front, and no President except Mr. Cleveland played a leading and decisive part in the quiet drama of our national life. Even Mr. Cleveland may be said to have owed his great role in affairs rather to his own native force and the confused politics of the time, than to any opportunity of leadership naturally afforded him by a system which had subordinated so many Presidents before him to Congress. The war with Spain again changed the balance of parts. Foreign questions became leading questions again, as they had been in the first days of the government, and in them the President was of necessity leader. Our new place in the affairs of the world has since that year of transformation kept him at the front of our government, where our own thoughts and the attention of men everywhere is centred upon him.

Both men and circumstances have created these contrasts in the administration and influence of the office of President. We have all been disciples of Montesquieu, but we have also been practical politicians. Mr. Bagehot once remarked that it was no proof of the excellence of the Constitution of the United States that the Americans had operated it with conspicuous success because the Americans could run any constitution successfully; and, while the compliment is altogether acceptable, it is certainly true that our practical sense is more noticeable than our theoretical consistency, and that, while we were once all constitutional lawyers, we are in these latter days apt to be very impatient of literal and dogmatic interpretations of constitutional principle.

The makers of the Constitution seem to have thought of the President as what the stricter Whig theorists wished the king to be: only the legal executive, the presiding and guiding authority in the application of law and the execution of policy. His veto upon legislation was only his 'check' on Congress,—was a power of restraint, not of guidance. He was empowered to prevent bad laws, but he was not to be given an opportunity to make good ones. As a matter of fact he has become very much more. He has become the leader of his party and the guide of the nation in political purpose, and therefore in legal action. The constitutional structure of the government has hampered and limited his action in these significant roles, but it has not prevented it. The influence of the President has varied with the men who have been Presidents and with the circumstances of their times, but the tendency has been unmistakably disclosed, and springs out of the very nature of government itself. It is merely the proof that our government is a living, organic thing, and must, like every other government, work out the close synthesis of active parts which can exist only when leadership is lodged in some one man or group of men. You cannot compound a successful government out of antagonisms. Greatly as the practice and influence of Presidents has varied, there can be no mistaking the fact that we have grown more and more inclined from generation to generation to look to the President as the unifying force in our complex system, the leader both of his party and of the nation. To do so is not inconsistent with the actual provisions of the Constitution; it is only inconsistent with a very mechanical theory of its meaning and intention. The Constitution contains no theories. It is as practical a document as Magna Carta.

The rôle of party leader is forced upon the President by the method of his selection. The theory of the makers of the Constitution may have been that the presidential electors would exercise a real choice, but it is hard to understand how, as experienced politicians, they can have expected anything of the kind. They did not provide that the electors should meet as one body for consultation and make deliberate choice of a President and Vice-President, but that they should meet "in their respective states" and cast their ballots in separate groups, without the possibility of consulting and without the least likelihood of agreeing, unless some such means as have actually been used were employed to suggest and determine their choice beforehand. It was the practice at first to make party nominations for the presidency by congressional caucus. Since the Democratic upheaval of General Jackson's time nominating conventions have taken the place of congressional caucuses; and the choice of Presidents by party conventions has had some very interesting results.

We are apt to think of the choice of nominating conventions as somewhat haphazard. We know, or think that we know, how their action is sometimes determined, and the knowledge makes us very uneasy. We know that there is no debate in nominating conventions, no discussion of the merits of the respective candidates, at which the country can sit as audience and assess the wisdom of the final choice. If there is any talking to be done, aside from the formal addresses of the temporary and permanent chairmen and of those who present the platform and the names of the several aspirants for nomination, the assembly adjourns. The talking that is to decide the result must be done in private committee rooms and behind the closed doors of the headquarters of the several state delegations to the convention. The intervals between sessions are filled with a very feverish activity. Messengers run from one headquarters to another until the small hours of the morning. Conference follows conference in a way that is likely to bring newspaper correspondents to the verge of despair, it being next to impossible to put the rumors together into any coherent story of what is going on. Only at the rooms of the national committee of the party is there any clear knowledge of the situation as a whole; and the excitement of the members of the convention rises from session to session under the sheer pressure of uncertainty. The final majority is compounded no outsider and few members can tell how.

Many influences, too, play upon nominating conventions, which seem mere winds of feeling. They sit in great halls, with galleries into which crowd thousands of spectators from all parts of the country, but chiefly, of course, from the place at which the convention sits, and the feeling of the galleries is transmitted to the floor. The cheers of mere spectators echo the names of popular candidates, and every excitement on the floor is enhanced a hundred fold in the galleries. Sudden gusts of impulse are apt to change the whole feeling of the convention, and offset in a moment the most careful arrangements of managing politicians. It has come to be a commonly accepted opinion that if the Republican convention of 1860 had not met in Chicago, it would have nominated Mr. Seward and not Mr. Lincoln. Mr. Seward was the acknowledged leader of the new party; had been its most telling spokesman; had given its tenets definition and currency. Mr. Lincoln had not been brought within view of the country as a whole until the other day, when he had given Mr. Douglas so hard a fight to keep his seat in the Senate, and had but just now given currency among thoughtful men to the striking phrases of the searching speeches he had made in debate with his practised antagonist. But the convention met in Illinois, amidst throngs of Mr. Lincoln's ardent friends and advocates. His managers saw to it that the galleries were properly filled with men who would cheer every mention of his name until the hail was shaken. Every influence of the place worked for him and he was chosen.

Thoughtful critics of our political practices have not allowed the excellence of the choice to blind them to the danger of the method. They have known too many examples of what the galleries have done to supplement the efforts of managing politicians to feel safe in the presence of processes which seem rather those of intrigue and impulse than those of sober choice. They can cite instances, moreover, of sudden, unlooked-for excitements on the floor of such bodies which have swept them from the control of all sober influences and hastened them to choices which no truly deliberative assembly could ever have made. There is no training school for Presidents, unless, as some governors have wished, it be looked for in the governorships of states; and nominating conventions have confined themselves in their selections to no class, have demanded of aspirants no particular experience or knowledge of affairs. They have nominated lawyers without political experience, soldiers, editors of newspapers, newspaper correspondents, whom they pleased, without regard to their lack of contact with affairs. It would seem as if their choices were almost matters of chance.

In reality there is much more method, much more definite purpose, much more deliberate choice in the extraordinary process than there seems to be. The leading spirits of the national committee of each party could give an account of the matter which would put a very different face on it and make the methods of nominating conventions seem, for all the undoubted elements of chance there are in them, on the whole very manageable. Moreover, the party that expects to win may be counted on to make a much more conservative and thoughtful selection of a candidate than the party that merely hopes to win. The haphazard selections which seem to discredit the system are generally made by conventions of the party unaccustomed to success. Success brings sober calculation and a sense of responsibility.

And it must be remembered also that our political system is not so coördinated as to supply a training for presidential aspirants or even to make it absolutely necessary that they should have had extended experience in public affairs. Certainly the country has never thought of members of Congress as in any particular degree fitted for the presidency. Even the Vice President is not afforded an opportunity to learn the duties of the office. The men best prepared, no doubt, are those who have been governors of states or members of cabinets. And yet even they are chosen for their respective offices generally by reason of a kind of fitness and availability which does not necessarily argue in them the size and power that would fit them for the greater office. In our earlier practice cabinet officers were regarded as in the natural line of succession to the presidency. Mr. Jefferson had been in General Washington's cabinet, Mr. Madison in Mr. Jefferson's, Mr. Monroe in Mr. Madison's; and generally it was the Secretary of State who was taken. But those were days when English precedent was strong upon us, when cabinets were expected to be made up of the political leaders of the party in power; and from their ranks subsequent candidates for the presidency were most likely to be selected. The practice, as we look back to it, seems eminently sensible, and we wonder why it should have been so soon departed from and apparently forgotten. We wonder, too, why eminent senators have not sometimes been chosen; why members of the House have so seldom commanded the attention of nominating conventions; why public life has never offered itself in any definite way as a preparation for the presidential office.

If the matter be looked at a little more closely, it will be seen that the office of President, as we have used and developed it, really does not demand actual experience in affairs so much as particular qualities of mind and character which we are at least as likely to find outside the ranks of our public men as within them. What is it that a nominating convention wants in the man it is to present to the country for its suffrages? A man who will be and who will seem to the country in some sort an embodiment of the character and purpose it wishes its government to have,—a man who understands his own day and the needs of the country, and who has the personality and the initiative to enforce his views both upon the people and upon Congress. It may seem an odd way to get such a man. It is even possible that nominating conventions and those who guide them do not realize entirely what it is that they do. But in simple fact the convention picks out a party leader from the body of the nation. Not that it expects its nominee to direct the interior government of the party and to supplant its already accredited and experienced spokesmen in Congress and in its state and national committees; but it does of necessity expect him to represent it before public opinion and to stand before the country as its representative man, as a true type of what the country may expect of the party itself in purpose and principle. It cannot but be led by him in the campaign; if he be elected, it cannot but acquiesce in his leadership of the government itself. What the country will demand of the candidate will be, not that he be an astute politician, skilled and practised in affairs, but that he be a man such as it can trust, in character, in intention, in knowledge of its needs, in perception of the best means by which those needs may be met, in capacity to prevail by reason of his own weight and integrity. Sometimes the country believes in a party, but more often it believes in a man; and conventions have often shown the instinct to perceive which it is that the country needs in a particular presidential year, a mere representative partisan, a military hero, or some one who will genuinely speak for the country itself, whatever be his training and antecedents. It is in this sense that the President has the role of party leader thrust upon him by the very method by which he is chosen.

As legal executive, his constitutional aspect, the President cannot be thought of alone. He cannot execute laws. Their actual daily execution must be taken care of by the several executive departments and by the now innumerable body of federal officials throughout the country. In respect of the strictly executive duties of his office the President may be said to administer the presidency in conjunction with the members of his cabinet, like the chairman of a commission. He is even of necessity much less active in the actual carrying out of the law than are his colleagues and advisers. It is therefore becoming more and more true, as the business of the government becomes more and more complex and extended, that the President is becoming more and more a political and less and less an executive officer. His executive powers are in commission, while his political powers more and more centre and accumulate upon him and are in their very nature personal and inalienable.

Only the larger sort of executive questions are brought to him. Departments which run with easy routine and whose transactions bring few questions of general policy to the surface may proceed with their business for months and even years together without demanding his attention; and no department is in any sense under his direct charge. Cabinet meetings do not discuss detail: they are concerned only with the larger matters of policy or expediency which important business is constantly disclosing. There are no more hours in the President's day than in another man's. If he is indeed the executive, he must act almost entirely by delegation, and is in the hands of his colleagues. He is likely to be praised if things go well, and blamed if they go wrong; but his only real control is of the persons to whom he deputes the performance of executive duties. It is through no fault or neglect of his that the duties apparently assigned to him by the Constitution have come to be his less conspicuous, less important duties, and that duties apparently not assigned to him at all chiefly occupy his time and energy. The one set of duties it has proved practically impossible for him to perform; the other it has proved impossible for him to escape.

He cannot escape being the leader of his party except by incapacity and lack of personal force, because he is at once the choice of the party and of the nation. He is the party nominee, and the only party nominee for whom the whole nation votes. Members of the House and Senate are representatives of localities, are voted for only by sections of voters, or by local bodies of electors like the members of the state legislatures. There is no national party choice except that of President. No one else represents the people as a whole, exercising a national choice; and inasmuch as his strictly executive duties are in fact subordinated, so far at any rate as all detail is concerned, the President represents not so much the party's governing efficiency as its controlling ideals and principles. He is not so much part of its organization as its vital link of connection with the thinking nation. He can dominate his party by being spokesman for the real sentiment and purpose of the country, by giving direction to opinion, by giving the country at once the information and the statements of policy which will enable it to form its judgments alike of parties and of men.

For he is also the political leader of the nation, or has it in his choice to be. The nation as a whole has chosen him, and is conscious that it has no other political spokesman. His is the only national voice in affairs. Let him once win the admiration and confidence of the country, and no other single force can withstand him, no combination of forces will easily overpower him. His position takes the imagination of the country. He is the representative of no constituency, but of the whole people. When he speaks in his true character, he speaks for no special interest. If he rightly interpret the national thought and boldly insist upon it, he is irresistible; and the country never feels the zest of action so much as when its President is of such insight and calibre. Its instinct is for unified action, and it craves a single leader. It is for this reason that it will often prefer to choose a man rather than a party. A President whom it trusts can not only lead it, but form it to his own views.

It is the extraordinary isolation imposed upon the President by our system that makes the character and opportunity of his office so extraordinary. In him are centred both opinion and party. He may stand, if he will, a little outside party and insist as if it were upon the general opinion. It is with the instinctive feeling that it is upon occasion such a man that the country wants that nominating conventions will often nominate men who are not their acknowledged leaders, but only such men as the country would like to see lead both its parties. The President may also, if he will, stand within the party counsels and use the advantage of his power and personal force to control its actual programs. He may be both the leader of his party and the leader of the nation, or he may be one or the other. If he lead the nation, his party can hardly resist him. His office is anything he has the sagacity and force to make it.

That is the reason why it has been one thing at one time, another at another. The Presidents who have not made themselves leaders have lived no more truly on that account in the spirit of the Constitution than those whose force has told in the determination of law and policy. No doubt Andrew Jackson overstepped the bounds meant to be set to the authority of his office. It was certainly in direct contravention of the spirit of the Constitution that he should have refused to respect and execute decisions of the Supreme Court of the United States, and no serious student of our history can righteously condone what he did in such matters on the ground that his intentions were upright and his principles pure. But the Constitution of the United States is not a mere lawyers' document: it is a vehicle of life, and its spirit is always the spirit of the age. Its prescriptions are clear and we know what they are; a written document makes lawyers of us all, and our duty as citizens should make us conscientious lawyers, reading the text of the Constitution without subtlety or sophistication; but life is always your last and most authoritative critic.

Some of our Presidents have deliberately held themselves off from using the full power they might legitimately have used, because of conscientious scruples, because they were more theorists than statesmen. They have held the strict literary theory of the Constitution, the Whig theory, the Newtonian theory, and have acted as if they thought that Pennsylvania Avenue should have been even longer than it is; that there should be no intimate communication of any kind between the Capitol and the White House; that the President as a man was no more at liberty to lead the houses of Congress by persuasion than he was at liberty as President to dominate them by authority,—supposing that he had, what he has not, authority enough to dominate them. But the makers of the Constitution were not enacting Whig theory, they were not making laws with the expectation that, not the laws themselves, but their opinions, known by future historians to lie back of them, should govern the constitutional action of the country. They were statesmen, not pedants, and their laws are sufficient to keep us to the paths they set us upon. The President is at liberty, both in law and conscience, to be as big a man as he can. His capacity will set the limit; and if Congress be overborne by him, it will be no fault of the makers of the Constitution,—it will be from no lack of constitutional powers on its part, but only because the President has the nation behind him, and Congress has not. He has no means of compelling Congress except through public opinion.

That I say he has no means of compelling Congress will show what I mean, and that my meaning has no touch of radicalism or iconoclasm in it. There are illegitimate means by which the President may influence the action of Congress. He may bargain with members, not only with regard to appointments, but also with regard to legislative measures. He may use his local patronage to assist members to get or retain their seats. He may interpose his powerful influence, in one covert way or another, in contests for places in the Senate. He may also overbear Congress by arbitrary acts which ignore the laws or virtually override them. He may even substitute his own orders for acts of Congress which he wants but cannot get. Such things are not only deeply immoral, they are destructive of the fundamental understandings of constitutional government and, therefore, of constitutional government itself. They are sure, moreover, in a country of free public opinion, to bring their own punishment, to destroy both the fame and the power of the man who dares to practice them. No honorable man includes such agencies in a sober exposition of the Constitution or allows himself to think of them when he speaks of the influences of "life" which govern each generation's use and interpretation of that great instrument, our sovereign guide and the object of our deepest reverence. Nothing in a system like ours can be constitutional which is immoral or which touches the good faith of those who have sworn to obey the fundamental law. The reprobation of all good men will always overwhelm such influences with shame and failure. But the personal force of the President is perfectly constitutional to any extent to which he chooses to exercise it, and it is by the clear logic of our constitutional practice that he has become alike the leader of his party and the leader of the nation.

The political powers of the President are not quite so obvious in their scope and character when we consider his relations with Congress as when we consider his relations to his party and to the nation. They need, therefore, a somewhat more critical examination. Leadership in government naturally belongs to its executive officers, who are daily in contact with practical conditions and exigencies and whose reputations alike for good judgment and for fidelity are at stake much more than are those of the members of the legislative body at every turn of the law's application. The law-making part of the government ought certainly to be very hospitable to the suggestions of the planning and acting part of it. Those Presidents who have felt themselves bound to adhere to the strict literary theory of the Constitution have scrupulously refrained from attempting to determine either the subjects or the character of legislation, except so far as they were obliged to decide for themselves, after Congress had acted, whether they should acquiesce in it or not. And yet the Constitution explicitly authorizes the President to recommend to Congress "such measures as he shall deem necessary and expedient," and it is not necessary to the integrity of even the literary theory of the Constitution to insist that such recommendations should be merely perfunctory. Certainly General Washington did not so regard them, and he stood much nearer the Whig theory than we do. A President's messages to Congress have no more weight or authority than their intrinsic reasonableness and importance give them: but that is their only constitutional limitation. The Constitution certainly does not forbid the President to back them up, as General Washington did, with such personal force and influence as he may possess. Some of our Presidents have felt the need, which unquestionably exists in our system, for some spokesman of the nation as a whole, in matters of legislation no less than in other matters, and have tried to supply Congress with the leadership of suggestion, backed by argument and by iteration and by every legitimate appeal to public opinion. Cabinet officers are shut out from Congress; the President himself has, by custom, no access to its floor; many long-established barriers of precedent, though not of law, hinder him from exercising any direct influence upon its deliberations; and yet he is undoubtedly the only spokesman of the whole people. They have again and again, as often as they were afforded the opportunity, manifested their satisfaction when he has boldly accepted the role of leader, to which the peculiar origin and character of his authority entitle him. The Constitution bids him speak, and times of stress and change must more and more thrust upon him the attitude of originator of policies.

His is the vital place of action in the system, whether he accept it as such or not, and the office is the measure of the man,—of his wisdom as well as of his force. His veto abundantly equips him to stay the hand of Congress when he will. It is seldom possible to pass a measure over his veto, and no President has hesitated to use the veto when his own judgment of the public good was seriously at issue with that of the houses. The veto has never been suffered to fall into even temporary disuse with us. In England it has ceased to exist, with the change in the character of the executive. There has been no veto since Anne's day, because ever since the reign of Anne the laws of England have been originated either by ministers who spoke the king's own will or by ministers whom the king did not dare gainsay; and in our own time the ministers who formulate the laws are themselves the executive of the nation; a veto would be a negative upon their own power. If bills pass of which they disapprove, they resign and give place to the leaders of those who approve them. The framers of the Constitution made in our President a more powerful, because a more isolated, king than the one they were imitating; and because the Constitution gave them their veto in such explicit terms, our Presidents have not hesitated to use it, even when it put their mere individual judgment against that of large majorities in both houses of Congress. And yet in the exercise of the power to suggest legislation, quite as explicitly conferred upon them by the Constitution, some of our Presidents have seemed to have a timid fear that they might offend some law of taste which had become a constitutional principle.

In one sense their messages to Congress have no more authority than the letters of any other citizen would have. Congress can heed or ignore them as it pleases; and there have been periods of our history when presidential messages were utterly without practical significance, perfunctory documents which few persons except the editors of newspapers took the trouble to read. But if the President has personal force and cares to exercise it, there is this tremendous difference between his messages and the views of any other citizen, either outside Congress or in it: that the whole country reads them and feels that the writer speaks with an authority and a responsibility which the people themselves have given him.

The history of our cabinets affords a striking illustration of the progress of the idea that the President is not merely the legal head but also the political leader of the nation. In the earlier days of the government it was customary for the President to fill his cabinet with the recognized leaders of his party. General Washington even tried the experiment which William of Orange tried at the very beginning of the era of cabinet government. He called to his aid the leaders of both political parties, associating Mr. Hamilton with Mr. Jefferson, on the theory that all views must be heard and considered in the conduct of the government. That was the day in which English precedent prevailed, and English cabinets were made up of the chief political characters of the day. But later years have witnessed a marked change in our practice, in this as in many other things. The old tradition was indeed slow in dying out. It persisted with considerable vitality at least until General Garfield's day, and may yet from time to time revive, for many functions of our cabinets justify it and make it desirable. But our later Presidents have apparently ceased to regard the cabinet as a council of party leaders such as the party they represent would have chosen. They look upon it rather as a body of personal advisers whom the President chooses from the ranks of those whom he personally trusts and prefers to look to for advice. Our recent Presidents have not sought their associates among those whom the fortunes of party contest have brought into prominence and influence, but have called their personal friends and business colleagues to cabinet positions, and men who have given proof of their efficiency in private, not in public, life,—bankers who had never had any place in the formal counsels of the party, eminent lawyers who had held aloof from politics, private secretaries who had shown an unusual sagacity and proficiency in handling public business; as if the President were himself alone the leader of his party, the members of his cabinet only his private advisers, at any rate advisers of his private choice. Mr. Cleveland may be said to have been the first President to make this conception of the cabinet prominent in his choices, and he did not do so until his second administration. Mr. Roosevelt has emphasized the idea.

Upon analysis it seems to mean this: the cabinet is an executive, not a political body. The President cannot himself be the actual executive; he must therefore find, to act in his stead, men of the best legal and business gifts, and depend upon them for the actual administration of the government in all its daily activities. If he seeks political advice of his executive colleagues, he seeks it because he relies upon their natural good sense and experienced judgment, upon their knowledge of the country and its business and social conditions, upon their sagacity as representative citizens of more than usual observation and discretion; not because they are supposed to have had any very intimate contact with politics or to have made a profession of public affairs. He has chosen, not representative politicians, but eminent representative citizens, selecting them rather for their special fitness for the great business posts to which he has assigned them than for their political experience, and looking to them for advice in the actual conduct of the government rather than in the shaping of political policy. They are, in his view, not necessarily political officers at all.

It may with a great deal of plausibility be argued that the Constitution looks upon the President himself in the same way. It does not seem to make him a prime minister or the leader of the nation's counsels. Some Presidents are, therefore, and some are not. It depends upon the man and his gifts. He may be like his cabinet, or he may be more than his cabinet. His office is a mere vantage ground from which he may be sure that effective words of advice and timely efforts at reform will gain telling momentum. He has the ear of the nation as of course, and a great person may use such an advantage greatly. If he use the opportunity, he may take his cabinet into partnership or not, as he pleases; and so its character may vary with his. Self-reliant men will regard their cabinets as executive councils; men less self-reliant or more prudent will regard them as also political councils, and will wish to call into them men who have earned the confidence of their party. The character of the cabinet may be made a nice index of the theory of the presidential office, as well as of the President's theory of party government; but the one view is, so far as I can see, as constitutional as the other.

One of the greatest of the President's powers I have not yet spoken of at all: his control, which is very absolute, of the foreign relations of the nation. The initiative in foreign affairs, which the President possesses without any restriction whatever, is virtually the power to control them absolutely. The President cannot conclude a treaty with a foreign power without the consent of the Senate, but he may guide every step of diplomacy, and to guide diplomacy is to determine what treaties must be made, if the faith and prestige of the government are to be maintained. He need disclose no step of negotiation until it is complete, and when in any critical matter it is completed the government is virtually committed. Whatever its disinclination, the Senate may feel itself committed also.

I have not dwelt upon this power of the President, because it has been decisively influential in determining the character and influence of the office at only two periods in our history; at the very first, when the government was young and had so to use its incipient force as to win the respect of the nations into whose family it had thrust itself, and in our own day when the results of the Spanish War, the ownership of distant possessions, and many sharp struggles for foreign trade make it necessary that we should turn our best talents to the task of dealing firmly, wisely, and justly with political and commercial rivals. The President can never again be the mere domestic figure he has been throughout so large a part of our history. The nation has risen to the first rank in power and resources. The other nations of the world look askance upon her, half in envy, half in fear, and wonder with a deep anxiety what she will do with her vast strength. They receive the frank professions of men like Mr. John Hay, whom we wholly trusted, with a grain of salt, and doubt what we were sure of, their truthfulness and sincerity, suspecting a hidden design under every utterance he makes. Our President must always, henceforth, be one of the great powers of the world, whether he act greatly and wisely or not, and the best statesmen we can produce will be needed to fill the office of Secretary of State. We have but begun to see the presidential office in this light; but it is the light which will more and more beat upon it, and more and more determine its character and its effect upon the politics of the nation. We can never hide our President again as a mere domestic officer. We can never again see him the mere executive he was in the thirties and forties. He must stand always at the front of our affairs, and the office will be as big and as influential as the man who occupies it.

How is it possible to sum up the duties and influence of such an office in such a system in comprehensive terms which will cover all its changeful aspects? In the view of the makers of the Constitution the President was to be legal executive; perhaps the leader of the nation; certainly not the leader of the party, at any rate while in office. But by the operation of forces inherent in the very nature of government he has become all three, and by inevitable consequence the most heavily burdened officer in the world. No other man's day is so full as his, so full of the responsibilities which tax mind and conscience alike and demand an inexhaustible vitality. The mere task of making appointments to office, which the Constitution imposes upon the President, has come near to breaking some of our Presidents down, because it is a never-ending task in a civil service not yet put upon a professional footing, confused with short terms of office, always forming and dissolving. And in proportion as the President ventures to use his opportunity to lead opinion and act as spokesman of the people in affairs the people stand ready to overwhelm him by running to him with every question, great and small. They are as eager to have him settle a literary question as a political; hear him as acquiescently with regard to matters of special expert knowledge as with regard to public affairs, and call upon him to quiet all troubles by his personal intervention. Men of ordinary physique and discretion cannot be Presidents and live, if the strain be not somehow relieved. We shall be obliged always to be picking our chief magistrates from among wise and prudent athletes,—a small class.

The future development of the presidency, therefore, must certainly, one would confidently predict, run along such lines as the President's later relations with his cabinet suggest. General Washington, partly out of unaffected modesty, no doubt, but also out of the sure practical instinct which he possessed in so unusual a degree, set an example which few of his successors seem to have followed in any systematic manner. He made constant and intimate use of his colleagues in every matter that he handled, seeking their assistance and advice by letter when they were at a distance and he could not obtain it in person. It is well known to all close students of our history that his greater state papers, even those which seem in some peculiar and intimate sense his personal utterances, are full of the ideas and the very phrases of the men about him whom he most trusted. His rough drafts came back to him from Mr. Hamilton and Mr. Madison in great part rephrased and rewritten, in many passages reconceived and given a new color. He thought and acted always by the light of counsel, with a will and definite choice of his own, but through the instrumentality of other minds as well as his own. The duties and responsibilities laid upon the President by the Constitution can be changed only by constitutional amendment,—a thing too difficult to attempt except upon some greater necessity than the relief of an overburdened office, even though that office be the greatest in the land; and it is to be doubted whether the deliberate opinion of the country would consent to make of the President a less powerful officer than he is. He can secure his own relief without shirking any real responsibility. Appointments, for example, he can, if he will, make more and more upon the advice and choice of his executive colleagues; every matter of detail not only, but also every minor matter of counsel or of general policy, he can more and more depend upon his chosen advisers to determine; he need reserve for himself only the larger matters of counsel and that general oversight of the business of the government and of the persons who conduct it which is not possible without intimate daily consultations, indeed, but which is possible without attempting the intolerable burden of direct control. This is, no doubt, the idea of their functions which most Presidents have entertained and which most Presidents suppose themselves to have acted on; but we have reason to believe that most of our Presidents have taken their duties too literally and have attempted the impossible. But we can safely predict that as the multitude of the President's duties increases, as it must with the growth and widening activities of the nation itself, the incumbents of the great office will more and more come to feel that they are administering it in its truest purpose and with greatest effect by regarding themselves as less and less executive officers and more and more directors of affairs and leaders of the nation,—men of counsel and of the sort of action that makes for enlightenment.

CHAPTER 8. PARTY GOVERNMENT IN THE UNITED STATES.

In order to understand the organization and operation of parties in the United States, it is necessary to turn once more to the theory upon which our federal and, for that matter, our state governments, also, were constructed. They were, in their make-up, Whig inventions. At the time our national government was erected, the Whig party in England was engaged in a very notable struggle to curb and regulate the power of the Crown. The struggle had begun long before the revolution which cut our politics asunder from the politics of England, and that revolution itself was only an acute manifestation of the great forces which were at work among thoughtful Englishmen everywhere. The revolution which separated America from England was part of a great Whig contest with the Crown for constitutional liberties. The leaders of that revolution held Whig doctrine; the greater Whig statesmen on the other side of the water recognized them as their allies and gave them their outspoken sympathy, perceiving that they were but fighting a battle which must sooner or later be fought in England, whether with arms or with votes and the more pacific strategy of politics. Every historian now sees that the radical changes made in the government of England during the nineteenth century were quickened and given assurance of success by the changes which had preceded them in America; that the leaders of the American Revolution had but taken precedence of the Whigs at home in bringing government into a new and responsible relationship to the people who were its subjects.

The theory of the Whigs in England did not go the length of seeking to destroy the power of the throne. It probably would not have gone that length in America if the throne had been on this side of the water, a domestic instead of a separate and distant power. The men in the old country to whom the American revolutionists showed the way sought only to offset the Crown with other influences,—influences of opinion acting through a reformed and purified representative chamber, whose consent not only should be necessary to the enactment of law, but the advice of whose leaders the king should find it necessary to heed; and the influences of judicial opinion acting through stable and independent courts. It was, as I have already pointed out, this theory of checks and balances, which I have called the Newtonian theory of government, that prevailed in the convention which framed the Constitution of the United States,—which prevailed over the very different theory of Hamilton, that government was not a thing which you could afford to tie up in a nice poise, as if it were to be held at an inactive equilibrium, but a thing which must every day act with straightforward and unquestionable power, with definite purpose and consistent force, choosing its policies and making good its authority, like a single organism,—the theory which would have seemed to Darwin the theory of nature itself, the nature of men as well as the nature of animal organisms. Dominated by the immediate forces and aspirations of their own day, ruled in thought and action by the great contest in which they had found themselves engaged, to hold the royal power off from arbitrary interference with their interests and their liberties, they allowed themselves to become more interested in providing checks to government than in supplying it with energy and securing to it the necessary certainty and consistency of action. They set legislature off against executive, and the courts against both, separated the three in sphere and power, and yet made the agreement of all three necessary to the operation of the government. The boast of the writers in the Federalist was of the perfection with which the convention at Philadelphia had interpreted Whig theory and embodied Whig dynamics in the Constitution. Mr. Hamilton's theory, that government was an affair of cooperative and harmonious forces, and that the danger of coordinate and coequal powers such as the framers of the Constitution had set up was that they might at their will pull in opposite directions and hold the government at a deadlock which no constitutional force could overcome and yet many situations might render inconvenient, if not hazardous, the temper and circumstances of the time gave public men little inclination to heed. Checks and balances were then the orthodox gospel of government.

The most serious success of the convention in applying Whig theory to the government they were constructing was the complete separation of Congress and the executive which they effected. The English Whigs fought for long to oust the Crown from the power and intimate influence it had had in the House of Commons through its control of members' seats and its corrupting power of patronage: they succeeded only in placing the leaders of the Commons itself in executive authority in the stead of the Crown. The real executive authority of the English government is vested in the ministers of the day, who are in effect a committee of the House of Commons, and legislature and executive work together under a common party organization. The one is only an agency of the other: the ministers act for their party in the House. The separation of parliament and the Crown which the reformers of the early part of the last century finally succeeded in effecting was not, in fact, a separation of the legislature from the executive, but only a separation of the real from the nominal executive. They entirely succeeded in making the king a modern "constitutional" monarch,—a monarch, that is, who, notwithstanding the dignity with which he is still surrounded and the very considerable influence which he can still exercise by reason of his station, his personal force, should he happen to have any, and his intimate access to the counsels of the executive ministry, merely "reigns" and does not govern. His choice of advisers the House of Commons dictates. But our constitution-makers did their work during the earlier part of the struggle, when it seemed merely a contest to offset the authority of the king with effectual checks, and long before it had become evident that the outcome would be the substitution of an executive which represented the popular house for one which did not. Having a free hand and a clean sheet of paper upon which to write, there was nothing to hinder the complete realization of their ideal. They succeeded in actually separating legislature and executive.

It may be that circumstances rendered their success more complete than they had intended. There is no reason to believe that they meant actually to exclude the President and his advisers from all intimate personal consultation with the houses in session. No doubt the President and the members of his cabinet could with perfect legal propriety and without any breach of the spirit of the Constitution attend the sessions of either the House or the Senate and take part in their discussions, at any rate to the extent of answering questions and explaining any measures which the President might see fit to urge in the messages which the Constitution explicitly authorizes him to send to Congress. But after a few brief attempts to institute a practice of that kind, in the early days of General Washington's administration, actual usage established another habit in respect of the intercourse between the executive and Congress, and later days have shown the houses very jealous of any attempt to establish such an intimacy. Executive officers would be most unwelcome in the houses. Their doors are shut against them. Only the door of a committee room here and there opens to receive them, and they enter only when they are invited.

In what I have said in a previous lecture of the remarkable and, in some respects, unexpected development of the President's influence and functions, I have already pointed out one of the most interesting and significant results of this absolute application of early Whig theory to the practice of our government. Its result has been that, so far as the government itself is concerned, there is but one national voice in the country, and that is the voice of the President. His isolation has quite unexpectedly been his exaltation. The House represents localities, is made up of individuals whose interest is the interest of separate and scattered constituencies, who are drawn together, indeed, under a master, the Speaker, but who are controlled by no national force except that of their party, a force outside the government rather than within it. The Senate represents in its turn regions and interests distinguished by many conflicting and contrasted purposes, united only by exterior party organization and a party spirit not generated within the chamber itself. Only the President represents the country as a whole, and the President himself is coöperatively bound to the houses only by the machinery and discipline of party, not as a person and functionary, but as a member of an outside organization which exists quite independently of the executive and legislature.

It is extraordinary the influence the early Whig theory of political dynamics has had amongst us and the far-reaching consequences which have ensued from it. It is far from being a democratic theory. It is, on the contrary, a theory whose avowed object, at any rate as applied in America, was to keep government at a sort of mechanical equipoise by means of a standing amicable contest among its several organic parts, each of which it seeks to make representative of a special interest in the nation. It is particularly intended to prevent the will of the people as a whole from having at any moment an unobstructed sweep and ascendency. And yet in every step we have taken with the intention of making our governments more democratic, we have punctiliously kept to Whig mechanics. The process shows itself most distinctly and most systematically in the structure of our state governments. We have supposed that the way to make executive offices democratic in character and motive was to separate them in authority,—to prescribe each officer's duties by statute, however petty and naturally subordinate in kind those duties might be, to put it to the voter to elect him separately, and to make him responsible, not to any superior officer set over him, but only to the courts,—thus making him a law unto himself so far as any other official is concerned. So far have we carried the theory of checks and balances, the theory of the independence of the several organs of government.

The operation of the system is worth looking into more closely for a moment. Not very long ago a mob of unmasked men rescued a prisoner with whom they sympathized from the sheriff of a county in one of our States. The circumstances of the rescue made it very evident that the sheriff had made no serious attempt to prevent the rescue. He had had reason to expect it, and had provided no sufficient armed guard for his prisoner. The case was so flagrant that the governor of the State wrote the sheriff a sharp letter of reprimand, censuring him very justly for his neglect of duty. The sheriff replied in an open letter in which he curtly bade the governor mind his own business. The sheriff was, he said, a servant of his county, responsible to its voters and not to the governor. And his impertinence was the law itself. The governor had no more authority over him than the youngest citizen. He was responsible only to the people of his own county, from whose ranks the mob had come which had taken his prisoner away from him. He could have been brought to book only by indictment and trial,—indictment at the instance of a district attorney elected on the same "ticket" with himself, by a grand jury of men who had voted for him, and trial by a petit jury of his neighbors, whose sympathy with the rescue might be presumed from the circumstances. This is Whig dynamics in its *reductio ad particulam*. It is a species of government in solution.

It can be solidified and drawn to system only by the external authority of party, an organization outside the government and independent of it. Not being drawn together by any system provided in our constitutions, being laid apart, on the contrary, in a sort of jealous dispersion and analysis by Whig theory enacted into law, it has been necessary to keep the several parts of the government in some kind of workable combination by outside pressure, by the closely knit imperative discipline of party, a body that has no constitutional cleavages and is free to tie itself into legislative and executive functions alike by its systematic control of the *personnel* of all branches of the government.

Fortunately, the federal executive is not dispersed into its many elements as the executive of each of our States is. The dispersion of our state executives runs from top to bottom. The governor has no cabinet. The executive officers of state associated with him in administration are elected as he is. Each refers his authority to particular statutes or particular clauses of the state constitution. Each is responsible politically to his constituents, the voters of the State, and, legally, to the courts and their juries. But in the federal government the executive is at least in itself a unit. Every one subordinate to the President is appointed by him and responsible to him, both legally and politically. He can control the *personnel* and the action of the whole of the great "department" of government of which he is the head. The Whig doctrine is insisted on only with regard to dealings of the legislature with the executive, and of the legislature or the executive with the courts. The three great functions of government are not to be merged or even drawn into organic coöperation, but are to be balanced against one another in a safe counterpoise. They are interdependent but organically disassociated; must coöperate, and yet are subject to no common authority.

The way in which the several branches of the federal government have been separately organized and given efficiency in the discharge of their own functions has only emphasized their separation and jealous independence. The effective organization of the House under its committees and its powerful Speaker, the organization of the Senate under its steering committees, the consolidation of the executive under the authority of the President, only render it the more feasible and the more likely that these several parts of the government will act with an all too effective consciousness of their distinct individuality and dignity, their distinct claim to be separately considered and severally obeyed in the shaping and conduct of affairs. They are not to be driven, and there is no machinery of which the Constitution knows anything by which they can be led and combined.

It is for that reason that we have had such an extraordinary development of party authority in the United States and have developed outside the government itself so elaborate and effective an organization of parties. They are absolutely necessary to hold the things thus disconnected and dispersed together and give some coherence to the action of political forces. There are, as I have already explained in another connection, so many officers to be elected that even the preparation of lists of candidates is too complicated and laborious a business to be undertaken by men busy about other things. Some one must make a profession of attending to it, must give it system and method. A few candidates for a few conspicuous offices which interested everybody, the voters themselves might select in the intervals of private business; but a multitude of candidates for offices great and small they cannot choose; and after they are chosen and elected to office they are still a multitude, and there must be somebody to look after them in the discharge of their functions, somebody to observe them closely in action, in order that they may be assessed against the time when they are to be judged. Each has his own little legal domain; there is no interdependence amongst them, no interior organization to hold them together. There must, therefore, be an exterior organization, voluntarily formed and independent of the law, whose object it shall be to bind them together in some sort of harmony and cooperation. That exterior organization is the political party. The hierarchy of its officers must supply the place of a hierarchy of legally constituted officials.

Nowhere else is the mere maintenance of the machinery of government so complex and difficult a matter as in the United States. It is not as if there were but a single government to be maintained and officered. There are the innumerable offices of States, of counties, of townships, of cities, to be filled; and it is only by elections, by the filling of offices, that parties test and maintain their hold upon public opinion. Their control of the opinion of the nation inevitably depends upon their hold on the many localities of which it is made up. If they lose their grip upon the petty choices which affect the daily life of counties and cities and States, they will inevitably lose their grip upon the greater matters, also, of which the action of the nation is made up. Parties get their coherence and prestige, their rootage and solidity, their mastery over men and events, from their command of detail, their control of the little tides that eventually flood the great channels of national action. No one realizes more completely the interdependence of municipal, state, and federal elections than do the party managers. Their parties cannot be one thing for the one set of elections and another for the other; and the complexity of the politician's task consists in the fact that, though from his point of view interdependent and intimately connected, the constantly recurring elections of a system under which everybody is elected are variously scattered in time and place and object.

We have made many efforts to separate local and national elections in time in order to separate them in spirit. Many local questions upon which the voters of particular cities or counties or States are called upon to vote have no connection whatever either in principle or in object with the national questions upon which the choice of congressmen and of presidential electors should turn. It is ideally desirable that the voter should be left free to choose the candidates of one party in local elections and the candidates of the opposite party in national elections. It is undoubtedly desirable that he should go further and separate matters of local administration from his choice of party altogether, choosing his local representatives upon their merits as men without regard to their party affiliations. We have hopefully made a score of efforts to obtain "nonpartisan" local political action. But such efforts always in the long run fail. Local parties cannot be one thing for one purpose and another for another without losing form and discipline altogether and becoming hopelessly fluid. Neither can parties form and re-form, now for this purpose and again for that, or be for one election one thing and for another another. Unless they can have local training and constant rehearsal of their parts, they will fail of coherent organization when they address themselves to the business of national elections. For national purposes they must regard themselves as parts of greater wholes, and it is impossible under such a system as our own that they should maintain their zest and interest in their business if their only objects are distant and general objects, without local rootage or illustration, centering in Congress and utterly disconnected with anything that they themselves handle. Local offices are indispensable to party discipline as rewards of local fidelity, as the visible and tangible objects of those who devote their time and energy to party organization and undertake to see to it that the full strength of the party vote is put forth when the several local sections of the party are called upon to unite for national purposes. If national politics are not to become a mere game of haphazard amidst which parties can make no calculations whatever, systematic and disciplined connections between local and national affairs are imperative, and some instrument must be found to effect them. Whatever their faults and abuses, party machines are absolutely necessary under our existing electoral arrangements, and are necessary chiefly for keeping the several segments of parties together. No party manager could piece local majorities together and make up a national majority, if local majorities were mustered upon non-partisan grounds. No party manager can keep his lieutenants to their business who has not control of local nominations. His lieutenants do not expect national rewards: their vital rootage is the rootage of local opportunity.

Just because, therefore, there is nowhere else in the world so complex and various an electoral machinery as in the United States, nowhere else in the world is party machinery so elaborate or so necessary. It is important to keep this in mind. Otherwise, when we analyze party action, we shall fall into the too common error of thinking that we are analyzing disease. As a matter of fact, the whole thing is just as normal and natural as any other political development. The part that party has played in this country has been both necessary and beneficial, and if bosses and secret managers are often undesirable persons, playing their parts for their own benefit or glorification rather than for the public good, they are at least the natural fruits of the tree. It has borne fruit good and bad, sweet and bitter, wholesome and corrupt, but it is native to our air and practice and can be uprooted only by an entire change of system.

All the peculiarities of party government in the United States are due to the too literal application of Whig doctrine, to the infinite multiplication of elective offices. There are two things to be done for which we have supplied no adequate legal or constitutional machinery: there are thousands of officials to he chosen and there are many disconnected parts of government to be brought into coöperation. "It may be laid down as a political maxim that whatever assigns to the people a power which they are naturally incapable of wielding takes it away from them." They have, under our Constitution and statutes, been assigned the power of filling innumerable elective offices; they are incapable of wielding that power because they have neither the time nor the necessary means of coöperative action; the power has therefore been taken away from them, not by law but by circumstances, and handed over to those who have the time and the inclination to supply the necessary organization; and the system of election has been transformed into a system of practically irresponsible appointment to office by private party managers,— irresponsible because our law has not yet been able to devise any means of making it responsible. It may also be laid down as a political maxim that when the several chief organs of government are separated by organic law and offset against each other in jealous seclusion, no common legal authority set over them, no necessary community of interest subsisting amongst them, no common origin or purpose dominating them, they must of necessity, if united at all, be united by pressure from without; and they must be united if government is to proceed. They cannot remain checked and balanced against one another; they must act, and act together. They must, therefore, of their own will or of mere necessity obey an outside master.

Both sets of dispersions, the dispersion of offices and the dispersion of functions and authorities, have coöperated to produce our parties, and their organization. Through their caucuses, their county conventions, their state conventions, their national conventions, instead of through legislatures and cabinets, they supply the indispensable means of agreement and coöperation, and direct the government of the country both in its policy and in its *personnel*. Their local managers make up the long and variegated lists of candidates made necessary under our would-be democratic practice; their caucuses and local conventions ratify the choice; their state and national conventions add declarations of principle and determine party policy. Only in the United States is party thus a distinct authority outside the formal government, expressing its purposes through its own separate and peculiar organs and permitted to dictate what Congress shall undertake and the national administration address itself to. Under every other system of government which is representative in character and which attempts to adjust the action of government to the wishes and interests of the people, the organization of parties is, in a sense, indistinguishable from the organs of the government itself. Party finds its organic lodgment in the national legislature and executive themselves. The several active parts of the government are closely united in organization for a common purpose, because they are under a common direction and themselves constitute the machinery of party control. Parties do not have to supply themselves with separate organs of their own outside the government and intended to dictate its policy, because such separate organs are unnecessary. The responsible organs of government are also the avowed organs of party. The action of opinion upon them is open and direct, not circuitous and secret.

It is interesting to observe that as a consequence the distinction we make between "politicians" and "statesmen" is peculiarly our own. In other countries where these words or their equivalents are used, the statesman differs from the politician only in capacity and in degree, and is distinguished as a public leader only in being a greater figure on the same stage, whereas with us politicians and statesmen differ in kind. A politician is a man who manages the organs of the party outside the open field of government, outside executive offices and legislative chambers, and who conveys the behests of party to those who hold the offices and make laws; while the statesman is the leader of public opinion, the immediate director (under the politicians) of executive or legislative policy, the diplomat, the recognized public servant. The politician, indeed, often holds public office and attempts the rôle of statesman as well, but, though the rôles may be combined, they are none the less sharply distinguishable. Party majorities which are actually in control of the whole legislative machinery, as party majorities in England are, determine party programs by the use of the government itself,—their leaders are at once "politicians" and "statesmen"; and, the function being public, the politician is more likely to be swallowed up in the statesman. But with us, who affect never to allow party majorities to get in complete control of governmental machinery if we can prevent it by constitutional obstacles, party programs are made up outside legislative chambers, by conventions constituted under the direction of independent politicians,—politicians, I mean, who are, at any rate in respect of that function, independent of the responsibilities of office and of public action; and these independent conventions, not charged with the responsibility of carrying out their programs, actually outline the policy of administrations and dictate the action of Congress, the irresponsible dictating to the responsible, and so, it may be, destroying the very responsibility itself. "The peculiarities of American party government are all due to this separation of party management from direct and immediate responsibility for the administration of the government."

The satisfactions of power must be very great to attract so many men of unusual gifts to attempt the hazardous and little honored business of party management. We have made it necessary that we should have "bosses" and that they and their lieutenants should assign offices by appointment, but it is a very difficult and precarious business which they undertake. It is difficult and hazardous not only because it is irregular and only partially protected by law, but also because the people look askance at it and often with a sudden disgust turn upon it and break it up, for a little while rendering it impossible. The reason for these occasional outbursts of discontent and resentment is evident and substantial enough. They come when the people happen to realize that under existing party machinery they have virtually no control at all over nominations for office, and that, having no real control over the choice of candidates, they are cut off from exercising real representative self-government,—that they have been solemnly taking part in a farce. But their revolt is only fitful and upon occasion. Reform associations arise, committees of fifty or seventy or a hundred are formed to set matters right and put government back into the hands of the people, but it is always found that no one can successfully supplant the carefully devised machinery of professional politicians without taking the same pains that they take, without devoting to the business the time and the enthusiasm for details which they devote to it, or supplant the politicians themselves without forming rival organizations as competent as theirs to keep an eye on the whole complicated process of elections and platforms, without, in short, themselves becoming in their turn professional politicians. It is an odd operation of the Whig system that it should make such party organizations at once necessary and disreputable, and I should say that in view of the legal arrangements which we have deliberately made, the disrepute in which professional politicians are held, is in spirit highly unconstitutional.

There can be and there need be no national boss like the local bosses of States and cities, because federal patronage is not distributed by election. Local bosses commonly control the selection of members of Congress because the congressional districts are local, and members of Congress are voted for by local ticket; but they cannot control federal appointments without the consent of the President. By same token, the President can, if he chooses, become national boss by the use of his enormous patronage, doling out his local gifts of place to local party managers in return for support and coöperation in the guidance and control of his party. His patronage touches every community in the United States. He can often by its use disconcert and even master the local managers of his own party by combining the arts of the politician with the duties of the statesman, and he can go far towards establishing a complete personal domination. He can even break party lines asunder and draw together combinations of his own devising. It is against this that our national civil service laws have been wisely directed.

But what really restrains him is his conspicuous position and the fact that opinion will hold him responsible for his use of his patronage. Local bosses are often very obscure persons. To the vast majority of the voters they are entirely unknown, and it is their desire to be as little in evidence as possible. They are often not themselves office-holders at all, and there is no way in which by mere elective processes they can be held responsible. But the President's appointments are public, and he alone by constitutional assignment is responsible for them. Such open responsibility sobers and restrains even where principle is lacking. Many a man who does not scruple to make in private political arrangements which will serve his own purposes will be very careful to be judicious in every act for which he is known to be singly responsible. Responsible appointments are always better than irresponsible. Responsible appointments are appointments made under scrutiny; irresponsible appointments are those made by private persons in private.

The machinery of party rule is nominally representative. The several assemblies and conventions through which the parties operate are supposed to be made up of delegates chosen by the voters of the party, to speak for them with a certain knowledge of what they want and expect. But here again the action of the voters themselves is hardly more than nominal. The lists of delegates are made up by the party managers as freely in all ordinary circumstances as are the lists of the candidates in whose selection they concur. To add the duty of really selecting delegates to the duty of selecting men for office already laid upon our voters by law would be only to add to the impossibility of their task, and to their confusion if they attempted to perform it. When difficulties arise in the process, rival bodies of delegates can always be chosen, and then the managing committees who are in charge of the party's affairs—the county committee, the state committee, or the national committee—can dictate which of the contesting delegations shall be admitted, which shall have their credentials accepted. It is to this necessity we have been brought by farming the functions of government out to outside parties. We have made the task of the voter hopeless and therefore impossible.

And yet at the best the control which party exercises over government is uncertain. There can be, whether for the voter or for the managing politician himself, little more than a presumption that what party managers propose and promise will be done, for the separation of authority between the several organs of government itself still stands in the way. Government is still in solution, and nothing may come to crystallization. But we may congratulate ourselves that we have succeeded as well as we have in giving our politics unity and coherence. We should have drifted sadly, should much oftener have been made to guess what the course of our politics should be, had we not constructed this singular and, on the whole, efficient machinery by which we have in all ordinary seasons contrived to hold the *personnel* and the policy of our government together.

Moreover, there is another use which parties thus thoroughly organized and universally active have served among us which has been of supreme importance. It is clear that without them it would hardly have been possible for the voters of the country to be united in truly national judgments upon national questions. For a hundred years or more we have been a nation in the making, and it would be hard to exaggerate the importance of the nationalizing influence of our great political parties. Without them, in a country so various as ours, with communities at every stage of development, separated into parts by the sharpest economic contrasts and social differences, with local problems and conditions of their own which seemed to give them a separate interest very difficult to combine with any other, full of keen rivalries and here and there cut athwart by deep-rooted prejudices, national opinions, national judgments, could never have been formulated or enforced without the instrumentality of well-disciplined parties which extended their organization in a close network over the whole country, and which had always their desire for office and for the power which office brings to urge as their conclusive reason,—a reason which every voter could understand,—why there should be agreement in opinion and in program as between section and section, whatever the temptation to divide and act separately, as their conclusive argument against local interest and preference. If local and national politics had ever been for long successfully divorced, this would have been impossible.

Students of our politics have not always sufficiently recognized the extraordinary part political parties have played in making a national life which might otherwise have been loose and diverse almost to the point of being inorganic a thing of definite coherence and common purpose. There is a sense in which our parties may be said to have been our real body politic. Not the authority of Congress, not the leadership of the President, but the discipline and zest of parties, has held us together, has made it possible for us to form and to carry out national programs. It is not merely that the utmost economic diversity has marked the development of the different parts of the country, and that their consciousness of different and

even rival and conflicting interests has rendered the sympathy between them imperfect, the likelihood of antagonism very great indeed. There have been social
differences, also, quite as marked. These social differences were no doubt themselves founded in economic diversity, but they cut much deeper than mere economic diversity of itself could have cut and made real sympathy unnatural, spontaneous coöperation between the portions of the country which they had offset
against one another extremely difficult, and, in the absence of party discipline,
extremely unlikely. The social contrast between the North and South before the
Civil War will occur to every one,—a contrast created, of course, by the existence
of the slave system in the South and deepened and elaborated by many another
influence, until the political partnership of the two regions became at last actually
impossible. And yet there was no exclusive southern party, no exclusive northern
party, until the war itself came. Until then each national party had a strong and
loyal following both North and South, and seemed to be conscious of no sectional
lines which need prevent cordial coöperation. The very interest which a section
with peculiar needs and objects of its own had in maintaining its proportional influence in the direction of the policy of the general government, in order both to
protect itself and to further such measures conceived in its own interest as it could
induce the partners to concede, made it eager to escape actual political isolation
and keep its representation in national party counsels.

And, though the contrast between the South with slavery and the other portions
of the country without it was the sharpest and most dangerous contrast that our
history has disclosed, many another crisis in our affairs has been accentuated by
differences of interest and of point of view almost as great. The feeling of the
communities beyond the Alleghanies towards the communities by the Atlantic
seaboard throughout all the time when foreign powers owned the southern outlet
of the great valley of the Mississippi; the feeling of the communities of the plains
towards the communities to the eastward which seemed to grudge them their development and to prefer the interest of the manufacturer to the interest of the
farmer; the feeling of the mining camps towards the regions of commerce and of
all the old order which got their wealth but did not understand or regard their
wishes in matters of local regulation and self-government; the circumstances in
which Territories were set up and the heats in which States were forged,—these
have been the difficulties and hazards of our national history, and it has been
nothing less than a marvel how the network of parties has taken up and broken
the restless strain of contest and jealousy, like an invisible network of kindly oil
upon the disordered waters of the sea.

It is in this vital sense that our national parties have been our veritable body
politic. The very compulsion of selfishness has made them serviceable; the very
play of self-interest has made them effective. In organization was their strength.
It brought them the rewards of local office, the command of patronage of many
kinds, the detailed control of opinion, the subtle mastery of every force of growth
and expansion. They strove for nothing so constantly or so watchfully as for the

compact, coöperative organization and action which served to hold the nation in their hands.

But we have come within sight of the end of the merely nationalizing process. Contrasts between region and region become every year less obvious, conflicts of interest less acute and disturbing. Party organization is no longer needed for the mere rudimentary task of holding the machinery together or giving it the sustenance of some common object, some single coöperative motive. The time is at hand when we can with safety examine the network of party in its detail and change its structure without imperilling its strength. This thing that has served us so well might now master us if we left it irresponsible. We must see to it that it is made responsible.

I have already explained in what sense and for what very sufficient reasons it is irresponsible. Party organizations appoint our elective officers, and we do not elect them. The chief obstacle to their reform, the chief thing that has stood in the way of making them amenable to opinion, controllable by independent opposition, is the reverence with which we have come to regard them. By binding us together at moments of crisis they have won our affectionate fealty. Because the Republican party "saved the Union," a whole generation went by, in many parts of the country, before men who had acted with it in a time of crisis could believe it possible for any "gentleman" or patriot to break away from it or oppose it, whatever its policy and however remote from anything it had originally professed or undertaken. Because the Democratic party had stood for state rights and a power freely dispersed among the people, because it had tried to avoid war and preserve the old harmony of the sections, men of the same fervor of sympathy in other parts of the country deemed it equally incredible that any man of breeding or of principle could turn his back upon it or act with any other political organization. The feeling lasted until lines of party division became equally fixed and artificial. But with changing generations feelings change. We are coming now to look upon our parties once more as instruments for progressive action, as means for handling the affairs of a new age. Sentimental reminiscence is less dominant over us. We are ready to study new uses for our parties and to adapt them to new standards and principles.

The principle of change, if change there is to be, should spring out of this question: Have we had enough of the literal translation of Whig theory into practice, into constitutions? Are we ready to make our legislatures and our executives our real bodies politic, instead of our parties? If we are, we must think less of checks and balances and more of coördinated power, less of separation of functions and more of the synthesis of action. If we are, we must decrease the number and complexity of the things the voter is called upon to do; concentrate his attention upon a few men whom he can make responsible, a few objects upon which he can easily centre his purpose; make parties his instruments and not his masters by an utter simplification of the things he is expected to look to.

Every test of principle or of program returns to our original conception of constitutional government. Every study of party must turn about our purpose to have real representative institutions. Constitutional government can be vital only when it is refreshed at every turn of affairs by a new and cordial and easily attained understanding between those who govern and those who are governed. It can be maintained only by genuine common counsel; and genuine common counsel can be obtained only by genuine representative institutions. A people who know their minds and can get real representatives to express them are a self-governed people, the practised masters of constitutional government.

"Wanted—A Party"*

A man must nowadays either belong to a party through mere force of habit, or else be puzzled to know what party he belongs to. Party platforms furnish no sort of chart by which he can shape his political course. Unless they are carefully labelled, be cannot tell which party speaks through them, for they all say much the same thing. If voters chose their party instead of happening into it, they would probably choose by the aid of two questions, namely, first, "What policy do we favor?" and, second, "Which party advocates that policy?" Perhaps it is fortunate, therefore, that so many drift to the ballot-box and so few choose; for, otherwise, multitudes would lose their votes before answering the second of these questions. They would practically disfranchise themselves if they waited to answer it. The professions of existing parties do not furnish any satisfactory reply to it; still less do their actions. Does any one favor civil service reform? The present act establishing competitive examinations and a commission was proposed by a democratic senator to a republican senate, was passed by that body and a democratic house, and signed by a republican president. The senator who proposed it was afterward cast aside by his constituency because of his reform sentiments. His measure is now administered, with full sympathy for its purposes, by a democratic president elected because of his record on this question; but it is covertly attacked in a democratic house, and openly sneered at in a republican senate; and the democratic chairman of the house committee on civil service reform fails of a renomination in North Carolina because of his fine reform work on that committee. Which party, then, advocates civil service reform?

Or turn to the question of federal aid to education in the states. Does some voter favor such aid? It was proposed in the senate by a republican, fathered in the house by a democrat, carried in the senate by a complex mixture of republican

---

* "Wanted,—A Party," *Boston Times*, September 26, 1886, p. 7. (Editor's note).

and democratic votes, and smothered in the house by no one knows whom. Is it the democrats or the republicans that would have national aid to education in the states?

Or, again, is it the tariff that is crucial? Does some new manufacturer in the South want the import duties kept up? Let him examine the record of proceedings in congress. Democratic revenue reformers are kept from even so much as introducing a bill by the opposition of democratic protectionists, and republicans assist both sides. Is the protectionist voter to be a democrat or a republican?

Is the silver question to be made a test? Each party is on both sides. Or labor problems? Which party is on any side with regard to that, except the side of profession which will catch the laborer's vote?

But why extend the perplexing recital? It is sadly confounding to think about so much confusion. And, be it observed, I am not speaking of these things in ridicule of our national parties, or in disgust with our national politics, nor yet in despair of our national institutions. I am simply gathering facts to serve as food for reflection, and in order to state what my own reflections upon them have been. My chief reflection has been, not that our national parties are in a state of disintegration; that is not a reflection. It is a mere patent fact. But that such a course of things is tending, so to say, to *individualize* our politics is a reflection, and one which seems worth exploring somewhat at large.

First, let me explain what I mean by the individualizing of our politics. I mean simply that the voter who exercises any choice at all, is being obliged to choose *men*, particular individuals, to tie to, instead of parties. Of course the conscientious voter always chose between men, between candidates, in voting; but formerly he could choose them as representing parties. Now he must choose them instead of parties. The feeling is: "No party means what it says; some men do seem to mean what they say; we will tie to them when we can." The last presidential election of course furnishes the most striking illustration of the operation of this feeling. The mugwump is the man who has cast loose from parties, which don't mean what they say, and offers to follow men who do speak with a purpose. Mr Cleveland is a democrat. But he was not elected because he was a democrat, but because the civil service of the country needed reforming, and he evidently meant to reform it, if given a chance. A man of that sort in the presidential chair would be worth any number of party platforms; a great number of discriminating voters accordingly followed him in preference to any party,—"irrespective of party," to use the orthodox phrase.

Mr. Cleveland's case was only a conspicuous one, however; it was not isolated. There is a yearly increasing number of mayors, governors, and congressmen holding their offices because of personal qualities or opinions pleasing to constituencies who do not stop to ask, in choosing them, whether the parties they formally represent possess like qualities or opinions.

Various reasons, historical and others, might be offered to explain this interesting but necessarily transitional state of affairs; as, for instance, that the republican party has outlived the purposes for which it was organized, and that the democratic party has ceased to be opposed to it in most matters, except in a Pickwickian sense. The republican party rendered the country some inestimable services, and the country, in natural gratitude, pensioned it with a quarter of a century of power. Meantime, the democratic party kicked its heels with what philosophy it could command on the cold outside of the offices, comforting itself with dignified repetitions of certain old and important constitutional principles which had all of a sudden apparently lost their old power as charms to conjure with. But the republican pension has run out now. It could not reasonably be claimed for a second generation. The pensioners, too, got intolerable as they grew old. We, accordingly, have a president who is a democrat in favor of civil service reform, and a congress which is nothing in particular and in favor of nothing unanimously, save large expenditures of money. The old parties, to put it in the vernacular, have "played out," and we are choosing here a man and there a man who means what he says, while waiting for a party which shall mean what *it* says.

The new parties which are hoped for in the future do not form readily or quickly for the same reason that the old parties have not adapted themselves to changed circumstances. Our system of government has supplied no official place, no place of actual authority, for leaders of parties. A party, consequently, must be a merely fortuitous concourse of atoms; and we must wait on the atoms. Even after it is formed, any party of ours must keep together rather by grace and enthusiasm than by vital organization. There is no ruling station in the government for its leaders. It must follow them rather for what they eloquently profess than for anything that they can actually do. The most leader-like post in politics is the speakership of the house of representatives, which is the most unsuitable place possible for a party captain. If we did not have a natural talent for forming parties, and it were not the fashion in all popular governments to have parties, it is to be seriously doubted whether we would not approximate that "natural society," of which some philosophers and some anarchists have dreamed, in which everybody would act for himself and nobody act, except accidentally, or through chance amiability, in concert with his neighbors.

There is, however, another and a better reason why we always have parties, and that is, that we have a splendid habit of all believing in certain great principles of human liberty and self-government, without being tamely all of one mind about the way in which those principles ought to be applied in particular cases. No time was ever bigger than this with unsolved problems as to the best ways in which to make liberty real and government helpful. Labor questions, financial questions, administrative questions must all tax the best thought of the country from this time on, until some clear purpose of reform, of financial reconstruction, or of governmental betterment is conceived by some group of men who mean what they say, who all mean the same thing, and who know how to say it, begin to speak their purpose, so that the nation will wake as at a new voice—a voice which calls with authority to duty and to action. Then a new party will be formed—and another party opposed to it. All that is wanting is a new, genuine and really meant purpose held by a few strong men of principle and boldness. That is a big "all," and it is still conspicuously wanting.

But the generations that really loved the old and now disintegrated parties is fast passing away. It is largely the new generation that wonders that any one ever doubted that the war was over—even sometimes wonders what the war was all about—that is compelling a clearing away of the worn-out formulas of the old dispensation and a hastening of something not stated to determine their politics. With the growth of this new generation we shall unquestionably witness the growth of new parties.

Part IV
Political and Administrative Leadership

"Leaders of Men"*

Those only are leaders of men, in the general eye, who lead in action. The title belongs, if the whole field of the world be justly viewed, no more rightfully to the men who lead in action than to those who lead in silent thought. A book is often quite as quickening a trumpet as any made of brass and sounded in the field. But it is the estimate of the world that bestows their meaning upon words: and that estimate is not often very far from the fact. The men who act stand nearer to the mass of men than do the men who write; and it is at their hands that new thought gets its translation into the crude language of deeds. The very crudity of that language of deeds exasperates the sensibilities of the author; and his exasperation proves the world's point—proves that, though he may be back of the leaders, he is not the leader. In his thought there was due and studied proportion; all limiting considerations were set in their right places as guards to ward off misapprehension. Every cadence of right utterance was made to sound in the careful phrases, in the perfect adjustments of sense. Just and measured reflection found full and fit expression. But when the thought is translated into action all its shadings disappear. It stands out a naked, lusty thing sure to rasp the sensibilities of every man of fastidious taste. Stripped for action, a thought must always shock those who cultivate the nicest fashions of literary dress, as authors do. But it is only when it thus stands forth in unabashed force that it can perform feats of strength in the arena round about which the great public sit as spectators, awarding the prizes by the suffrage of their applause.

Here, unquestionably, we come upon the heart of the perennial misunderstanding between the men who write and the men who act. The men who write love

---

* "Leaders of Men," in *Leaders of Men*, edited by T. H. Vail Motter (Princeton University Press, 1952); this address was originally delivered by Wilson on several occasions in 1889 and 1890. (Editor's note).

proportion, the men who act must strike out practicable lines of action and neglect proportion. This would seem sufficiently to explain the well-nigh universal repugnance felt by literary men towards democracy. The arguments which induce popular action must always be broad and obvious arguments: only a very gross substance of concrete conception can make any impression on the minds of the masses; they must get their ideas very absolutely put, and are much readier to receive a half-truth which they can understand than a whole truth which has too many sides to be seen all at once. How can any man whose method is the method of artistic completeness of thought and expression, whose mood is the mood of contemplation, for a moment understand or tolerate the majority whose purpose and practice it is to strike out broad, rough-hewn policies, whose mood is the mood of action? The great stream of freedom, which

"broadens down
from precedent to precedent,"

is not a clear mountain current such as the fastidious man of chastened thought likes to drink from: it is polluted with not a few of the coarse elements of the gross world on its banks; it is heavy with the drainage of a very material universe.

One of the nicest tests of the repugnance felt by the literary nature for the sort of leadership and action which commends itself to the world of common men may be applied by asking some author of careful, studious thought to utter his ideas to a mass-meeting from a platform occupied by representative citizens. He shrinks from it as he would shrink from being publicly dissected! Even to hear someone else, given to apt public speech, reproduce his thoughts in a way to make them acceptable to an audience is often a mild, sometimes an acute, form of torture for him. If the world would really know his thoughts for what they are, let them go to his written words, con his phrases, join paragraph with paragraph, chapter with chapter: then, the whole form and fashion of his conceptions impressed upon their minds, they will know him as no platform speaker could make him known. Of course such preferences greatly limit his audience: not many out of the great multitudes who crowd about him buy his books. But, if the few who can understand, read and are convinced, will not his thoughts finally leaven the mass?

The true leader of men is equipped by lacking certain sensibilities which the literary man, when analyzed, is found to have as a chief part of his make-up. He lacks that subtle power of sympathy that enables the men who write the great works of the imagination to put their minds under the spell of a thousand motives not their own but the living force in those whom they interpret. He could not write fiction. He could not conceive *The Ring and the Book*—the impersonation of a half score points of view. An imaginative realization of other natures and minds than his own is as impossible for him, as his own commanding, dominating frame of mind and character are impossible for the sensitive seer whose imagination can give life to a thousand characters. Mr. Browning could no more be a statesman—

if statesmen are to be popular leaders also—than Mr. Disraeli could write a novel. Mr. Browning can see from everybody's point of view—no intellectual sympathy comes amiss to him: Mr. Disraeli can see from no point of view but his own—and the characters he put in those works of his which were meant to be novels move as puppets to his will, as the men he governed did. They are his mouthpieces—as little like themselves as were the Tory squires in the Commons like themselves after they became his chess-men.

One of the most interesting and suggestive criticisms made upon Mr. Gladstone's leadership during the life of his ministries was that he was not decisive in the House of Commons as Palmerston and Peel had been before him. He could not help seeing two sides of a question: the force of objections evidently told upon him, and his conclusions seemed the result of a nice balance of considerations, not the commands of an unhesitating conviction. A party likes to be led by very absolute opinions: it chills it to hear it admitted that there is some reason on the other side. Mr. Peel saw both sides of some questions; but he never saw them both at once. He saw now one, and afterwards, by slow, honest conversion, the others. Mr. Gladstone's transparent honesty adds to his moral weight with the people as a leader of opposition, for in opposition only the whole attitude is significant. Particulars of position and policy tell upon a governing party, on the other hand, and for them the consistency of unhesitating opinion counts as an element of success and prestige.

That the leader of men must have such sympathetic insight as shall enable him to know quite unerringly the motives which move other men in the mass is of course self-evident; but this insight which he must have is not the Shakespearean insight. It need not pierce the particular secrets of individual men: it need only know what it is that lies waiting to be stirred in the minds and purposes of groups and masses of men. Besides it is not a sympathy that serves, but is a sympathy whose power is to command, to command by knowing its instrument. The seer, whose function is imaginative interpretation, is the man of science; the leader is the mechanic. The chemist knows his materials interpretatively: he can make subtlest analysis of all their affinities, of all their antipathies; can give you the point of view of every gas or metal or liquid with regard to every other liquid or gas or metal; he can marry, he can divorce, he can destroy them. He could suppose fictitious cases with regard to the conduct of the elements which would appear most clever and probable to other chemists: would appear witty and credible, doubtless, to the elements themselves, could they know. But the mining-engineer's point of view is very different. He, too, must know chemical properties, but only in order that he may use them—only in order to have the right sort of explosion at the right place. So, too, the mechanic's point of view must be quite different from that of the physicist. He must know what his tools can do and what they will stand; but he must be something more than interpreter of their qualities—and something quite different. "It is the general opinion of locomotive superintendents that it is not essential that the men who run locomotives should be good mechanics. Brunel, the distinguished civil engineer, said that he never would trust himself to run a locomotive because he was sure to think of some problem relating to his profession which would distract his attention from the engine. It is probably a similar reason which unfits good mechanics for being good locomotive runners."[1]

Imagine Thackeray leading the House of Commons, or Mr. Lowell on the stump! How comically would their very genius defeat them! The special gift of these two men is a critical understanding of other men, their fallible fellow-creatures. How could their keen humorous sense of what was transpiring in the breasts of their followers and fellow-partisans be held back from banter? How could they take the mass seriously—themselves refrain from laughter and also from the temptation of provoking it? Thackeray argue patiently and respectfully with a dense country member, equipped with nothing but diverting scruples and laughable prejudices? Impossible. As well ask a biologist to treat a cat or a rabbit as if it were a pet with no admirable machinery inside to tempt the dissecting knife.

The competent leader of men cares little for the interior niceties of other people's characters: he cares much—everything for the external uses to which they may be put. His will seeks the lines of least resistance; but the whole question with him is a question as to the application of force. There are men to be moved: how shall he move them? He supplies the power; others supply only the materials upon which that power operates. The power will fail if it be misapplied; it will be misapplied if it be not suitable both in its character and in its method to the nature of the materials upon which it is spent; but that nature is, after all, only its means. It is the power which dictates, dominates; the materials yield. Men are as clay in the hands of the consummate leader.

It often happens that the leader displays a sagacity and an insight in the handling of men in the mass which quite baffle the wits of the shrewdest analyst of individual character. Men in the mass differ from men as individuals. A man who knows, and keenly knows, every man in town may yet fail to understand a mob or a mass-meeting of his fellow-townsmen. Just as the whole tone and method suitable for a public speech are foreign to the tone and method proper in individual, face to face dealings with separate men, so is the art of leading different from the art of writing novels.

Some of the gifts and qualities which most commend the literary man to success would inevitably doom the would-be leader to failure. One could wish no better proof and example of this than is furnished by the career of that most notable of great Irishmen, Edmund Burke. Everyone knows that Burke's life was spent in Parliament, and everyone knows that the eloquence he poured forth there is as deathless as our literature; and yet everyone is left to wonder that he was of so little consequence in the actual direction of affairs. How noble a figure in the

---

[1] *Scribner's Magazine*, vol. IV, p. 192. "American Locomotives and Cars."

history of English politics: how large a man, how commanding a mind; and yet how ineffectual in the work of bringing men to turn their faces as he would have them, toward the high purposes he had ever in view. We hear with astonishment that after the delivery of that consummate speech on the Nabob of Arcot's debts, which everybody has read, Pitt and Grenville easily agree that they need not trouble themselves to make any reply. His speech on conciliation with America is not only wise beyond precedent in the annals of debate but marches with a force of phrase which, it would seen must have been irresistible—and yet we know that it emptied the House of all audience. You remember what Goldsmith playfully suggested for Burke's epitaph:

> "Here lies our good Edmund, whose genius was such,
> We scarcely can praise it, or blame it, too much;
> Who, too deep for his hearers, still went on refining,
> And thought of convincing while they thought of dining:
> Though equal to all things, for all things unfit,
> Too nice for a statesman, too proud for a wit;
> For a patriot too cool; for a drudge disobedient,
> And too fond of the right to pursue the expedient.
> In short, 'twas his fate, unemploy'd, or in place, sir,
> To eat mutton cold, and cut blocks with a razor."

Certainly this is too small a measure for so big a man, as Goldsmith himself would have been the first to admit; but the description is almost as true as it is clever. It is better to read Burke than to have heard him; and the thoughts which miscarried in the parliaments of George III have had their triumphs in parliaments of a later day—have established themselves at the heart of such policies as are liberalizing the world. His power was literary, not forensic; he was no leader of men; he was an organizer of thought, but not of party victories. "Burke is a wise man," said Fox, "but he is wise too soon." He was wise also too much. He went on from the wisdom of to-day to the wisdom of to-morrow, to the wisdom which is for all time: and it was impossible he should be followed so far. Men want the wisdom which they are expected to apply to be obvious and conveniently limited in amount. They want a thoroughly reliable article, with very simple adjustments and manifest present uses. Elaborate it—increase the expenditure of thought necessary to obtain it—and they will decline to listen to any propositions concerning it. You must keep it in stock for the use of the next generation.

Men are not led by being told what they don't know. Persuasion is a force, but not information; and persuasion is accomplished by creeping into the confidence of those you would lead. Their confidence is gained by qualities which they can recognize, by arguments which they can assimilate: by the things which find easy entrance into their minds and are easily transmitted to the palms of their hands or the ends of their walking-sticks in the shape of applause. Burke's thoughts penetrate the mind and possess the heart of the quiet student; his style of saying things fills the attention as if it were finest music; but they are not thoughts to be shouted over; it is not a style to ravish the ear of the voter at the hustings. If you would be a leader of men, you must lead your own generation, not the next. Your playing must be good now, while the play is on the boards and the audience in the seats: it will not get you the repute of a great actor to have excellences discovered in you afterwards. Burke's genius made conservative men uneasy. How could a man be safe who had so many ideas?

Englishmen of the present generation wonder that England should have been ruled once by John Addington, a man about whom nothing was accentuated but his dullness; by Mr. Perceval, a sort of Tory squire without blood or any irregularity; by Lord Castlereagh, whose speaking was so bad as to drive his hearers to assume that there must be some great purpose lurking behind its amorphous masses somewhere simply because it was inconceivable that there should be in it so little purpose as it revealed. Accustomed to the persistent power of Gladstone, the epigrammatic variety of Disraeli, the piquant indiscretions of Salisbury, they naturally marvel that they could have been interested enough in such men to heed or follow them. But after all the Englishman has not changed. He still prefers Northcote to more exciting financiers; still listens to a mild young Scotchman acquiescently touching weighty Irish affairs; still thinks Lord Hartington, who cannot speak with point safer than Sir Vernon Harcourt who can; still has a sneaking liking for prosy Mr. W. H. Smith, the successful newsvender, and a sneaking distrust of successful men of thought like Mr. John Morley. He is made as uncomfortable and as indignant by the vagaries of Lord Randolph Churchill as he once was, in times he has forgotten, by the equally bumptious young Disraeli. The story is told of a thoroughgoing old country Tory of the time when Pitt was displaced by Addington that, going to tell a friend of the formation of a new ministry by that excellent mediocrity, he repeated with unction the whole list of commonplace men who were to constitute the new Government, and then, rubbing his hands in demonstrative satisfaction, exclaimed, "Well, thank God, we have at last got a ministry without one of those confounded men of genius in it!" Cobden was doubtless right when he said that "the only way in which the soul of a great nation can be stirred, is by appealing to its sympathies with a true principle in its unalloyed simplicity," and that it was "necessary for the concentration of a people's mind that an individual should become the incarnation of a principle"; but the emphasis must be laid on the "unalloyed simplicity" of the principle. It will not do to incarnate too many ideas at a time if you are to be universally understood and numerously followed.

Cobden himself is an excellent case in point. Embodying the true principle of unhampered commerce "in its unalloyed simplicity," he became a power in England second to none. Never before he mounted the platform had England so steadily yielded to argument, so completely thawed under persuasion. Cobden was singularly equipped for leadership—especially for leadership of this practical, business-like kind. He had nothing in him of the literary mind, which conceives images and is dominated by associations: he conceived only facts, and was dominated by programs of reform. Going to Greece, he found Ilissus and Cephissus, the famed streams of Attica, ridiculous rivulets and wondered that the world should pause so often to study such Lilliputian states as classical Hellas contained when there were the politics of the United States and the vast rivers and mountains of the new continents to think about. "What famous puffers those old Greeks were!" he exclaims.

He journeyed to Egypt and sat beside Mehemet Ali, one of the fiercest warriors and most accomplished tyrants of our century, with an eye open to the fact that the royal viceroy was a somewhat fat personage who fell into blunders when he boasted of the cotton crops of the land he had under his heel; seeing also that his conductor and introducer, Col. C., had hit upon the wrong resource in beginning the conversation by a reference to the excellent weather in a latitude "where uninterrupted sunshine prevails for seven years together." Nothing in means of travel, in the manners and resources of the countries he visited, or in the remarks of the people he met upon practical matters escaped him. He is in Constantinople, and notes that Mr. Perkins, whoever he may have been, "is opposed to the belief in the regeneration of the Turk." His diary chronicles, under date at Malta, that Waghorn said that the English admirals were all too old and that that accounted for the service being less efficient than formerly. He keeps the world of practical details under constant cross-examination. And when, in later days, the great anti-corn-law League is in the heat of its task of reforming the English tariff, how seriously this earnest man takes the vast fairs, the colossal bazaars and all the other homely, bourgeois machinery by means of which the League keeps itself supplied at once with funds for its work and with that large measure of popular attention necessary to its success. This is the organizer! who is incapable of being fatigued by the commonplace—or amused by it—and who is thoroughly in love with working at a single idea.

Mark the simplicity and directness of the arguments and ideas of such men. The motives which they urge are elemental; the morality which they seek to enforce is large and obvious; the policy they emphasize, purged of all subtlety. They give you the fine gold of truth in the nugget, not cunningly beaten into elaborate shapes and chased with intricate patterns. "If oratory were a business and not an art," says Mr. Justin McCarthy, "then it might be contended reasonably enough that Mr. Cobden was one of the greatest orators England has ever known. Nothing could exceed the persuasiveness of his style. His manner was simple, sweet and earnest. It persuaded by convincing. It was transparently sincere." In a word, its simplicity and clearness gave it entrance into the minds of his auditors, its sincerity into their hearts.

But we see the same things in the oratory of Bright, with whom oratory was not a business but an art. Hear him appeal to his constituents in Birmingham, that capital of the spirit of gain, touching what he deemed an iniquitous foreign policy:

> "I believe," he exclaims, "there is no permanent greatness in a nation except it be based upon morality. I do not care for military greatness or military renown. I care for the condition of the people among whom I live. There is no man in England who is less likely to speak irreverently of the Crown and Monarchy of England than I am; but crowns, coronets, mitres, military display, the pomp of war, wide colonies, and a huge empire, are, in my view, all trifles light as air, and not worth considering, unless with them you can have a fair share of comfort, contentment, and happiness among the great body of the people. Palaces, baronial castles, great halls, stately mansions, do not make a nation. The nation in every country dwells in the cottage; and unless the light of your constitution can shine there, unless the beauty of your legislation and the excellence of your statesmanship are impressed there on the feelings and conditions of the people, rely upon it you have yet to learn the duties of government....
>
> "You can mould opinion, you can create political power—you cannot think a good thought on this subject and communicate it to your neighbours— you cannot make these points topics of discussion in your social circles and more general meetings, without affecting sensibly and speedily the course which the Government of your country will pursue. May I ask you, then, to believe, as I do most devoutly believe, that the moral law was not written for men alone in their individual character, but that it was written as well for nations, and for nations great as this of which we are citizens. If nations reject and deride that moral law, there is a penalty which will inevitably follow. It may not come at once, it may not come in our lifetime; but, rely upon it, the great Italian poet is not a poet only, but a prophet, when he says—
>
> 'The sword of heaven is not in haste to smite,
> Nor yet doth linger.'
>
> We have experience, we have beacons, we have landmarks enough. We know what the past has cost us, we know how much and how far we have wandered, but we are not left without a guide. It is true we have not, as an ancient people had, Urim and Thummim—those oraculous gems on Aaron's breast—from which to take counsel, but we have the unchangeable and eternal principles of the moral law to guide us, and only so far as we walk by that guidance can we be permanently a great nation, or our people a happy people."

How simple, how evident it all is—how commonplace the motives appealed to—how old the moral maxim—how obvious every consideration urged! And yet how effective such a passage is—how it carries!—what a thrill of life and of power there is in it. As simple as the quiet argument of Cobden, though more alight with passionate feeling. As direct and unpretentious as a bit of conversation, though elevated above the level of conversation by a sweep of accumulating phrase such as may be made effectual for the throwing down of strongholds.

Style has of course a great deal to do with such effects in popular oratory. Armies do not win battles by sword-fencing, but by the fierce cut of the sabre, the direct volley of musketry, the straightforward argument of artillery, the impetuous dash of cavalry. And it is in the same way that oratorical battles are won: not by the nice refinements of statement, the deft sword-play of dialectic fence, but by the straight and speedy thrusts of speech sent through and through the gross and obvious frame of a subject. It must be clear and always clear what the sentences would be about. They must be advanced with the firm tread of disciplined march. Their meaning must be clear and loud.

There is much also in physical gifts, as everybody knows. The popular orator should be satisfying to the eye and to the ear: broad, sturdy, clear-eyed, musically voiced, like John Bright; built with the stature and mien of a Norse god, like Webster; towering, imperious, persuading by voice and carriage, like Clay; or vast, rugged, fulminating, like O'Connell, fit for a Celtic Olympus.

It is easy to call a man like Daniel O'Connell a demagogue, but it is juster to see in him a born leader of men. We remember him as the agitator, simple, loud, incessant, a bit turbulent, not a little coarse also, full of flouts and jibes, bitter and abusive, in headlong pursuit of the aims of Irish liberty. We ought to remember him as the ardent supporter of every policy that made for English and for human liberty also, a friend of reform when reform was unpopular, a champion of oppressed classes who had almost no one else to speak for them, a battler for what was liberal and enlightened and against what was unfair and prejudiced, all along the line. He was no courter of popularity: but his heart was the heart of his people: their cause and their hopes were his. He was not their slave, nor were they his dupes. He was their mouthpiece. And what a mouth-piece! Nature seems to have planned him for utterance. His figure and influence loom truly grand as we look back to him standing, as he so often did, before concourses mustered, scores of thousands strong, upon the open heath to hear and to protest of Ireland's wrongs.

> "His Titan strength must touch what gave it birth;
> Hear him to mobs, and on his mother earth!"

Here is the testimony of one who saw one of those immeasurable assemblies stand round about the giant Celt and saw the Master wield his spell:

> "Methought no clarion could have sent its sound
> Even to the centre of the hosts around;
> And as I thought rose the sonorous swell,
> As from some church-tower swings the silvery bell.

Aloft and clear, from airy tide to tide,
It glided, easy as a bird may glide;
To the last verge of that vast audience sent,
It play'd with each wild passion as it went;
Now stirred the uproar, now the murmur still'd,
And sobs or laughter answer'd as it will'd.
Then did I know what spells of infinite choice,
To rouse or lull, has the sweet human voice;
Then did I seem to seize the sudden clue
To the grand troublous Life Antique—to view
Under the rock-stand of Demosthenes,
Mutable Athens heave her noisy seas."

This huge organization, this thrilling voice, ringing out clear and effectual over vast multitudes were, it would seem, too big, too voluminous for Parliament. There no channels offered which were broad and free enough to give effective course to the crude force of the man. The gross and obvious force of him shocked sensitive, slow, and decorous men, not accustomed to having sense served up to them with a shout. The open heath was needed to contain O'Connell. But even in Parliament where the decorum and reserve of debate offered him no effective play, his honesty, his ardor for liberty, his good humour, his transparent genuineness won for O'Connell at last almost his due meed of respect. The qualities that made him irresistible with the people won him regard, if not influence, with the people's representatives.

The whole question of leadership receives a sharp practical test in a popular legislative assembly. The revolutions which have changed the whole principle and method of government within the last hundred years have created a new kind of leadership in legislation: a leadership which is not yet, perhaps, fully understood. It used to be thought that legislation was an affair proper to be conducted only by the few who were instructed for the benefit of the many who were uninstructed: that statesmanship was a function of origination for which only trained and instructed men were fit. Those who actually conducted legislation and undertook affairs were rather whimsically chosen by Fortune to illustrate this theory, but such was the ruling thought in politics. The Sovereignty of the People, however, that great modern principle of politics, has erected a different conception—or, if so be that, in the slowness of our thought, we hang on to the old conception, has created a very different practice. When we are angry with public men nowadays we charge them with subserving instead of forming and directing public opinion. It is to be suspected that when we make such charges we are suffering our standards of judgment to lag behind our politics. When an Englishman declares that Mr. Gladstone is truckling to public opinion in his Irish policy, he surely cannot expect us to despise Mr. Gladstone on that account, even if the declaration be true, inasmuch as it is now quite indisputably the last part of the Nineteenth Century, and the nineteenth is a century, we know, which has established the principle that public opinion must be truckled to (if you will use a disagreeable word) in the conduct of government. A man, surely, would not fish for votes (if that be what Mr. Gladstone is doing) among the minority—particularly if he be in his eightieth year and in need of getting the votes at once if he is to get them at all. He must believe, at any rate, that he is throwing his bait among the majority. And it is a dignified proposition with us—is it not?—that as is the majority, so ought the government to be.

Pray do not misunderstand me. I am not radical. I would not for the world be instrumental in discrediting the ancient and honorable pastime of abusing demagogues. Demagogues were quite evidently, it seems to me, meant for abuse, if we are to argue by exclusion: for assuredly they were never known to serve any other useful purpose. I will follow the hounds any day in pursuit of one of the wily, doubling rascals, however rough the country to be ridden over! But you must allow me to make my condemnations tally with my theory of government. Is Irish opinion ripe for Home Rule, as the Liberals claim? Very well then: let them have Home Rule. Every community, says my political philosophy, should be governed for its own interests, not for the satisfaction of any other community.

Still I seem radical, without in reality being so. I advance my explanation, therefore, another step. Society is not a crowd, but an organism; and, like every organism, it must grow as a whole or else be deformed. The world is agreed, too, that it is an organism also in this, that it will die unless it be vital in every part. That is the only line of reasoning by which we can really establish the majority in legitimate authority. This organic whole, Society, is made up, obviously, for the most part, of the majority. It grows by the development of its aptitudes and desires, and under their guidance. The evolution of its institutions must take place by slow modification and nice all-round adjustment. And all this is but a careful and abstract way of saying that no reform may succeed for which the major thought of the nation is not prepared: that the instructed few may not be safe leaders, except in so far as they have communicated their instruction to the many, except in so far as they have transmuted their thought into a common, a popular thought.

Let us fairly distinguish, therefore, the peculiar and delicate duties of the popular leader from the not very peculiar or delicate crimes of the demagogue. Leadership, for the statesman, is interpretation. He must read the common thought: he must test and calculate very circumspectly the preparation of the nation for the next move in the progress of politics. If he fairly hit the popular thought, when we have missed it, are we to say that he is a demagogue? The nice point is to distinguish the firm and progressive popular thought from the momentary and whimsical popular mood, the transitory or mistaken popular passion. But it is fatally easy to blame or misunderstand the statesman. Our temperament is one of logic, let us say. We hold that one and one make two and we see no salvation for the people except they receive the truth. The statesman is of another opinion. One and one doubtless make two, he is ready to admit, but the people think that one and one make more than two and until they see otherwise we shall have to legislate on that supposition. This is not to talk nonsense. The Roman augurs very soon discovered that sacred fowls drank water and pecked grain with no sage intent of prophecy, but from motives quite mundane and simple. But it would have been a revolution to say so and act so in the face of a people who believed otherwise, and executive policy had to proceed on the theory of a divine method of fowl digestion. The divinity that once did hedge a king, grows—not now very high about the latest Hohenzollern—not so high but that one may see that he is a bumptious young gentleman slenderly equipped with wisdom or discretion. But who that prefers growth to revolution would propose that legislation in Germany proceed independently of this hereditary accident?

In no case may we safely hurry the organism away from its habit: for it is held together by that habit, and by it is enabled to perform its functions completely. The constituent habit of a people inheres in its thought, and to that thought legislation—even the legislation that advances and modifies habit—must keep very near. The ear of the leader must ring with the voices of the people. He cannot be of the school of the prophets; he must be of the number of those who studiously serve the slow-paced daily need.

In what, then, does political leadership consist? It is leadership in conduct, and leadership in conduct must discern and strengthen the tendencies that make for development. The legislative leader must perceive the direction of the nation's permanent forces and must feel the speed of their operation. There is initiative here, but not novelty; there are old thoughts, but a progressive application of them. There is such initiative as we may conceive the man part of the mythical centaur to have exercised. Doubtless the centaur acted not as a man, but as a horse would act, the head conceiving only such things as were possible for the performance of its lower and nether, equine, parts. He never dared to climb where hoofs could gain no sure foothold: and he knew that there were four feet, not two, to be provided with standing-room. There must have been the caper of the beast in all his schemes. He would have had as much respect for a blacksmith as for a haberdasher. He must have had the standards of the stable rather than the standards of the drawing-room. The headship of the mind over the body is a like headship for all of us; it is observant of possibility and of physical environment.

The inventing mind is impatient of such restraints: the aspiring soul has at all times longed to be loosed from the body. But such are the conditions of organic life. If the body is to be put off, dissolution must be endured. As the conceiving mind is tenant of the body, so is the conceiving legislator tenant of that greater body, Society. Practical leadership may not beckon to the slow masses of men from beyond some dim, unexplored space or some intervening chasm: it must daily feel the road that leads to the goal proposed, knowing that it is a slow, a very slow, evolution to wings, and that for the present, and for a very long future also, Society must walk, dependent upon practicable paths, incapable of scaling sudden, precipitous heights, a road-breaker, not a fowl of the air. In the words of the Master, Burke, "to follow, not to force, the public inclination—to give a direction, a form, a technical dress, and a specific sanction, to the general sense of the community, is the true end of legislation." That general sense of the community may wait to be aroused, and the statesman must arouse it; may be inchoate and vague, and the statesman must formulate and make it explicit. But he cannot, and should not, do more. The forces of the public thought may be blind: he must lend them sight; they may blunder: he must set them right. He can do something to create such forces of opinion; but it is a creation of forms, not of substance, and without such forces at his back he can do nothing effective.

This function of interpretation, this careful exclusion of individual origination it is that makes it difficult for the impatient original mind to distinguish the popular statesman from the demagogue. The demagogue sees and seeks self-interest in an acquiescent reading of that part of the public thought upon which he depends for votes; the statesman, also reading the common inclination, also, when he reads aright, obtains the votes that keep him in power. But if you will justly observe the two, you will find the one trimming to the inclinations of the moment, the other obedient to the permanent purposes of the public mind. The one adjusts his sails to the breeze of the day; the other makes his plans to ripen with the slow progress of the years. While the one solicitously watches the capricious changes of the weather, the other diligently sows the grains in their seasons. The one ministers to himself, the other to the race.

To the literary temperament leadership in both kinds is impossible. The literary mind conceives images, images rounded, perfect, ideal; unlimited, unvaried by accident. It craves outlooks. It handles such stuff as dreams are made of. It is not guided by principles, as statesmen conceive principles, but by conceptions. Principles, as statesmen conceive them, are threads to the labyrinth of circumstances; principles, as the literary mind holds them, are unities. Throw the conceiving mind, habituated to contemplating wholes, into the arena of politics, and it seems to itself to be standing upon shifting sands, where no sure foothold and no upright posture are possible. Its ideals are to it more real and solid than any actuality of the world in which men are managed.

The late Mr. Matthew Arnold was wont now and again to furnish excellent illustration of these points. In the presence of the acute political crisis in Ireland, he urged that no radical remedy be undertaken, except the very radical remedy of changing the characters of the English people. What was needed was not Home Rule for Ireland but a sounder home conscience and less Philistinism in England. "Wait," he said, in effect, "don't legislate. Let me talk to these middle classes a little more, and then, without radical measures of relief, they will treat Ireland in the true human spirit." Doubtless he was right. When America was discontented, and, because of the resistance by England of Home Rule, began to clamour for home sovereignty, the truest remedy would have been, not revolution, but the enlightenment of the English people. But the process of enlightenment was slow; the injustice was pressing: and revolution came on apace. Unquestionably culture is the best cure for anarchy; but anarchy is swifter than her adversary. Culture lags behind the practicable remedy.

There is a familiar anecdote that belongs just here. The captain of a Mississippi steamboat had made fast to the shore because of a thick fog lying upon the river. The fog lay low and dense upon the surface of the water, but overhead all was clear. A cloudless sky showed a thousand points of starry light. An impatient passenger inquired the cause of the delay. "We can't see to steer," said the captain. "But all's clear overhead," suggested the passenger, "you can see the North Star." "Yes," replied the officer, "but we are not going that way." Politics must follow the actual windings of the channel of the river: if it steer by the stars it will run aground.

You may say that if all this be truth: if practical political thought may not run in straight lines, but must twist and turn through all the sinuous paths of various circumstance, then compromise is the true gospel of politics. I cannot wholly gainsay the proposition. But it depends almost altogether upon how you conceive and define compromise whether it seem hateful or not—whether it be hateful or not. I understand the biologists to say that all growth is a process of compromise: a compromise of the vital forces within the organism with the physical forces without, which constitute its environment. Yet growth is not dishonest. Neither need compromise in politics be dishonest—if only it be progressive. Is not compromise the law of Society in all things? Do we not in all dealings adjust views, compound differences, placate antagonisms? Uncompromising thought is the luxury of the closeted recluse. Untrammelled reasoning is the indulgence of the philosopher, of the dreamer of sweet dreams. We make always a sharp distinction between the literature of conduct and the literature of the imagination. "Poetic justice" we recognize as being quite out of the common run of experience.

Nevertheless, leadership does not always wear the harness of compromise. Once and again one of those great Influences which we call a Cause arises in the midst of the nation. Men of strenuous minds and high ideals come forward with a sort of gentle majesty as champions of a political or moral principle. They wear no armour; they bestride no chargers; they only speak their thought, in season and out of season. But the attacks they sustain are more cruel than the collisions of arms. Their souls are pierced with a thousand keen arrows of obloquy. Friends desert and despise them. They stand alone: and oftentimes are made bitter by their isolation. They are doing nothing less than defy public opinion, and shall they convert it by blows? Yes, presently the forces of the popular thought hesitate, waver, seem to doubt their power to subdue a half score stubborn minds. Again a little while and they have yielded. Masses come over to the side of the reform. Resistance is left to the minority and such as will not be converted are crushed.

What has happened? Has it been given to a handful of men to revolutionize by the foolishness of preaching the whole thought of a nation and of an epoch? By no means. None but Christian doctrine was ever permitted to dig entirely new channels for human thought, and turn that thought quickly about from its old courses; and even Christianity came only "in the fullness of time" and has had a triumph as slow-paced as history itself.

No cause is born out of its time. Every successful reform movement has had as its efficient cry some principle of equity or morality already accepted well-nigh universally, but not yet universally applied in the affairs of life. Every such movement has been the awakening of a people to see a new field for old principles. These men who stood alone at the inception of the movement and whose voices then seemed as it were the voices of men crying in the wilderness, have in reality been simply the more sensitive organs of Society—the parts first awakened to consciousness of a situation. With the start and irritation of a rude and sudden summons from sleep, Society resents the disturbance of its restful unconsciousness, and for a moment racks itself with hasty passion. But, once get it completely aroused, it will sanely meet the necessities of conduct revealed by the hour of its awakening.

Great reformers do not, indeed, observe times and circumstances. Theirs is not a service of opportunity. They have no thought for occasion, no capacity for compromise. But they are none the less produced by occasions. They are early vehicles of the Spirit of the Age. They are born of the very times that oppose them: their success is the acknowledgment of their legitimacy. For how many centuries had the world heard single, isolated voices summoning it to religious toleration before that toleration became inevitable, because not to have had it would have been an anomaly, an anachronism. It was postponed till it should fit into the world's whole system—and only in this latter time did its advocates become leaders. Did not Protestantism come first to Germany, which had already unconsciously drifted very far away from Rome? Did not parliamentary reform come in England only as the tardy completion of tendencies long established and long drilled for success? Were not the Corn Laws repealed because they were a belated remnant of an effete system of economy and politics? Did not the abolition of slavery come just in the nick of time to restore to a system already sorely deranged the symmetry and wholeness of its original plan? In every case what took place was the destruction of an anomaly, the wiping out of an anachronism. Does not every historian of insight perceive the timeliness of these reforms? Is it not the judgment of history that they were the products of a period, that there was laid upon their originators, not the gift of creation, but in a superior degree the gift of insight, the spirit of their age? It was theirs to hear the inarticulate voices that stir in the night-watches, apprising the lonely sentinel of what the day will bring forth.

Turn to religious leaders, and similar principles will be found to govern their rise and influence. Of course among religious leaders there is one type which stands out above all the rest, catching the eye of the world. This is the type to which Bernard of Clairvaux, Calvin, and Savonarola belong. Of course Bernard was no Protestant reformer, as Calvin was, and Savonarola played the part towards the Church neither of Calvin nor of Bernard. But I do not now speak of ecclesiastical reform; I speak simply of leadership. There is one transcendent feature in which these three men are alike. Each spoke to his generation of righteousness and judgment to come. Each withstood men because of their sins, and each himself dominated because of eloquence and purity and personal force.

Perhaps there is no beauty in any career that may justly be compared with the beauty which was wrought into the life of the saintly abbot of Clairvaux, the man who, without self-assertion, was yet raised to rule, first over his fellows in the Church, afterwards once and again over kings and in the affairs of nations, because he feared God but not man, because he loved righteousness and hated the wrong. When caught in the entanglements of fierce international disputes, men called to quiet Clairvaux for help, and there came out of the cloister a man simple in mien and habit, simple also in life and purpose, but bearing upon his sweet, grave face a stamp of godly courage that sent to the heart of the haughtiest among men a thrill of awe; a man, regarding his fellow-men with a calm gaze that nevertheless glowed with a clear perception of the truth that held the proudest in check. Pride and self-will broke against the spirit of this quiet man as if they were the mist and he the rock. He stood in the midst of his generation a master, a living rebuke to sin, a lively inspiration to good.

There is much less of grace, but there is no less of power in the figure of Savonarola, the pale, burning man who substituted a pulpit for the throne of the Medici, who made the dimly lighted church where were to be heard the Oracles of God the only centre of power. How excellent, and how terrible, is the force of the man, lashing Florence into obedience with the quick whips of his almost inspired utterances! And then there is Calvin, ruler and priest of Geneva: how singular and how elevated is the place such men hold among the greater figures and forces of history! Theirs, it would seem, was a leadership of rebuke. With how stern a menace did they apprise men of their sins and constrain them to their duty. Their sceptre was a scourge of small whips; their words purified as with flame; they were supreme by reason of the spirit that was in them.

And yet it does not seem to me that even these men escape from the analysis which must be made of all leadership. I have said that no man thinking thoughts born out of time can succeed in leading his generation, and that successful leadership is a product of sympathy, not of antagonism. I do not believe that any man can lead who does not act, whether it be consciously or unconsciously, under the impulse of a profound sympathy with those whom he leads—a sympathy which is insight—an insight which is of the heart rather than of the intellect. The law unto every such leader as these whom we now have in mind is the law of love. In the face of Savonarola, marked and hollowed as it is by the fierce flames of his nature, solemn, sombre, cast in the moulds of anxious fear rather than in the moulds of hope, is nevertheless to be seen a mask for an inward beauty of tenderness. The sensitiveness of a woman lurks in the stern features, not to be identified with any one of them, and yet not to be overlooked. In Calvin, too, love is the sanction of justice. And in Bernard it is love that reigns, not enmity towards his fellow-men. Such men incarnate the consciences of the men whom they rule. They compel obedience, not so much by reason of fear as by reason of their infallible analysis of character. Men know that they speak justice, and obey by instinct. By methods which would infallibly alienate individuals they master multitudes, and that is their indisputable title to be named leaders of men.

It is a long cry from Savonarola and Calvin to Voltaire, but it is to Voltaire that I at this point find it convenient to resort for illustration and comment. The transition is the more abrupt because I cannot claim leadership for Voltaire in any of the senses to which I have limited the word. But there are literary men, nevertheless, who fail of being leaders only for the lack of initiative in action; who have the thought, but not the executive parts of leaders; whose minds, if we may put it so, contain all the materials for leadership, but whose wills spend their force, not upon men, but upon paper. Standing, as they do, half way between the men who act and the men who merely think and imagine, they may very neatly serve our present purpose, of differentiating leaders from the quieter race of those who content themselves with thought. And of this class Voltaire was a perfect type.

Our slow world spends its time catching up with the ideas of its best minds. It would seem that in almost every generation men are born who embody the projected consciousness of their time and people. Their thought runs forward apace into the regions whither the race is advancing, but where it will not for many a weary day arrive. A few generations, and that point, thus early descried, is passed; the new thoughts of one age are the commonplaces of the next. Such is the literary function: it reads the present fragments of thought as completed wholes, and thus enables the fragments, no doubt, in due time to achieve their completion. There are, on the other hand, again, other periods which we call periods of critical thought; and these do not project their ideas as wholes, but speak them incomplete, as parts. Whoever can hit the latent conceptions of such a period will receive immediate recognition: he is simply the articulate utterance of itself.

Such a man, of such fortune, was Voltaire. No important distinction can be drawn between his mind and the mind of France in the period in which he lived — except, no doubt, that the mind of France was diffused, Voltaire's concentrated. It was an Englishman, doubtless, who said he would like to slap Voltaire's face, for then he could feel that he had given France the affront direct. I suppose we cannot imagine how happy it must have made a Frenchman of the last century to laugh with Voltaire. His hits are indeed palpable: no literary swordsman but must applaud them. The speed of his style, too, and the swift critical destructiveness of it are in the highest degree exhilarating and admirable. It is capital sport to ride a tilt with him against some belated superstition, to see him unseat priest and courtier alike in his dashing overthrow of shams. But for us it is not vital sport. The things that he killed are now long dead; the things he found it impossible to slay, still triumph over all opponents — are grown old in conquest. But for a Frenchman of the last century the thing was being done. To read Voltaire must have made him feel that he was reading his own thoughts; laughing his own laugh; speaking his own scorn; speeding his own present impulses. Voltaire shocked political and ecclesiastical magnates, but he rejoiced the general mind of

France. The men whom he attacked felt at once and instinctively that this was not the premonitory flash from a distant storm, but a bolt from short range; that the danger was immediate, the need for the cover of authority an instantaneous need. No wonder the people of Paris took the horses from Voltaire's coach and themselves dragged him through the streets; the load ought to have been light, as light as the carriage, for they were pulling themselves. The old man inside was presently to die, and carry away with him the spirit of the Eighteenth Century. If Voltaire seriously doubted the existence of a future life, we have no grounds for wonder. It is hard to think of him in any world but this. It is awkward to conceive the Eighteenth Century given a place in either of the realms of eternity. It would chill the one; it would surely liberalize the other. That singular century does not seem to belong in the line of succession to any immortality.

Men who hit the critical, floating thought of their age, seem to me leaders in all but initiative. They are not ahead of their age. They do not conceive its thoughts in future wholes: they snatch it in its present parts. They gather to a head each characteristic sentiment of their day. They are listened to; they would be followed, if they would but lead.

There are some qualities of the mind of Thomas Carlyle which seem to place him in this class. To speak of him is to go a good part of the way back to the great preachers of whom I have spoken. Carlyle was the apostle of a vague sort of lay religion, as imperative as Calvinism, though less provocative of organization—a religion with a sanction but without a hierarchy. He was not all preacher. He was something less than a prophet, and yet something more than a Jeremiah. He throbbed as much as a Scotch peasant could with the pulses of the Nineteenth Century. He was hotly moved by its forces; he felt with a keenness which reached the pitch of suffering the puissant influences abroad in his day. He withstood them, it is true; he would have beaten many of them back with denunciations; but there is a deep significance in his fierce longing for action, in his keen desire to lead. It is noteworthy that there is no wholeness in his thought, as in most products of the literary mind there would be; its parts are *disjecta membra*. His ideas are flashes brought forth by his hot contact with the forces of thought active about him. With almost inarticulate fervour he seems once and again to break forth with the very spirit of our century on his lips.

It would of course be absurd to compare Carlyle with Voltaire, the spiritual man with the intellectual; and yet it seems to me that Carlyle is as representative of the spiritual aspects of our own century as Voltaire was of all the mental aspects of his own very different age. Incoherent and impossible in his proposition of measures, sadly needing interpretation to the common mind even in his utterance of the thoughts brought to him out of his century, eager often to revert to old standards of action, a figure rugged, amorphous, needing to be explained, he was yet the voice of his own age, not a prophet of the next. In his writings are thrown up, as if by a convulsion of nature, the hidden things of the modern mind. Those who lead may well look and learn. His mind is a sub-soil plow and in its furrows may crops be sown.

If there were no other quality which marked the absence of any practical gift of leadership in Carlyle, his fierce impatience would be sufficient evidence. The dynamics of leadership lie in persuasion, and persuasion is never impatient. "You are poor fishers of men," it has been said of a certain class of preachers; "you do not go fishing with a rod and a line, and with the patient sagacity of the true sportsman. You use a telegraph pole and a cable: with these you savagely beat the water and bid men bite or be damned. And you expect they will be caught!"

What a lesson it is in the organic wholeness of Society, this study of leadership! How subtle and delicate is the growth of the organism, and how difficult initiative in it! Where is rashness? It is excluded. And raw invention? It is discredited. How, as we look about us into the great maze of Society, see its solidarity, its complexity, its restless forces surging amidst its delicate tissues, its hazards and its exalted hopes—how can we but be filled with awe! Many are the functions that enter into its quick unresting life. There is the lonely seer, seeking the truths that shall stand permanent and endure; the poet, tracing all perfected lines of beauty, sounding full-voiced all notes of love or hope, of duty or gladness; the toilers in the world's massy stuffs, moulders of metals, forgers of steel, refiners of gold; there are the winds of commerce, the errors and despairs of war; the old things and the new: the vast things that dominate and the small things that constitute the world; passions of men, loves of women; the things that are visible and which pass away and the things which are invisible and eternal. And in the midst of all stands the leader, gathering, as best he can, the thoughts that are completed—that are perceived—that have told upon the common mind; judging also of the work that is now at length ready to be completed; reckoning the gathered gain; perceiving the fruits of toil and of war—and combining all these into words of progress, into acts of recognition and completion. Who shall say that this is not an exalted function? Who shall doubt or dispraise the title of leadership?

Shall we wonder, either, if the leader be a man open at all points to all men, ready to break into coarse laughter with the Rabelaisian vulgar; ready also to prose with the moralist and the reformer; with an eye of tolerance and shrewd appreciation for life of every mode and degree; a sort of sensitive dial registering all forces that move upon the face of Society? I do not conceive the leader a trimmer, weak to yield what clamour claims, but the deeply human man, quick to know and to do the things that the hour and his nation need.

"The Study of Administration"*

I suppose that no practical science is ever studied where there is no need to know it. The very fact, therefore, that the eminently practical science of administration is finding its way into college courses in this country would prove that this country needs to know more about administration, were such proof of the fact required to make out a case. It need not be said, how ever, that we do not look into college programmes for proof of this fact. It is a thing almost taken for granted among us, that the present movement called civil service reform must, after the accomplishment of its first purpose, expand into efforts to improve, not the *personnel* only, but also the organization and methods of our government offices: because it is plain that their organization and methods need improvement only less than their *personnel*. It is the object of administrative study to discover, first, what government can properly and successfully do, and, secondly, how it can do these proper things with the utmost possible efficiency and at the least possible cost either of money or of energy. On both these points there is obviously much need of light among us; and only careful study can supply that light.

Before entering on that study, however, it is needful:

1. To take some account of what others have done in the same line; that is to say, of the history of the study.
2. To ascertain just what is its subject-matter.
3. To determine just what are the best methods by which to develop it, and the most clarifying political conceptions to carry with us into it.

Unless we know and settle these things, we shall set out without chart or compass.

* "The Study of Administration," *Political Science Quarterly II* (July 1887): 197–222. (Editor's note).

I.

The science of administration is the latest fruit of that study of the science of politics which was begun some twenty-two hundred years ago. It is a birth of our own century, almost of our own generation.

Why was it so late in coming? Why did it wait till this too busy century of ours to demand attention for itself? Administration is the most obvious part of government; it is government in action; it is the executive, the operative, the most visible side of government, and is of course as old as government itself. It is government in action, and one might very naturally expect to find that government in action had arrested the attention and provoked the scrutiny of writers of politics very early in the history of systematic thought.

But such was not the case. No one wrote systematically of administration as a branch of the science of government until the present century had passed its first youth and had begun to put forth its characteristic flower of systematic knowledge. Up to our own day all the political writers whom we now read had thought, argued, dogmatized only about the *constitution* of government; about the nature of the state, the essence and seat of sovereignty, popular power and kingly prerogative; about the greatest meanings lying at the heart of government, and the high ends set before the purpose of government by man's nature and man's aims. The central field of controversy was that great field of theory in which monarchy rode tilt against democracy, in which oligarchy would have built for itself strongholds of privilege, and in which tyranny sought opportunity to make good its claim to receive submission from all competitors. Amidst this high warfare of principles, administration could command no pause for its own consideration. The question was always: Who shall make law, and what shall that law be? The other question, how law should be administered with enlightenment, with equity, with speed, and without friction, was put aside as "practical detail" which clerks could arrange after doctors had agreed upon principles.

That political philosophy took this direction was of course no accident, no chance preference or perverse whim of political philosophers. The philosophy of any time is, as Hegel says, "nothing but the spirit of that time expressed in abstract thought"; and political philosophy, like philosophy of every other kind, has only held up the mirror to contemporary affairs. The trouble in early times was almost altogether about the constitution of government; and consequently that was what engrossed men's thoughts. There was little or no trouble about administration,—at least little that was heeded by administrators. The functions of government were simple, because life itself was simple. Government went about imperatively and compelled men, without thought of consulting their wishes. There was no complex system of public revenues and public debts to puzzle financiers; there were, consequently, no financiers to be puzzled. No one who possessed power was long at a loss how to use it. The great and only question was: Who shall possess it? Populations were of manageable numbers; property was of simple sorts. There were plenty of farms, but no stocks and bonds: more cattle than vested interests.

I have said that all this was true of "early times"; but it was substantially true also of comparatively late times. One does not have to look back of the last century for the beginnings of the present complexities of trade and perplexities of commercial speculation, nor for the portentous birth of national debts. Good Queen Bess, doubtless, thought that the monopolies of the sixteenth century were hard enough to handle without burning her hands; but they are not remembered in the presence of the giant monopolies of the nineteenth century. When Blackstone lamented that corporations had no bodies to be kicked and no souls to be damned, he was anticipating the proper time for such regrets by full a century. The perennial discords between master and workmen which now so often disturb industrial society began before the Black Death and the Statute of Laborers; but never before our own day did they assume such ominous proportions as they wear now. In brief, if difficulties of governmental action are to be seen gathering in other centuries, they are to be seen culminating in our own.

This is the reason why administrative tasks have nowadays to be so studiously and systematically adjusted to carefully tested standards of policy, the reason why we are having now what we never had before, a science of administration. The weightier debates of constitutional principle are even yet by no means concluded; but they are no longer of more immediate practical moment than questions of administration. It is getting to be harder to *run* a constitution than to frame one.

Here is Mr. Bagehot's graphic, whimsical way of depicting the difference between the old and the new in administration:

> In early times, when a despot wishes to govern a distant province, he sends down a satrap on a grand horse, and other people on little horses; and very little is heard of the satrap again unless he send back some of the little people to tell what he has been doing. No great labour of superintendence is possible. Common rumour and casual report are the sources of intelligence. If it seems certain that the province is in a bad state, satrap No. 1 is recalled, and satrap No. 2 sent out in his stead. In civilized countries the process is different. You erect a bureau in the province you want to govern; you make it write letters and copy letters; it sends home eight reports *per diem* to the head bureau in St. Petersburg. Nobody does a sum in the province without some one doing the same sum in the capital, to "check" him, and see that he does it correctly. The consequence of this is, to throw on the heads of departments an amount of reading and labour which can only be accomplished by the greatest natural aptitude, the most efficient training, the most firm and regular industry.[1]

There is scarcely a single duty of government which was once simple which is not now complex; government once had but a few masters; it now has scores of

[1] Essay on William Pitt.

masters. Majorities formerly only underwent government; they now conduct government. Where government once might follow the whims of a court, it must now follow the views of a nation.

And those views are steadily widening to new conceptions of state duty; so that, at the same time that the functions of government are every day becoming more complex and difficult, they are also vastly multiplying in number. Administration is everywhere putting its hands to new undertakings. The utility, cheapness, and success of the government's postal service, for instance, point towards the early establishment of governmental control of the telegraph system. Or, even if our government is not to follow the lead of the governments of Europe in buying or building both telegraph and railroad lines, no one can doubt that in some way it must make itself master of masterful corporations. The creation of national commissioners of railroads, in addition to the older state commissions, involves a very important and delicate extension of administrative functions. Whatever hold of authority state or federal governments are to take upon corporations, there must follow cares and responsibilities which will require not a little wisdom, knowledge, and experience. Such things must be studied in order to be well done. And these, as I have said, are only a few of the doors which are being opened to offices of government. The idea of the state and the consequent ideal of its duty are undergoing noteworthy change; and "the idea of the state is the conscience of administration." Seeing every day new things which the state ought to do, the next thing is to see clearly how it ought to do them.

This is why there should be a science of administration which shall seek to straighten the paths of government, to make its business less unbusinesslike, to strengthen and purify its organization, and to crown its duties with dutifulness. This is one reason why there is such a science.

But where has this science grown up? Surely not on this side the sea. Not much impartial scientific method is to be discerned in our administrative practices. The poisonous atmosphere of city government, the crooked secrets of state administration, the confusion, sinecurism, and corruption ever and again discovered in the bureaux at Washington forbid us to believe that any clear conceptions of what constitutes good administration are as yet very widely current in the United States. No; American writers have hitherto taken no very important part in the advancement of this science. It has found its doctors in Europe. It is not of our making; it is a foreign science, speaking very little of the language of English or American principle. It employs only foreign tongues; it utters none but what are to our minds alien ideas. Its aims, its examples, its conditions, are almost exclusively grounded in the histories of foreign races, in the precedents of foreign systems, in the lessons of foreign revolutions. It has been developed by French and German professors, and is consequently in all parts adapted to the needs of a compact state, and made to fit highly centralized forms of government; whereas, to answer our purposes, it must be adapted, not to a simple and compact, but to a complex and multiform state, and made to fit highly decentralized forms of government. If we would employ it, we must Americanize it, and that not formally, in language merely, but radically, in thought, principle, and aim as well. It must learn our constitutions by heart; must get the bureaucratic fever out of its veins; must inhale much free American air.

If an explanation be sought why a science manifestly so susceptible of being made useful to all governments alike should have received attention first in Europe, where government has long been a monopoly, rather than in England or the United States, where government has long been a common franchise, the reason will doubtless be found to be twofold: first, that in Europe, just because government was independent of popular assent, there was more governing to be done; and, second, that the desire to keep government a monopoly made the monopolists interested in discovering the least irritating means of governing. They were, besides, few enough to adopt means promptly.

It will be instructive to look into this matter a little more closely. In speaking of European governments I do not, of course, include England. She has not refused to change with the times. She has simply tempered the severity of the transition from a polity of aristocratic privilege to a system of democratic power by slow measures of constitutional reform which, without preventing revolution, has confined it to paths of peace. But the countries of the continent for a long time desperately struggled against all change, and would have diverted revolution by softening the asperities of absolute government. They sought so to perfect their machinery as to destroy all wearing friction, so to sweeten their methods with consideration for the interests of the governed as to placate all hindering hatred, and so assiduously and opportunely to offer their aid to all classes of undertakings as to render themselves indispensable to the industrious. They did at last give the people constitutions and the franchise; but even after that they obtained leave to continue despotic by becoming paternal. They made themselves too efficient to be dispensed with, too smoothly operative to be noticed, too enlightened to be inconsiderately questioned, too benevolent to be suspected, too powerful to be coped with. All this has required study; and they have closely studied it.

On this side the sea we, the while, had known no great difficulties of government. With a new country, in which there was room and remunerative employment for everybody, with liberal principles of government and unlimited skill in practical politics, we were long exempted from the need of being anxiously careful about plans and methods of administration. We have naturally been slow to see the use or significance of those many volumes of learned research and painstaking examination into the ways and means of conducting government which the presses of Europe have been sending to our libraries. Like a lusty child, government with us has expanded in nature and grown great in stature, but has also become awkward in movement. The vigor and increase of its life has been altogether out of proportion to its skill in living. It has gained strength, but it has not acquired deportment. Great, therefore, as has been our advantage over the countries of Europe in point of ease and health of constitutional development, now that the time for more careful administrative adjustments and larger administrative knowledge has come to us, we are at a signal disadvantage as compared with the transatlantic nations; and this for reasons which I shall try to make clear.

Judging by the constitutional histories of the chief nations of the modern world, there may be said to be three periods of growth through which government has passed in all the most highly developed of existing systems, and through which it promises to pass in all the rest. The first of these periods is that of absolute rulers, and of an administrative system adapted to absolute rule; the second is that in which constitutions are framed to do away with absolute rulers and substitute popular control, and in which administration is neglected for these higher concerns; and the third is that in which the sovereign people undertake to develop administration under this new constitution which has brought them into power.

Those governments are now in the lead in administrative practice which had rulers still absolute but also enlightened when those modern days of political illumination came in which it was made evident to all but the blind that governors are properly only the servants of the governed. In such governments administration has been organized to subserve the general weal with the simplicity and effectiveness vouchsafed only to the undertakings of a single will.

Such was the case in Prussia, for instance, where administration has been most studied and most nearly perfected. Frederic the Great, stern and masterful as was his rule, still sincerely professed to regard himself as only the chief servant of the state, to consider his great office a public trust; and it was he who, building upon the foundations laid by his father, began to organize the public service of Prussia as in very earnest a service of the public. His no less absolute successor, Frederic William III, under the inspiration of Stein, again, in his turn, advanced the work still further, planning many of the broader structural features which give firmness and form to Prussian administration to-day. Almost the whole of the admirable system has been developed by kingly initiative.

Of similar origin was the practice, if not the plan, of modern French administration, with its symmetrical divisions of territory and its orderly gradations of office. The days of the Revolution—of the Constituent Assembly—were days of constitution-*writing*, but they can hardly be called days of constitution-*making*. The Revolution heralded a period of constitutional development,—the entrance of France upon the second of those periods which I have enumerated,—but it did not itself inaugurate such a period. It interrupted and unsettled absolutism, but did not destroy it. Napoleon succeeded the monarchs of France, to exercise a power as unrestricted as they had ever possessed.

The recasting of French administration by Napoleon is, therefore, my second example of the perfecting of civil machinery by the single will of an absolute ruler before the dawn of a constitutional era. No corporate, popular will could ever have effected arrangements such as those which Napoleon commanded. Arrangements so simple at the expense of local prejudice, so logical in their indifference to popular choice, might be decreed by a Constituent Assembly, but could be established only by the unlimited authority of a despot. The system of the year VIII was ruthlessly thorough and heartlessly perfect. It was, besides, in large part, a return to the despotism that had been overthrown.

Among those nations, on the other hand, which entered upon a season of constitution-making and popular reform before administration had received the impress of liberal principle, administrative improvement has been tardy and half-done. Once a nation has embarked in the business of manufacturing constitutions, it finds it exceedingly difficult to close out that business and open for the public a bureau of skilled, economical administration. There seems to be no end to the tinkering of constitutions. Your ordinary constitution will last you hardly ten years without repairs or additions; and the time for administrative detail comes late.

Here, of course, our examples are England and our own country. In the days of the Angevin kings, before constitutional life had taken root in the Great Charter, legal and administrative reforms began to proceed with sense and vigor under the impulse of Henry II's shrewd, busy, pushing, indomitable spirit and purpose; and kingly initiative seemed destined in England, as elsewhere, to shape governmental growth at its will. But impulsive, errant Richard and weak, despicable John were not the men to carry out such schemes as their father's. Administrative development gave place in their reigns to Constitutional struggles; and Parliament became king before any English monarch had had the practical genius or the enlightened conscience to devise just and lasting forms for the civil service of the state.

The English race, consequently, has long and successfully studied the art of curbing executive power to the constant neglect of the art of perfecting executive methods. It has exercised itself much more in controlling than in energizing government. It has been more concerned to render government just and moderate than to make it facile, well-ordered and effective. English and American political history has been a history, not of administrative development, but of legislative oversight,—not of progress in governmental organization, but of advance in law-making and political criticism. Consequently, we have reached a time when administrative study and creation are imperatively necessary to the well-being of our governments saddled with the habits of a long period of constitution-making. That period has practically closed, so far as the establishment of essential principles is concerned, but we cannot shake off its atmosphere. We go on criticizing when we ought to be creating. We have reached the third of the periods I have mentioned,—the period, namely, when the people have to develop administration in accordance with the Constitutions they won for themselves in a previous period of struggle with absolute power; but we are not prepared for the tasks of the new period.

Such an explanation seems to afford the only escape from blank astonishment at the fact that, in spite of our vast advantages in point of political liberty, and above all in point of practical political skill and sagacity, so many nations are ahead of us in administrative organization and administrative skill. Why, for instance, have we but just begun purifying a civil service which was rotten full fifty years ago? To say that slavery diverted us is but to repeat what I have said—that flaws in our constitution delayed us.

Of course all reasonable preference would declare for this English and American course of politics rather than for that of any European country. We should not like to have had Prussia's history for the sake of having Prussia's administrative skill; and Prussia's particular system of administration would quite suffocate us. It is better to be untrained and free than to be servile and systematic. Still there is no denying that it would be better yet to be both free in spirit and proficient in practice. It is this even more reasonable preference which impels us to discover what there may be to hinder or delay us in naturalizing this much-to-be-desired science of administration.

What, then, is there to prevent?

Well, principally, popular sovereignty. It is harder for democracy to organize administration than for monarchy. The very completeness of our most cherished political successes in the past embarrasses us. We have enthroned public opinion; and it is forbidden us to hope during its reign for any quick schooling of the sovereign in executive expertness or in the conditions of perfect functional balance in government. The very fact that we have realized popular rule in its fulness has made the task of *organizing* that rule just so much the more difficult. In order to make any advance at all we must instruct and persuade a multitudinous monarch called public opinion,—a much less feasible undertaking than to influence a single monarch called a king. An individual sovereign will adopt a simple plan and carry it out directly: he will have but one opinion, and he will embody that one opinion in one command. But this other sovereign, the people, will have a score of differing opinions. They can agree upon nothing simple: advance must be made through compromise, by a compounding of differences, by a trimming of plans and a suppression of too straightforward principles. There will be a succession of resolves running through a course of years, a dropping fire of commands running through a whole gamut of modifications.

In government, as in virtue, the hardest of hard things is to make progress. Formerly the reason for this was that the single person who was sovereign was generally either selfish, ignorant, timid, or a fool,—albeit there was now and again one who was wise. Nowadays the reason is that the many, the people, who are sovereign have no single ear which one can approach, and are selfish, ignorant, timid, stubborn, or foolish with the selfishness, the ignorances, the stubbornnesses, the timidities, or the follies of several thousand persons,—albeit there are hundreds who are wise. Once the advantage of the reformer was that the sovereign's mind had a definite locality, that it was contained in one man's head, and that consequently it could be gotten at; though it was his disadvantage that that mind learned only reluctantly or only in small quantities, or was under the influence of some one who let it learn only the wrong things. Now, on the contrary, the reformer is bewildered by the fact that the sovereign's mind has no definite locality, but is contained in a voting majority of several million heads; and embarrassed by the fact that the mind of this sovereign also is under the influence of favorites, who are none the less favorites in a good old-fashioned sense of the word because they are not persons but preconceived opinions; *i.e.*, prejudices which are not to be reasoned with because they are not the children of reason.

Wherever regard for public opinion is a first principle of government, practical reform must be slow and all reform must be full of compromises. For wherever public opinion exists it must rule. This is now an axiom half the world over, and will presently come to be believed even in Russia. Whoever would effect a change in a modern constitutional government must first educate his fellow-citizens to want *some* change. That done, he must persuade them to want the particular change he wants. He must first make public opinion willing to listen and then see to it that it listen to the right things. He must stir it up to search for an opinion, and then manage to put the right opinion in its way.

The first step is not less difficult than the second. With opinions, possession is more than nine points of the law. It is next to impossible to dislodge them. Institutions which one generation regards as only a makeshift approximation to the realization of a principle, the next generation honors as the nearest possible approximation to that principle, and the next worships as the principle itself. It takes scarcely three generations for the apotheosis. The grandson accepts his grandfather's hesitating experiment as an integral part of the fixed constitution of nature.

Even if we had clear insight into all the political past, and could form out of perfectly instructed heads a few steady, infallible, placidly wise maxims of government into which all sound political doctrine would be ultimately resolvable, *would the country act on them*? That is the question. The bulk of mankind is rigidly unphilosophical, and nowadays the bulk of mankind votes. A truth must become not only plain but also commonplace before it will be seen by the people who go to their work very early in the morning; and not to act upon it must involve great and pinching inconveniences before these same people will make up their minds to act upon it.

And where is this unphilosophical bulk of mankind more multifarious in its composition than in the United States? To know the public mind of this country, one must know the mind, not of Americans of the older stocks only, but also of Irishmen, of Germans, of negroes. In order to get a footing for new doctrine, one must influence minds cast in every mould of race, minds inheriting every bias of environment, warped by the histories of a score of different nations, warmed or chilled, closed or expanded by almost every climate of the globe.

So much, then, for the history of the study of administration, and the peculiarly difficult conditions under which, entering upon it when we do, we must undertake it. What, now, is the subject-matter of this study, and what are its characteristic objects?

II.

The field of administration is a field of business. It is removed from the hurry and strife of politics; it at most points stands apart even from the debatable ground of constitutional study. It is a part of political life only as the methods of the counting-house are a part of the life of society; only as machinery is part of the manufactured product. But it is, at the same time, raised very far above the dull level of mere technical detail by the fact that through its greater principles it is directly connected with the lasting maxims of political wisdom, the permanent truths of political progress.

The object of administrative study is to rescue executive methods from the confusion and costliness of empirical experiment and set them upon foundations laid deep in stable principle.

It is for this reason that we must regard civil-service reform in its present stages as but a prelude to a fuller administrative reform. We are now rectifying methods of appointment; we must go on to adjust executive functions more fitly and to prescribe better methods of executive organization and action. Civil-service reform is thus but a moral preparation for what is to follow. It is clearing the moral atmosphere of official life by establishing the sanctity of public office as a public trust, and, by making the service unpartisan, it is opening the way for making it businesslike. By sweetening its motives it is rendering it capable of improving its methods of work.

Let me expand a little what I have said of the province of administration. Most important to be observed is the truth already so much and so fortunately insisted upon by our civil-service reformers; namely, that administration lies outside the proper sphere of *politics*. Administrative questions are not political questions. Although politics sets the tasks for administration, it should not be suffered to manipulate its offices.

This is distinction of high authority; eminent German writers insist upon it as of course. Bluntschli,[2] for instance, bids us separate administration alike from politics and from law. Politics, he says, is state activity "in things great and universal," while "administration, on the other hand," is "the activity of the state in individual and small things. Politics is thus the special province of the statesman, administration of the technical official." "Policy does nothing without the aid of administration"; but administration is not therefore politics. But we do not require German authority for this position; this discrimination between administration and politics is now, happily, too obvious to need further discussion.

There is another distinction which must be worked into all our conclusions, which, though but another side of that between administration and politics, is not quite so easy to keep sight of: I mean the distinction between *constitutional* and administrative questions, between those governmental adjustments which are es-

---

[2] [Johann K. Bluntschli,] Politik [als *Wissenschaft*], S[ection] 467.

sential to constitutional principle and those which are merely instrumental to the possibly changing purposes of a wisely adapting convenience.

One cannot easily make clear to every one just where administration resides in the various departments of any practicable government without entering upon particulars so numerous as to confuse and distinctions so minute as to distract. No lines of demarcation, setting apart administrative from non-administrative functions, can be run between this and that department of government without being run up hill and down dale, over dizzy heights of distinction and through dense jungles of statutory enactment, hither and thither around "ifs" and "buts," "whens" and "howevers," until they become altogether lost to the common eye not accustomed to this sort of surveying, and consequently not acquainted with the use of the theodolite of logical discernment. A great deal of administration goes about *incognito* to most of the world, being confounded now with political "management," and again with constitutional principle.

Perhaps this ease of confusion may explain such utterances as that of Niebuhr's: "Liberty," he says, "depends incomparably more upon administration than upon constitution." At first sight this appears to be largely true. Apparently facility in the actual exercise of liberty does depend more upon administrative arrangements than upon constitutional guarantees; although constitutional guarantees alone secure the existence of liberty. But—upon second thought—is even so much as this true? Liberty no more consists in easy functional movement than intelligence consists in the ease and vigor with which the limbs of a strong man move. The principles that rule within the man, or the constitution, are the vital springs of liberty or servitude. Because independence and subjection are without chains, are lightened by every easy-working device of considerate, paternal government, they are not thereby transformed into liberty. Liberty cannot live apart from constitutional principle; and no administration, however perfect and liberal its methods, can give men more than a poor counterfeit of liberty if it rest upon illiberal principles of government.

A clear view of the difference between the province of constitutional law and the province of administrative function ought to leave no room for misconception; and it is possible to name some roughly definite criteria upon which such a view can be built. Public administration is detailed and systematic execution of public law. Every particular application of general law is an act of administration. The assessment and raising of taxes, for instance, the hanging of a criminal, the transportation and delivery of the mails, the equipment and recruiting of the army and navy, *etc.*, are all obviously acts of administration; but the general laws which direct these things to be done are as obviously outside of and above administration. The broad plans of governmental action are not administrative; the detailed execution of such plans is administrative. Constitutions, therefore, properly concern themselves only with those instrumentalities of government which are to control general law. Our federal constitution observes this principle in saying nothing of even the greatest of the purely executive offices, and speaking only of that President of the Union who was to share the legislative and policy-making functions of government, only of those judges of highest jurisdiction who were to interpret and guard its principles, and not of those who were merely to give utterance to them.

This is not quite the distinction between Will and answering Deed, because the administrator should have and does have a will of his own in the choice of means for accomplishing his work. He is not and ought not to be a mere passive instrument. The distinction is between general plans and special means.

There is, indeed, one point at which administrative studies trench on constitutional ground—or at least upon what seems constitutional ground. The study of administration, philosophically viewed, is closely connected with the study of the proper distribution of constitutional authority. To be efficient it must discover the simplest arrangements by which responsibility can be unmistakably fixed upon officials; the best way of dividing authority without hampering it, and responsibility without obscuring it. And this question of the distribution of authority, when taken into the sphere of the higher, the originating functions of government, is obviously a central constitutional question. If administrative study can discover the best principles upon which to base such distribution, it will have done constitutional study an invaluable service. Montesquieu did not, I am convinced, say the last word on this head.

To discover the best principle for the distribution of authority is of greater importance, possibly, under a democratic system, where officials serve many masters, than under others where they serve but a few. All sovereigns are suspicious of their servants, and the sovereign people is no exception to the rule; but how is its suspicion to be allayed by *knowledge*? If that suspicion could but be clarified into wise vigilance, it would be altogether salutary; if that vigilance could be aided by the unmistakable placing of responsibility, it would be altogether beneficent. Suspicion in itself is never healthful either in the private or in the public mind. *Trust is strength* in all relations of life; and, as it is the office of the constitutional reformer to create conditions of trustfulness, so it is the office of the administrative organizer to fit administration with conditions of clear-cut responsibility which shall insure trustworthiness.

And let me say that large powers and unhampered discretion seem to me the indispensable conditions of responsibility. Public attention must be easily directed, in each case of good or bad administration, to just the man deserving of praise or blame. There is no danger in power, if only it be not irresponsible. If it be divided, dealt out in shares to many, it is obscured; and if it be obscured, it is made irresponsible. But if it be centred in heads of the service and in heads of branches of the service, it is easily watched and brought to book. If to keep his office a man must achieve open and honest success, and if at the same time he feels himself intrusted with large freedom of discretion, the greater his power the less likely is he to abuse it, the more is he nerved and sobered and elevated by it. The less his power, the more safely obscure and unnoticed does he feel his position to be, and the more readily does he relapse into remissness.

Just here we manifestly emerge upon the field of that still larger question,—the proper relations between public opinion and administration.

To whom is official trustworthiness to be disclosed, and by whom is it to be rewarded? Is the official to look to the public for his meed of praise and his push of promotion, or only to his superior in office? Are the people to be called in to settle administrative discipline as they are called in to settle constitutional principles? These questions evidently find their root in what is undoubtedly the fundamental problem of this whole study. That problem is: What part shall public opinion take in the conduct of administration?

The right answer seems to be, that public opinion shall play the part of authoritative critic.

But the *method* by which its authority shall be made to tell? Our peculiar American difficulty in organizing administration is not the danger of losing liberty, but the danger of not being able or willing to separate its essentials from its accidents. Our success is made doubtful by that besetting error of ours, the error of trying to do too much by vote. Self-government does not consist in having a hand in everything, any more than housekeeping consists necessarily in cooking dinner with one's own hands. The cook must be trusted with a large discretion as to the management of the fires and the ovens.

In those countries in which public opinion has yet to be instructed in its privileges, yet to be accustomed to having its own way, this question as to the province of public opinion is much more readily soluble than in this country, where public opinion is wide awake and quite intent upon having its own way anyhow. It is pathetic to see a whole book written by a German professor of political science for the purpose of saying to his countrymen, "Please try to have an opinion about national affairs"; but a public which is so modest may at least be expected to be very docile and acquiescent in learning what things it has *not* a right to think and speak about imperatively. It may be sluggish, but it will not be meddlesome. It will submit to be instructed before it tries to instruct. Its political education will come before its political activity. In trying to instruct our own public opinion, we are dealing with a pupil apt to think itself quite sufficiently instructed beforehand.

The problem is to make public opinion efficient without suffering it to be meddlesome. Directly exercised, in the oversight of the daily details and in the choice of the daily means of government, public criticism is of course a clumsy nuisance, a rustic handling delicate machinery. But as superintending the greater forces of formative policy alike in politics and administration, public criticism is altogether safe and beneficent, altogether indispensable. Let administrative study find the best means for giving public criticism this control and for shutting it out from all other interference.

But is the whole duty of administrative study done when it has taught the people what sort of administration to desire and demand, and how to get what they demand? Ought it not to go on to drill candidates for the public service?

There is an admirable movement towards universal political education now afoot in this country. The time will soon come when no college of respectability can afford to do without a well-filled chair of political science. But the education thus imparted will go but a certain length. It will multiply the number of intelligent critics of government, but it will create no competent body of administrators. It will prepare the way for the development of a sure-footed understanding of the general principles of government, but it will not necessarily foster skill in conducting government. It is an education which will equip legislators, perhaps, but not executive officials. If we are to improve public opinion, which is the motive power of government, we must prepare better officials as the *apparatus* of government. If we are to put in new boilers and to mend the fires which drive our governmental machinery, we must not leave the old wheels and joints and valves and bands to creak and buzz and clatter on as best they may at bidding of the new force. We must put in new running parts wherever there is the least lack of strength or adjustment. It will be necessary to organize democracy by sending up to the competitive examinations for the civil service men definitely prepared for standing liberal tests as to technical knowledge. A technically schooled civil service will presently have become indispensable.

I know that a corps of civil servants prepared by a special schooling and drilled, after appointment, into a perfected organization, with appropriate hierarchy and characteristic discipline, seems to a great many very thoughtful persons to contain elements which might combine to make an offensive official class,— a distinct, semi-corporate body with sympathies divorced from those of a progressive, free-spirited people, and with hearts narrowed to the meanness of a bigoted officialism. Certainly such a class would be altogether hateful and harmful in the United States. Any measures calculated to produce it would for us be measures of reaction and of folly.

But to fear the creation of a domineering, illiberal officialism as a result of the studies I am here proposing is to miss altogether the principle upon which I wish most to insist. That principle is, that administration in the United States must be at all points sensitive to public opinion. A body of thoroughly trained officials serving during good behavior we must have in any case: that is a plain business necessity. But the apprehension that such a body will be anything un-American clears away the moment it is asked, What is to constitute good behavior? For that question obviously carries its own answer on its face. Steady, hearty allegiance to the policy of the government they serve will constitute good behavior. That *policy* will have no taint of officialism about it. It will not be the creation of permanent officials, but of statesmen whose responsibility to public opinion will be direct and inevitable. Bureaucracy can exist only where the whole service of the state is removed from the common political life of the people, its chiefs as well as its rank and file. Its motives, its objects, its policy, its standards, must be bureaucratic. It would be difficult to point out any examples of impudent exclusiveness and arbitrariness on the part of officials doing service under a chief of department who really served the people, as all our chiefs of departments must be made to do. It would be easy, on the other hand, to adduce other instances like that of the influence of Stein in Prussia, where the leadership of one statesman imbued with true public spirit transformed arrogant and perfunctory bureaux into public-spirited instruments of just government.

The ideal for us is a civil service cultured and self-sufficient enough to act with sense and vigor, and yet so intimately connected with the popular thought, by means of elections and constant public counsel, as to find arbitrariness of class spirit quite out of the question.

III.

Having thus viewed in some sort the subject-matter and the objects of this study of administration, what are we to conclude as to the methods best suited to it — the points of view most advantageous for it?

Government is so near us, so much a thing of our daily familiar handling, that we can with difficulty see the need of any philosophical study of it, or the exact point of such study, should it be undertaken. We have been on our feet too long to study now the art of walking. We are a practical people, made so apt, so adept in self-government by centuries of experimental drill that we are scarcely any longer capable of perceiving the awkwardness of the particular system we may be using, just because it is so easy for us to use any system. We do not study the art of governing: we govern. But mere unschooled genius for affairs will not save us from sad blunders in administration. Though democrats by long inheritance and re-peated choice, we are still rather crude democrats. Old as democracy is, its orga-nization on a basis of modern ideas and conditions is still an unaccomplished work. The democratic state has yet to be equipped for carrying those enormous burdens of administration which the needs of this industrial and trading age are so fast accumulating. Without comparative studies in government we cannot rid our-selves of the misconception that administration stands upon an essentially differ-ent basis in a democratic state from that on which it stands in a non-democratic state.

After such study we could grant democracy the sufficient honor of ultimately determining by debate all essential questions affecting the public weal, of basing all structures of policy upon the major will; but we would have found but one rule of good administration for all governments alike. So far as administrative func-tions are concerned, all governments have a strong structural likeness; more than that, if they are to be uniformly useful and efficient, they *must* have a strong struc-tural likeness. A free man has the same bodily organs, the same executive parts, as the slave, however different may be his motives, his services, his energies. Monarchies and democracies, radically different as they are in other respects, have in reality much the same business to look to.

It is abundantly safe nowadays to insist upon this actual likeness of all gov-ernments, because these are days when abuses of power are easily exposed and arrested, in countries like our own, by a bold, alert, inquisitive, detective public thought and a sturdy popular self-dependence such as never existed before. We are slow to appreciate this; but it is easy to appreciate it. Try to imagine personal government in the United States. It is like trying to imagine a national worship of Zeus. Our imaginations are too modern for the feat.

But, besides being safe, it is necessary to see that for all governments alike the legitimate ends of administration are the same, in order not to be frightened at the idea of looking into foreign systems of administration for instruction and suggestion; in order to get rid of the apprehension that we might perchance blindly borrow something incompatible with our principles. That man is blindly astray who denounces attempts to transplant foreign systems into this country. It is impossible: they simply would not grow here. But why should we not use such parts of foreign contrivances as we want, if they be in any way serviceable? We are in no danger of using them in a foreign way. We borrowed rice, but we do not eat it with chopsticks. We borrowed our whole political language from England, but we leave the words "king" and "lords" out of it. What did we ever originate, except the action of the federal government upon individuals and some of the functions of the federal supreme court?

We can borrow the science of administration with safety and profit if only we read all fundamental differences of condition into its essential tenets. We have only to filter it through our constitutions, only to put it over a slow fire of criticism and distil away its foreign gases.

I know that there is a sneaking fear in some conscientiously patriotic minds that studies of European systems might signalize some foreign methods as better than some American methods; and the fear is easily to be understood. But it would scarcely be avowed in just any company.

It is the more necessary to insist upon thus putting away all prejudices against looking anywhere in the world but at home for suggestions in this study, because nowhere else in the whole field of politics, it would seem, can we make use of the historical, comparative method more safely than in this province of administration. Perhaps the more novel the forms we study the better. We shall the sooner learn the peculiarities of our own methods. We can never learn either our own weaknesses or our own virtues by comparing ourselves with ourselves. We are too used to the appearance and procedure of our own system to see its true significance. Perhaps even the English system is too much like our own to be used to the most profit in illustration. It is best on the whole to get entirely away from our own atmosphere and to be most careful in examining such systems as those of France and Germany. Seeing our own institutions through such *media*, we see ourselves as foreigners might see us were they to look at us without preconceptions. Of ourselves, so long as we know only ourselves, we know nothing.

Let it be noted that it is the distinction, already drawn, between administration and politics which makes the comparative method so safe in the field of administration. When we study the administrative systems of France and Germany, knowing that we are not in search of *political* principles, we need not care a peppercorn for the constitutional or political reasons which Frenchmen or Germans give for their practices when explaining them to us. If I see a murderous fellow sharpening a knife cleverly, I can borrow his way of sharpening the knife without borrowing his probable intention to commit murder with it; and so, if I see a monarchist dyed in the wool managing a public bureau well, I can learn his business methods without changing one of my republican spots. He may serve his king; I will continue to serve the people; but I should like to serve my sovereign as well as he serves his. By keeping this distinction in view,—that is, by studying administration as a means of putting our own politics into convenient practice, as a means of making what is democratically politic towards all administratively possible towards each,—we are on perfectly safe ground, and can learn without error what foreign systems have to teach us. We thus devise an adjusting weight for our comparative method of study. We can thus scrutinize the anatomy of foreign governments without fear of getting any of their diseases into our veins; dissect alien systems without apprehension of blood-poisoning.

Our own politics must be the touchstone for all theories. The principles on which to base a science of administration for America must be principles which have democratic policy very much at heart. And, to suit American habit, all general theories must, as theories, keep modestly in the background, not in open argument only, but even in our own minds,—lest opinions satisfactory only to the standards of the library should be dogmatically used, as if they must be quite as satisfactory to the standards of practical politics as well. Doctrinaire devices must be postponed to tested practices. Arrangements not only sanctioned by conclusive experience elsewhere but also congenial to American habit must be preferred without hesitation to theoretical perfection. In a word, steady, practical statesmanship must come first, closet doctrine second. The cosmopolitan what-to-do must always be commanded by the American how-to-do-it.

Our duty is, to supply the best possible life to a *federal* organization, to systems within systems; to make town, city, county, state, and federal governments live with a like strength and an equally assured healthfulness, keeping each unquestionably its own master and yet making all interdependent and co-operative, combining independence with mutual helpfulness. The task is great and important enough to attract the best minds.

This interlacing of local self-government with federal self-government is quite a modern conception. It is not like the arrangements of imperial federation in Germany. There local government is not yet, fully, local *self*-government. The bureaucrat is everywhere busy. His efficiency springs out of *esprit de corps*, out of care to make ingratiating obeisance to the authority of a superior, or, at best, out of the soil of a sensitive conscience. He serves, not the public, but an irresponsible minister. The question for us is, how shall our series of governments within governments be so administered that it shall always be to the interest of the public officer to serve, not his superior alone but the community also, with the best efforts of his talents and the soberest service of his conscience? How shall such service be made to his commonest interest by contributing abundantly to his sustenance, to his dearest interest by furthering his ambition, and to his highest interest by advancing his honor and establishing his character? And how shall this be done alike for the local part and for the national whole?

If we solve this problem we shall again pilot the world. There is a tendency—is there not?—a tendency as yet dim, but already steadily impulsive and clearly destined to prevail, towards, first the confederation of parts of empires like the British, and finally of great states themselves. Instead of centralization of power, there is to be wide union with tolerated divisions of prerogative. This is a tendency towards the American type—of governments joined with governments for the pursuit of common purposes, in honorary equality and honorable subordination. Like principles of civil liberty are everywhere fostering like methods of government; and if comparative studies of the ways and means of government should enable us to offer suggestions which will practicably combine openness and vigor in the administration of such governments with ready docility to all serious, well-sustained public criticism, they will have approved themselves worthy to be ranked among the highest and most fruitful of the great departments of political study. That they will issue in such suggestions I confidently hope.

Woodrow Wilson.

Part V
Foreign Policy

"War Message to Congress"*

April 2, 1917

Gentlemen of the Congress,—I have called the Congress into extraordinary session because there are serious, very serious, choices of policy to be made, and made immediately, which it was neither right nor constitutionally permissible that I should assume the responsibility of making.

On the 3d of February last I officially laid before you the extraordinary announcement of the Imperial German Government that on and after the first day of February it was its purpose to put aside all restraints of law or of humanity and use its submarines to sink every vessel that sought to approach either the ports of Great Britain and Ireland or the western coasts of Europe or any of the ports controlled by the enemies of Germany within the Mediterranean. That had seemed to be the object of the German submarine warfare earlier in the war, but since April of last year the Imperial Government had somewhat restrained the commanders of its undersea craft in conformity with its promise then given to us that passenger boats should not be sunk and that due warning would be given to all other vessels which its submarines might seek to destroy, when no resistance was offered or escape attempted, and care taken that their crews were given at least a fair chance to save their lives in their open boats.

The precautions taken were meager and haphazard enough, as was proved in distressing instance after instance in the progress of the cruel and unmanly business, but a certain degree of restraint was observed.

The new policy has swept every restriction aside. Vessels of every kind, whatever their flag, their character, their cargo, their destination, their errand, have been ruthlessly sent to the bottom without warning and without thought of help

* Titled by Wilson "We Must Accept War," in Wilson, *In Our First Year of War: Messages and Addresses to the Congress and the People, March 5, 1917, to January 8, 1918* (New York: Harper & Brothers Publishers, 1918), 9–25. Wilson's subheadings have been omitted. (Editor's note).

or mercy for those on board, the vessels of friendly neutrals along with those of belligerents. Even hospital ships and ships carrying relief to the sorely bereaved and stricken people of Belgium, though the latter were provided with safe conduct through the proscribed areas by the German Government itself and were distinguished by unmistakable marks of identity, have been sunk with the same reckless lack of compassion or of principle.

I was for a little while unable to believe that such things would in fact be done by any government that had hitherto subscribed to the humane practices of civilized nations. International law had its origin in the attempt to set up some law which would be respected and observed upon the seas, where no nation had right of dominion and where lay the free highways of the world. By painful stage after stage has that law been built up, with meager enough results, indeed, after all was accomplished that could be accomplished, but always with a clear view, at least, of what the heart and conscience of mankind demanded.

This minimum of right the German Government has swept aside under the plea of retaliation and necessity and because it had no weapons which it could use at sea except these which it is impossible to employ as it is employing them without throwing to the winds all scruples of humanity or of respect for the understandings that were supposed to underlie the intercourse of the world.

I am not now thinking of the loss of property involved, immense and serious as that is, but only of the wanton and wholesale destruction of the lives of noncombatants, men, women, and children, engaged in pursuits which have always, even in the darkest periods of modern history, been deemed innocent and legitimate. Property can be paid for; the lives of peaceful and innocent people cannot be.

The present German submarine warfare against commerce is a warfare against mankind. It is a war against all nations. American ships have been sunk, American lives taken, in ways which it has stirred us very deeply to learn of, but the ships and people of other neutral and friendly nations have been sunk and overwhelmed in the waters in the same way. There has been no discrimination. The challenge is to all mankind. Each nation must decide for itself how it will meet it. The choice we make for ourselves must be made with a moderation of counsel and a temperateness of judgment befitting our character and our motives as a nation. We must put excited feeling away.

Our motive will not be revenge or the victorious assertion of the physical might of the nation, but only the vindication of right, of human right, of which we are only a single champion.

When I addressed the Congress on the twenty-sixth of February last I thought that it would suffice to assert our neutral rights with arms, our right to use the seas against unlawful interference, our right to keep our people safe against unlawful violence. But armed neutrality, it now appears, is impracticable. Because submarines are in effect outlaws when used as the German submarines have been used against merchant shipping, it is impossible to defend ships against their attacks as the law of nations has assumed that merchantmen would defend themselves against privateers or cruisers, visible craft giving chase upon the open sea.

It is common prudence in such circumstances, grim necessity, indeed, to endeavor to destroy them before they have shown their own intention. They must be dealt with upon sight, if dealt with at all.

The German Government denies the right of neutrals to use arms at all within the areas of the sea which it has proscribed, even in the defense of rights which no modern publicist has ever before questioned their right to defend. The intimation is conveyed that the armed guards which we have placed on our merchant ships will be treated as beyond the pale of law and subject to be dealt with as pirates would be.

Armed neutrality is ineffectual enough at best; in such circumstances and in the face of such pretensions it is worse than ineffectual: it is likely only to produce what it was meant to prevent; it is practically certain to draw us into the war without either the rights or the effectiveness of belligerents.

There is one choice we cannot make, we are incapable of making: we will not choose the path of submission and suffer the most sacred rights of our nation and our people to be ignored or violated. The wrongs against which we now array ourselves are no common wrongs; they cut to the very roots of human life.

With a profound sense of the solemn and even tragical character of the step I am taking and of the grave responsibilities which it involves, but in unhesitating obedience to what I deem my constitutional duty, I advise that the Congress declare the recent course of the Imperial German Government to be in fact nothing less than war against the government and people of the United States; that it formally accept the status of belligerent which has thus been thrust upon it; and that it take immediate steps not only to put the country in a more thorough state of defense but also to exert all its power and employ all its resources to bring the Government of the German Empire to terms and end the war.

What this will involve is clear. It will involve the utmost practicable cooperation in counsel and action with the governments now at war with Germany, and, as incident to that, the extension to those governments of the most liberal financial credits, in order that our resources may so far as possible be added to theirs.

It will involve the organization and mobilization of all the material resources of the country to supply the materials of war and serve the incidental needs of the nation in the most abundant and yet the most economical and efficient way possible.

It will involve the immediate full equipment of the navy in all respects but particularly in supplying it with the best means of dealing with the enemy's submarines.

It will involve the immediate addition to the armed forces of the United States already provided for by law in case of war at least five hundred thousand men, who should, in my opinion, be chosen upon the principle of universal liability to service, and also the authorization of subsequent additional increments of equal force so soon as they may be needed and can be handled in training.

It will involve also, of course, the granting of adequate credits to the Government, sustained, I hope, so far as they can equitably be sustained by the present generation, by well conceived taxation. I say sustained so far as may be equitable by taxation because it seems to me that it would be most unwise to base the credits which will now be necessary entirely on money borrowed.

It is our duty, I most respectfully urge, to protect our people so far as we may against the very serious hardships and evils which would be likely to arise out of the inflation which would be produced by vast loans.

In carrying out the measures by which these things are to be accomplished we should keep constantly in mind the wisdom of interfering as little as possible in our own preparation and in the equipment of our own military forces with the duty,—for it will be a very practical duty,—of supplying the nations already at war with Germany with the materials which they can obtain only from us or by our assistance. They are in the field and we should help them in every way to be effective there.

I shall take the liberty of suggesting, through the several executive departments of the Government, for the consideration of your committees, measures for the accomplishment of the several objects I have mentioned. I hope that it will be your pleasure to deal with them as having been framed after very careful thought by the branch of the Government upon which the responsibility of conducting the war and safeguarding the nation will most directly fall.

While we do these things, these deeply momentous things, let us be very clear, and make very clear to all the world what our motives and our objects are. My own thought has not been driven from its habitual and normal course by the unhappy events of the last two months, and I do not believe that the thought of the nation has been altered or clouded by them.

I have exactly the same things in mind now that I had in mind when I addressed the Senate on the 22nd of January last; the same that I had in mind when I addressed the Congress on the 3d of February and on the 26th of February.

Our object now, as then, is to vindicate the principles of peace and justice in the life of the world as against selfish and autocratic power and to set up amongst the really free and self-governed peoples of the world such a concert of purpose and of action as will henceforth ensure the observance of those principles.

Neutrality is no longer feasible or desirable where the peace of the world is involved and the freedom of its peoples, and the menace to that peace and freedom lies in the existence of autocratic governments backed by organized force which is controlled wholly by their will, not by the will of their people. We have seen the last of neutrality in such circumstances.

We are at the beginning of an age in which it will be insisted that the same standards of conduct and of responsibility for wrong done shall be observed among nations and their governments that are observed among the individual citizens of civilized states.

We have no quarrel with the German people. We have no feeling towards them but one of sympathy and friendship. It was not upon their impulse that their government acted in entering this war. It was not with their previous knowledge or approval.

It was a war determined upon as wars used to be determined upon in the old, unhappy days when peoples were nowhere consulted by their rulers and wars were provoked and waged in the interest of dynasties or of little groups of ambitious men who were accustomed to use their fellow-men as pawns and tools.

Self-governed nations do not fill their neighbor states with spies or set the course of intrigue to bring about some critical posture of affairs which will give them an opportunity to strike and make conquest. Such designs can be successfully worked out only under cover and where no one has the right to ask questions.

Cunningly contrived plans of deception or aggression, carried, it may be, from generation to generation, can be worked out and kept from the light only within the privacy of courts or behind the carefully guarded confidences of a narrow and privileged class. They are happily impossible where public opinion commands and insists upon full information concerning all the nation's affairs.

A steadfast concert for peace can never be maintained except by a partnership of democratic nations. No autocratic government could be trusted to keep faith within it or observe its covenants. It must be a league of honor, a partnership of opinion. Intrigue would eat its vitals away; the plottings of inner circles who could plan what they would and render account to no one would be a corruption seated at its very heart. Only free peoples can hold their purpose and their honor steady to a common end and prefer the interests of mankind to any narrow interest of their own.

Does not every American feel that assurance has been added to our hope for the future peace of the world by the wonderful and heartening things that have been happening within the last few weeks in Russia?

Russia was known by those who knew it best to have been always in fact democratic at heart, in all the vital habits of her thought, in all the intimate relationships of her people that spoke their natural instinct, their habitual attitude towards life.

The autocracy that crowned the summit of her political structure, long as it had stood and terrible as was the reality of its power, was not in fact Russian in origin, character, or purpose; and now it has been shaken off and the great, generous Russian people have been added in all their naive majesty and might to the forces that are fighting for freedom in the world, for justice, and for peace. Here is a fit partner for a league of honor.

One of the things that has served to convince us that the Prussian autocracy was not and could never be our friend is that from the very outset of the present war it has filled our unsuspecting communities and even our offices of government with spies and set criminal intrigues everywhere afoot against our national unity of counsel, our peace within and without, our industries and our commerce.

Indeed it is now evident that its spies were here even before the war began; and it is unhappily not a matter of conjecture but a fact proved in our courts of justice that the intrigues which have more than once come perilously near to disturbing the peace and dislocating the industries of the country have been carried on at the instigation, with the support, and even under the personal direction of official agents of the Imperial Government accredited to the Government of the United States.

Even in checking these things and trying to extirpate them we have sought to put the most generous interpretation possible upon them because we knew that their source lay, not in any hostile feeling or purpose of the German people towards us (who were, no doubt as ignorant of them as we ourselves were), but only in the selfish designs of a Government that did what it pleased and told its people nothing. But they have played their part in serving to convince us at last that that Government entertains no real friendship for us and means to act against our peace and security at its convenience. That it means to stir up enemies against us at our very doors the intercepted note to the German Minister at Mexico City is eloquent evidence.

We are accepting this challenge of hostile purpose because we know that in such a government, following such methods, we can never have a friend; and that in the presence of its organized power, always lying in wait to accomplish we know not what purpose, there can be no assured security for the democratic governments of the world.

We are now about to accept gauge of battle with this natural foe to liberty and shall, if necessary, spend the whole force of the nation to check and nullify its pretensions and its power. We are glad, now that we see the facts with no veil of false pretense about them, to fight thus for the ultimate peace of the world and for the liberation of its peoples, the German peoples included: for the rights of nations great and small and the privilege of men everywhere to choose their way of life and of obedience. The world must be made safe for democracy. Its peace must be planted upon the tested foundations of political liberty.

We have no selfish ends to serve. We desire no conquest, no dominion. We seek no indemnities for ourselves, no material compensation for the sacrifices we shall freely make. We are but one of the champions of the rights of mankind. We shall be satisfied when those rights have been made as secure as the faith and the freedom of nations can make them.

Just because we fight without rancor and without selfish object, seeking nothing for ourselves but what we shall wish to share with all free peoples, we shall, I feel confident, conduct our operations as belligerents without passion and ourselves observe with proud punctilio the principles of right and of fair play we profess to be fighting for.

I have said nothing of the governments allied with the Imperial Government of Germany because they have not made war upon us or challenged us to defend our right and our honor.

The Austro-Hungarian Government has, indeed, avowed its unqualified endorsement and acceptance of the reckless and lawless submarine warfare adopted now without disguise by the Imperial German Government, and it has therefore not been possible for this Government to receive Count Tarnowski, the Ambassador recently accredited to this Government by the Imperial and Royal Government of Austria-Hungary; but that Government has not actually engaged in warfare against citizens of the United States on the seas, and I take the liberty, for the present at least, of postponing a discussion of our relations with the authorities at Vienna.

We enter this war only where we are clearly forced into it because there are no other means of defending our rights.

It will be all the easier for us to conduct ourselves as belligerents in a high spirit of right and fairness because we act without animus, not in enmity towards a people or with the desire to bring any injury or disadvantage upon them, but only in armed opposition to an irresponsible government which has thrown aside all considerations of humanity and of right and is running amuck.

We are, let me say again, the sincere friends of the German people, and shall desire nothing so much as the early re-establishment of intimate relations of mutual advantage between us,—however hard it may be for them, for the time being, to believe that this is spoken from our hearts. We have borne with their present government through all these bitter months because of that friendship,—exercising a patience and forbearance which would otherwise have been impossible.

We shall, happily, still have an opportunity to prove that friendship in our daily attitude and actions towards the millions of men and women of German birth and native sympathy who live amongst us and share our life, and we shall be proud to prove it towards all who are in fact loyal to their neighbors and to the Government in the hour of test. They are, most of them, as true and loyal Americans as if they had never known any other fealty or allegiance. They will be prompt to stand with us in rebuking and restraining the few who may be of a different mind and purpose. If there should be disloyalty, it will be dealt with with a firm hand of stern repression; but, if it lifts its head at all, it will lift it only here and there and without countenance except from a lawless and malignant few.

It is a distressing and oppressive duty, Gentlemen of the Congress, which I have performed in thus addressing you. There are, it may be, many months of fiery trial and sacrifice ahead of us. It is a fearful thing to lead this great peaceful people into war, into the most terrible and disastrous of all wars, civilization itself seeming to be in the balance. But the right is more precious than peace, and we shall fight for the things which we have always carried nearest our hearts,—for democracy, for the right of those who submit to authority to have a voice in their own governments, for the rights and liberties of small nations, for a universal dominion of right by such a concert of free peoples as shall bring peace and safety to all nations and make the world itself at last free.

To such a task we can dedicate our lives and our fortunes, everything that we are and everything that we have, with the pride of those who know that the day has come when America is privileged to spend her blood and her might for the principles that gave her birth and happiness and the peace which she has treasured. God helping her, she can do no other.

"Fourteen Points"*

January 8, 1918

Gentlemen of the Congress, – Once more, as repeatedly before, the spokesmen of the Central Empires have indicated their desire to discuss the objects of the war and the possible bases of a general peace. Parleys have been in progress at Brest-Litovsk between representatives of the Central Powers, to which the attention of all the belligerents has been invited for the purpose of ascertaining whether it may be possible to extend these parleys into a general conference with regard to terms of peace and settlement.

The Russian representatives presented not only a perfectly definite statement of the principles upon which they would be willing to conclude peace, but also an equally definite program of the concrete application of those principles. The representatives of the Central Powers, on their part, presented an outline of settlement which, if much less definite, seemed susceptible of liberal interpretation until their specific program of practical terms was added. That program proposed no concessions at all either to the sovereignty of Russia or to the preferences of the populations with whose fortunes it dealt, but meant, in a word, that the Central Empires were to keep every foot of territory their armed forces had occupied,—every province, every city, every point of vantage,—as a permanent addition to their territories and their power. It is a reasonable conjecture that the general principles of settlement which they at first suggested originated with the more liberal statesmen of Germany and Austria, the men who have begun to feel the force of their own peoples' thought and purpose, while the concrete terms of actual settlement came from the military leaders who have no thought but to keep what they have got. The negotiations have been broken off. The Russian

---

* Titled by Wilson "The Terms of Peace," in Wilson, *In Our First Year of War: Messages and Addresses to the Congress and the People, March 5, 1917, to January 8, 1918* (New York: Harper & Brothers Publishers, 1918), 150–61. Wilson's subheadings have been omitted. (Editor's note).

representatives were sincere and in earnest. They cannot entertain such proposals of conquest and domination.

The whole incident is full of significance. It is also full of perplexity. With whom are the Russian representatives dealing? For whom are the representatives of the Central Empires speaking? Are they speaking for the majorities of their respective parliaments or for the minority parties, that military and imperialistic minority which has so far dominated their whole policy and controlled the affairs of Turkey and of the Balkan states which have felt obliged to become their associates in this war? The Russian representatives have insisted, very justly, very wisely, and in the true spirit of modern democracy, that the conferences they have been holding with the Teutonic and Turkish statesmen should be held within open, not closed doors, and all the world has been audience, as was desired.

To whom have we been listening, then? To those who speak the spirit and intention of the Resolutions of the German Reichstag of the ninth of July last, the spirit and intention of the liberal leaders and parties of Germany, or to those who resist and defy that spirit and intention and insist upon conquest and subjugation? Or are we listening, in fact, to both, unreconciled and in open and hopeless contradiction? These are very serious and pregnant questions. Upon the answer to them depends the peace of the world.

But, whatever the results of the parleys at Brest-Litovsk, whatever the confusions of counsel and of purpose in the utterances of the spokesmen of the Central Empires, they have again attempted to acquaint the world with their objects in the war and have again challenged their adversaries to say what their objects are and what sort of settlement they would deem just and satisfactory. There is no good reason why that challenge should not be responded to, and responded to with the utmost candor. We did not wait for it. Not once, but again and again, we have laid our whole thought and purpose before the world, not in general terms only, but each time with sufficient definition to make it clear what sort of definitive terms of settlement must necessarily spring out of them.

Within the last week Mr. Lloyd George has spoken with admirable candor and in admirable spirit for the people and Government of Great Britain. There is no confusion of counsel among the adversaries of the Central Powers, no uncertainty of principle, no vagueness of detail. The only secrecy of counsel, the only lack of fearless frankness, the only failure to make definite statement of the objects of the war, lies with Germany and her Allies. The issues of life and death hang upon these definitions. No statesman who has the least conception of his responsibility ought for a moment to permit himself to continue this tragical and appalling outpouring of blood and treasure unless he is sure beyond a peradventure that the objects of the vital sacrifice are part and parcel of the very life of Society and that the people for whom he speaks think them right and imperative as he does.

There is, moreover, a voice calling for these definitions of principle and of purpose which is, it seems to me, more thrilling and more compelling than any of the many moving voices with which the troubled air of the world is filled. It is the voice of the Russian people. They are prostrate and all but helpless, it would seem, before the grim power of Germany, which has hitherto known no relenting and no pity. Their power, apparently, is shattered. And yet their soul is not subservient. They will not yield either in principle or in action. Their conception of what is right, of what is humane and honorable for them to accept, has been stated with a frankness, a largeness of view, a generosity of spirit, and a universal human sympathy which must challenge the admiration of every friend of mankind; and they have refused to compound their ideals or desert others that they themselves may be safe.

They call to us to say what it is that we desire, – in what, if in anything, our purpose and our spirit differ from theirs; and I believe that the people of the United States would wish me to respond, with utter simplicity and frankness. Whether their present leaders believe it or not, it is our heartfelt desire and hope that some way may be opened whereby we may be privileged to assist the people of Russia to attain their utmost hope of liberty and ordered peace.

It will be our wish and purpose that the processes of peace, when they are begun, shall be absolutely open and that they shall involve and permit henceforth no secret understandings of any kind. The day of conquest and aggrandizement is gone by; so is also the day of secret covenants entered into in the interest of particular governments and likely at some unlooked-for moment to upset the peace of the world. It is this happy fact, now clear to the view of every public man whose thoughts do not still linger in an age that is dead and gone, which makes it possible for every nation whose purposes are consistent with justice and the peace of the world to avow now or at any other time the objects it has in view.

We entered this war because violations of right had occurred which touched us to the quick and made the life of our own people impossible unless they were corrected and the world secured once for all against their recurrence. What we demand in this war, therefore, is nothing peculiar to ourselves. It is that the world be made fit and safe to live in; and particularly that it be made safe for every peace-loving nation which, like our own, wishes to live its own life, determine its own institutions, be assured of justice and fair dealing by the other peoples of the world as against force and selfish aggression. All the peoples of the world are in effect partners in this interest, and for our own part we see very clearly that unless justice be done to others it will not be done to us.

The program of the world's peace, therefore, is our program; and that program, the only possible program, as we see it, is this:

I. Open covenants of peace, openly arrived at, after which there shall be no private international understandings of any kind but diplomacy shall proceed always frankly and in the public view.

II. Absolute freedom of navigation upon the seas, outside territorial waters, alike in peace and in war, except as the seas may be closed in whole or in part by international action for the enforcement of international covenants.

III. The removal, so far as possible, of all economic barriers and the establishment of an equality of trade conditions among all the nations consenting to the peace and associating themselves for its maintenance.

IV. Adequate guarantees given and taken that national armaments will be reduced to the lowest point consistent with domestic safety.

V. A free, open-minded, and absolutely impartial adjustment of all colonial claims, based upon a strict observance of the principle that in determining all such questions of sovereignty the interests of the populations concerned must have equal weight with the equitable claims of the government whose title is to be determined.

VI. The evacuation of all Russian territory and such a settlement of all questions affecting Russia as will secure the best and freest cooperation of the other nations of the world in obtaining for her an unhampered and unembarrassed opportunity for the independent determination of her own political development and national policy and assure her of a sincere welcome into the society of free nations under institutions of her own choosing; and, more than a welcome, assistance also of every kind that she may need and may herself desire. The treatment accorded Russia by her sister nations in the months to come will be the acid test of their good will, of their comprehension of her needs as distinguished from their own interests, and of their intelligent and unselfish sympathy.

VII. Belgium, the whole world will agree, must be evacuated and restored, without any attempt to limit the sovereignty which she enjoys in common with all other free nations. No other single act will serve as this will serve to restore confidence among the nations in the laws which they have themselves set and determined for the government of their relations with one another. Without this healing act the whole structure and validity of international law is forever impaired.

VIII. All French territory should be freed and the invaded portions restored, and the wrong done to France by Prussia in 1871 in the matter of Alsace-Lorraine, which has unsettled the peace of the world for nearly fifty years, should be righted, in order that peace may once more be made secure in the interests of all.

IX. A readjustment of the frontiers of Italy should be effected along clearly recognizable lines of nationality.

X. The peoples of Austria-Hungary, whose place among the nations we wish to see safeguarded and assured, should be accorded the freest opportunity of autonomous development.

XI. Rumania, Serbia, and Montenegro should be evacuated; occupied territories restored; Serbia accorded free and secure access to the sea; and the relations of the several Balkan states to one another determined by friendly counsel along historically established lines of allegiance and nationality; and international guarantees of the political and economic independence and territorial integrity of the several Balkan states should be entered into.

XII. The Turkish portions of the present Ottoman Empire should be assured a secure sovereignty, but the other nationalities which are now under Turkish rule should be assured an undoubted security of life and an absolutely unmolested opportunity of autonomous development, and the Dardanelles should be permanently opened as a free passage to the ships and commerce of all nations under international guarantees.

XIII. An independent Polish state should be erected which should include the territories inhabited by indisputably Polish populations, which should be assured a free and secure access to the sea, and whose political and economic independence and territorial integrity should be guaranteed by international covenant.

XIV. A general association of nations must be formed under specific covenants for the purpose of affording mutual guarantees of political independence and territorial integrity to great and small states alike.

In regard to these essential rectifications of wrong and assertions of right we feel ourselves to be intimate partners of all the governments and peoples associated together against the Imperialists. We cannot be separated in interest or divided in purpose. We stand together until the end.

For such arrangements and covenants we are willing to fight and to continue to fight until they are achieved; but only because we wish the right to prevail and desire a just and stable peace such as can be secured only by removing the chief provocations to war, which this program does remove. We have no jealousy of German greatness, and there is nothing in this program that impairs it. We grudge her no achievement or distinction of learning or of pacific enterprise, such as have made her record very bright and very enviable. We do not wish to injure her or to block in any way her legitimate influence or power. We do not wish to fight her either with arms or with hostile arrangements of trade if she is willing to associate herself with us and the other peace-loving nations of the world in covenants of justice and law and fair dealing. We wish her only to accept a place of equality among the peoples of the world,—the new world in which we now live,—instead of a place of mastery.

Neither do we presume to suggest to her any alteration or modification of her institutions. But it is necessary, we must frankly say, and necessary as a preliminary to any intelligent dealings with her on our part, that we should know whom her spokesmen speak for when they speak to us, whether for the Reichstag majority or for the military party and the men whose creed is imperial domination.

We have spoken now, surely, in terms too concrete to admit of any further doubt or question. An evident principle runs through the whole program I have outlined. It is the principle of justice to all peoples and nationalities, and their right to live on equal terms of liberty and safety with one another, whether they be strong or weak. Unless this principle be made its foundation no part of the structure of international justice can stand. The people of the United States could act upon no other principle; and to the vindication of this principle they are ready to devote their lives, their honor, and everything that they possess. The moral climax of this the culminating and final war for human liberty has come, and they are ready to put their own strength, their own highest purpose, their own integrity and devotion to the test.

APPENDIX
CHRONOLOGY OF WILSON'S ACADEMIC
WORK AND OTHER SELECTED EVENTS

Works that can be found in this volume are indicated with an asterisk(*). For works not available in this volume, but available instead in the 69-volume Papers of Woodrow Wilson *(ed. Arthur S. Link, Princeton University Press, 1966–1993), I have provided the volume and page numbers from that collection, which I have abbreviated as "PWW."*

Dec. 28, 1856	Thomas Woodrow Wilson born in Staunton, Virginia.
1858	Wilson family moves to Augusta, Georgia.
1870	Wilson family moves to Columbia, South Carolina.
1873–1874	Wilson enters Davidson College, North Carolina. Withdraws due to "ill health."
1875	Enters Princeton.
1876–1878	Aug/1876 "Work-Day Religion" (PWW 1:176-8)
	* Aug/1876 "Christ's Army"
	Sep/1876 "A Christian Statesman" (PWW 1:188-9)
	* Dec/1876 "Christian Progress"
	Jan/1878 "Some Thoughts on the Present State of Public Affairs" (PWW 1:347-54)
June 1879	Graduates from Princeton.
	* Aug/1879 "Cabinet Govt in the U.S."
	Sep/1879 "Self-Government in France" (PWW 1:515-39)
Sep. 1879	Enters University of Virginia Law School.
	Oct/1879 "Congressional Govt" (PWW 1:548-74)
	Mar/1880 "John Bright" (PWW 1:608-21)
	Apr/1880 "Mr. Gladstone, A Character Sketch" (PWW 1:624-42)

Dec. 1880	Withdraws from UVA Law School b/c of "ill health."
1881	Residing with parents, continues to study law.

Feb/1881 "Stray Thoughts from the South" (PWW 2:19-25, 26-31)

Mar/1881 "What can be done for Constitutional Liberty" (PWW 2:33-40)

1882	Opens law practice w/ Edward I. Renick in Atlanta.

Dec/1882 "Government by Debate" (PWW 2:159-275)

Sep. 1883	Enters Johns Hopkins University for graduate study in history & political science.

Jan/1884 "Committee or Cabinet Government?" (PWW 2:614-40)

Jan–Sep/1884 *Congressional Government* written

* Jan/1885 *Congressional Government* published

June 24, 1885	Marries Ellen Louise Axson at Savannah, Georgia.
Sep. 1885	Leaves Johns Hopkins without degree, becomes Assoc Prof. of History at Bryn Mawr College.

Nov/1885 "The 'Courtesy of the Senate'" (PWW 5:44-48)

Nov/1885 "The Art of Governing" (PWW 5:50-4)

Dec/1885 "The Modern Democratic State"

Feb/1886 "Responsible Government under the Constitution" (PWW 5:107-24)

* Nov/1886 "The Study of Administration"

1886	Earns Ph.D. with *Congressional Government* accepted as dissertation.

Nov/1886 "Of the Study of Politics"

* Aug/1887 "Socialism and Democracy"

Jan/1888 "Taxation and Appropriation" (PWW 5:653-6)

Feb. 1888	Begins annual 5-week lectureship at Johns Hopkins on administration (continues through 1897).
Sep. 1888	Undertakes new position as Professor at Wesleyan University.

* Jun/1889 *The State*

* Jun/1890 "Leaders of Men"

Sep. 1890	Undertakes new position as Professor of Jurisprudence & Political Economy at Princeton.

Oct/1890 "The English Constitution" (PWW 7:12-44)

Sep/1891 "The Study of Politics" (PWW 7:278-84)

Nov/1891 "Political Sovereignty" (PWW 7:325-41)

Dec/1891 "Democracy" (PWW 7:345-69)

1893 *Division & Reunion*

Mar/1893 "Mr. Cleveland's Cabinet" (PWW 8:160-78)

1893 *An Old Master, and Other Political Essays*

1896 *Mere Literature* (collection of essays)

1896 *George Washington*

1897	Final year of annual 5-week lectureship on administration at Johns Hopkins.
1897–1902	Apr/1897 "The Making of the Nation" (PWW 10:217-36) Jun/1897 "On Being Human" (PWW 10:245-59) Aug/1897 "Leaderless Government" (PWW 10:288-304) Feb/1898 Lectures at Johns Hopkins on Burke, Bagehot, and Maine (PWW 10:408-61) Aug/1900 Preface to the 15th Edition of *Congressional Government* (PWW 11:567-71) 1902 *A History of the American People*
Oct. 25, 1902	Inaugurated President of Princeton University.
1907–1908	Apr/1907 Lectures at Columbia University that are later published as *Constitutional Government* * Jul/1907 "The Author & Signers of the Declaration of Independence" Aug/1907 "A Credo" (PWW 17:335-38) * 1908 Publication of *Constitutional Government in the United States*
Sep. 15, 1910	Nominated as Democratic candidate for Governor of New Jersey.
Nov. 8, 1910	Elected Governor of New Jersey (inaugurated 1/17/1911).
July 2, 1912	Nominated as Democratic candidate for President of the United States.
Nov. 5, 1912	Elected President of the United States (inaugurated 3/4/1913). * 1913 Publication of *The New Freedom*
Nov. 7, 1916	Re-elected President of the United States (inaugurated 3/5/1917).
Apr. 2, 1917	Asks for a declaration of war (signs war resolution 4/6/1917).
Jan. 8, 1918	Fourteen Points address to Congress.
Nov. 11, 1918	Armistice proclaimed.
June 28, 1919	Signs Treaty of Versailles.
Sep 3–26, 1919	Speaking tour on behalf of Treaty; collapses after Pueblo speech on 9/26 and returns to Washington.
March 4, 1921	End of Wilson's presidency; President Harding inaugurated.
Feb. 3, 1924	Wilson's death.

SELECTED BIBLIOGRAPHY

What follows is not a comprehensive bibliography of scholarly work on Wilson. Instead, I have selected works which strike me as most directly relevant to the study of Wilson's political thought. The bibliography does not, for the most part, include the many important historical accounts. For a comprehensive bibliographic essay, the most recent of which I am aware is the one included in Kendrick A. Clements, The Presidency of Woodrow Wilson *(Lawrence, KS: University Press of Kansas, 1992).*

Bimes, Terri, and Stephen Skowronek. "Woodrow Wilson's Critique of Popular Leadership: Reassessing the Modern-Traditional Divide in Presidential History." *Polity* 29:1 (Fall 1996): 27–63.

Bishirjian, Richard J. "Croly, Wilson, and the American Civil Religion." *Modern Age* (Winter 1979): 33–38.

Blumenthal, Henry. "Woodrow Wilson and the Race Question." *The Journal of Negro History* (January 1963): 1–10.

Brownlow, Louis. "Woodrow Wilson and Public Administration." *Public Administration Review* 16 (1956): 77–81.

Butler, Gregory S. "Visions of a Nation Transformed: Modernity and Ideology in Wilson's Political Thought." *Journal of Church and State* 39 (Winter 1997): 37–51.

Ceaser, James W. *Presidential Selection: Theory and Development*, 170–212. Princeton: Princeton University Press, 1979.

Ceaser, James W., Glen E. Thurow, Jeffrey K. Tulis, Joseph M. Bessette. "The Rise of the Rhetorical Presidency." *Presidential Studies Quarterly* 11 (Spring 1981): 158–71.

Claeys, Eric R. "The Living Commerce Clause: Federalism in Progressive Political Theory and the Commerce Clause after *Lopez* and *Morrison*." *William and Mary Bill of Rights Journal* 11 (January 2003): 403–63.

Clements, Kendrick A. *The Presidency of Woodrow Wilson* (Lawrence, KS: University Press of Kansas, 1992).

———. "Woodrow Wilson and Administrative Reform." *Presidential Studies Quarterly* 28:2 (Spring 1998): 320–36.

Clor, Harry. "Woodrow Wilson." In *American Political Thought: The Philosophic Dimension of American Statesmanship*, ed. Morton J. Frisch and Richard G. Stevens. Dubuque, IA: Kendall/Hunt, 1976 (orig. pub. 1971), 191–218.

Connelly, William F., Jr., "Introduction" to Wilson, *Congressional Government*. Somerset, NJ: Transaction, 2002.

Cooper, Phillip J. "The Wilsonian Dichotomy in Administrative Law." In *Politics and Administration: Woodrow Wilson and American Public Administration*, ed. Jack Rabin and James S. Bowman, 79–94. New York: Marcel Dekker, 1984.

Cronon, E. David. "Introduction" to *The Political Thought of Woodrow Wilson*, ed. Cronon. Indianapolis: The Bobbs-Merrill Company, Inc., 1965.

Cuff, Robert D. "Wilson and Weber: Bourgeois Critics in an Organized Age." *Public Administration Review* 38 (May/June 1978): 240–44.

Derthick, Martha, and John J. Dinan, "Progressivism and Federalism." In *Progressivism and the New Democracy*, ed. Sidney M. Milkis and Jerome M. Mileur, 81–102. Amherst: University of Massachusetts Press, 1999.

Doig, Jameson W. "'If I See a Murderous Fellow Sharpening a Knife Cleverly . . .': The Wilsonian Dichotomy and the Public Authority Tradition." *Public Administration Review* 43 (July/August 1983): 292–304.

Eden, Robert. "Opinion Leadership and the Problem of Executive Power: Woodrow Wilson's Original Position." *Review of Politics* 57 (Summer 1995): 483–503.

———. *Political Leadership and Nihilism: A Study of Weber and Nietzsche*, 1–35. Tampa: University of South Florida Press, 1983.

———. "The Rhetorical Presidency and the Eclipse of Executive Power: Woodrow Wilson's *Constitutional Government in the United States*." *Polity* 18:3 (Spring 1996): 357–78.

Eidelberg, Paul. *A Discourse on Statesmanship: The Design and Transformation of the American Polity*, 279–362. Urbana, IL: University of Illinois Press, 1974.

Eisenach, Eldon J. *The Lost Promise of Progressivism*. Lawrence, KS: University Press of Kansas, 1994.

Gaughan, Anthony. "Woodrow Wilson and the Legacy of the Civil War." *Civil War History* 43:3 (1977): 225–42.

Gillman, Howard. "The Constitution Besieged: TR, Taft, and Wilson on the Virtue and Efficacy of a Faction-Free Republic." *Presidential Studies Quarterly* 19 (Winter 1989): 179–201.

Kesler, Charles R. "The Public Philosophy of the New Freedom and the New Deal." In *The New Deal and Its Legacy*, ed. Robert Eden, 155–66. New York: Greenwood Press, 1989.

———. "Separation of Powers and the Administrative State." In *The Imperial Congress*, ed. Gordon S. Jones and John A. Marini, 20–40. New York: Pharos Books, 1988.

———. "Woodrow Wilson and the Statesmanship of Progress." In *Natural Right and Political Right*, ed. Thomas B. Silver and Peter W. Schramm, 103–27. Durham, NC: Carolina Academic Press, 1984.

Kirwan, Kent A. "The Crisis of Identity in the Study of Public Administration: Woodrow Wilson." *Polity* 9 (Spring 1977): 321–43.

———. "Historicism and Statesmanship in the Reform Argument of Woodrow Wilson." *Interpretation* (September 1981): 339–51.

Link, Arthur S. "Woodrow Wilson: The American as Southerner." *The Journal of Southern History* 36:1 (February 1970): 3–17.

Longaker, Richard P. "Woodrow Wilson and the Presidency." In *The Philosophy and Policies of Woodrow Wilson*, ed. Earl Latham, 67–81. Chicago: University of Chicago Press, 1958.

Marini, John A. *The Politics of Budget Control*, 39–66. Washington: Crane Russak, 1992.

Marion, David E. "Alexander Hamilton and Woodrow Wilson on the Spirit and Form of a Responsible Republican Government." *Review of Politics* 42:3 (July 1980): 309–27.

Miewald, Robert D. "The Origins of Wilson's Thought: The German Tradition and the Organic State." In *Politics and Administration*, ed. Rabin and Bowman, 17–30.

Milkis, Sidney M. "Introduction: Progressivism, Then and Now." In *Progressivism and the New Democracy*, ed. Milkis and Mileur, 1–39.

———. *Political Parties and Constitutional Government*, 42–71. Baltimore: The Johns Hopkins University Press, 1999.

———. *The President and the Parties: The Transformation of the American Party System Since the New Deal*, 21–51. New York: Oxford University Press, 1993.

Pearson, Sidney A., Jr. "Introduction" to Wilson, *Constitutional Government in the United States*. Somerset, NJ: Transaction, 2001.

Pestritto, Ronald J. "Woodrow Wilson, American History, and the Advent of Progressivism." In *Challenges to the American Founding: Slavery, Historicism, and Progressivism in the Nineteenth Century*, ed. Pestritto and Thomas G. West, 265–96. Lanham, MD: Lexington Books, 2005.

———. "Woodrow Wilson, the Organic State, and American Republicanism." In *History of American Political Thought*, ed. Bryan-Paul Frost and Jeffrey Sikkenga, 549–68. Lanham, MD: Lexington Books, 2003.

———. *Woodrow Wilson and the Roots of Modern Liberalism*. Lanham, MD: Rowman & Littlefield, 2005.

Rohr, John A. "The Constitutional World of Woodrow Wilson." In *Politics and Administration*, ed. Rabin and Bowman, 31–49.

Ruiz, George W. "The Ideological Convergence of Theodore Roosevelt and Woodrow Wilson." *Presidential Studies Quarterly* 19 (Winter 1989): 159–77.

Stid, Daniel D. *The President as Statesman: Woodrow Wilson and the Constitution*. Lawrence, KS: University Press of Kansas, 1998.

Stillman, Richard J., II. "Woodrow Wilson and the Study of Administration: A New Look at an Old Essay." *American Political Science Review* 67 (June 1973): 582–88.

Thorsen, Niels Aage. *The Political Thought of Woodrow Wilson 1875–1910*. Princeton: Princeton University Press, 1988.

Tulis, Jeffrey K. *The Rhetorical Presidency*, 117–44. Princeton: Princeton University Press, 1987.

Turner, Henry A. "Woodrow Wilson: Exponent of Executive Leadership." *The Western Political Quarterly* 4 (1951): 97–115.

Van Riper, Paul P. "The American Administrative State: Wilson and the Founders—An Unorthodox View." *Public Administration Review* 43 (November/December 1983): 477–90.

Walker, Larry. "Woodrow Wilson, Progressive Reform, and Public Administration." *Political Science Quarterly* 104:3 (1989): 509–25.

Walker, Larry, and Jeremy F. Plant, "Woodrow Wilson and the Federal System." In *Politics and Administration*, ed. Rabin and Bowman, 119–32.

Wolfe, Christopher. "Woodrow Wilson: Interpreting the Constitution." *Review of Politics* 41 (January 1979): 121–42.

Young, Roland. "Woodrow Wilson's *Congressional Government* Reconsidered." In *Philosophy and Policies of Woodrow Wilson*, ed. Latham, 201–13.

Zentner, Scot J. "Caesarism and the American Presidency." *Southeastern Political Science Review* 24:4 (December 1996): 629–53.

——. "Liberalism and Executive Power: Woodrow Wilson and the American Founders." *Polity* 26:4 (Summer 1994): 579–99.

——. "President and Party in the Thought of Woodrow Wilson." *Presidential Studies Quarterly* 26:3 (Summer 1996): 666–77.

Index

About the Editor

Ronald J. Pestritto is Associate Professor of Politics at the University of Dallas and a Research Fellow of the Claremont Institute for the Study of Statesmanship and Political Philosophy. His books include *Woodrow Wilson and the Roots of Modern Liberalism* (Rowman & Littlefield, 2005).